AF897604

A Text Book Of

NETWORK AND INFORMATION SECURITY

(22620)

Semester - VI

THIRD YEAR DIPLOMA IN COMPUTER ENGINEERING AND INFORMATION TECHNOLOGY GROUP

As Per MSBTE's 'I' Scheme Syllabus

Mrs. Mrunal P. Fatangare
M. E. (Computer)
HOD, Information Technology Department
MAEER,s MIT Polytechnic, Pune

Mrs. Pallavi U. Nehete
M.E. (I.T.)
Lecturer, Information Technology Department
MAEER,s MIT Polytechnic, Pune

NIRALI PRAKASHAN
ADVANCEMENT OF KNOWLEDGE

N4399

NETWORK AND INFORMATION SECURITY **ISBN 978-93-89825-46-6**

First Edition : December 2019

© : Author

The text of this publication, or any part thereof, should not be reproduced or transmitted in any form or stored in any computer storage system or device for distribution including photocopy, recording, taping or information retrieval system or reproduced on any disc, tape, perforated media or other information storage device etc., without the written permission of Author with whom the rights are reserved. Breach of this condition is liable for legal action.

Every effort has been made to avoid errors or omissions in this publication. In spite of this, errors may have crept in. Any mistake, error or discrepancy so noted and shall be brought to our notice shall be taken care of in the next edition. It is notified that neither the publisher nor the author or seller shall be responsible for any damage or loss of action to any one, of any kind, in any manner, therefrom.

Published By :
NIRALI PRAKASHAN
Abhyudaya Pragati, 1312, Shivaji Nagar
Off J.M. Road, PUNE – 411005
Tel - (020) 25512336/37/39, Fax - (020) 25511379
Email : niralipune@pragationline.com

➢ DISTRIBUTION CENTRES

PUNE

Nirali Prakashan (For orders within Pune) : 119, Budhwar Peth, Jogeshwari Mandir Lane, Pune 411002, Maharashtra
Tel : (020) 2445 2044, Fax : (020) 2445 1538; Mobile : 9657703145
Email : niralilocal@pragationline.com

Nirali Prakashan (For orders outside Pune) : S. No. 28/27, Dhayari, Near Asian College Pune 411041
Tel : (020) 24690204 Fax : (020) 24690316; Mobile : 9657703143
Email : bookorder@pragationline.com

MUMBAI

Nirali Prakashan : 385, S.V.P. Road, Rasdhara Co-op. Hsg. Society Ltd.,
Girgaum, Mumbai 400004, Maharashtra; Mobile : 9320129587
Tel : (022) 2385 6339 / 2386 9976, Fax : (022) 2386 9976
Email : niralimumbai@pragationline.com

➢ DISTRIBUTION BRANCHES

JALGAON

Nirali Prakashan : 34, V. V. Golani Market, Navi Peth, Jalgaon 425001, Maharashtra,
Tel : (0257) 222 0395, Mob : 94234 91860; Email : niralijalgaon@pragationline.com

KOLHAPUR

Nirali Prakashan : New Mahadvar Road, Kedar Plaza, 1st Floor Opp. IDBI Bank, Kolhapur 416 012
Maharashtra. Mob : 9850046155; Email : niralikolhapur@pragationline.com

NAGPUR

Nirali Prakashan : Above Maratha Mandir, Shop No. 3, First Floor,
Rani Jhanshi Square, Sitabuldi, Nagpur 440012, Maharashtra
Tel : (0712) 254 7129; Email : niralinagpur@pragationline.com

DELHI

Nirali Prakashan : 4593/15, Basement, Agarwal Lane, Ansari Road, Daryaganj
Near Times of India Building, New Delhi 110002 Mob : 08505972553
Email : niralidelhi@pragationline.com

BENGALURU

Nirali Prakashan : Maitri Ground Floor, Jaya Apartments, No. 99, 6th Cross, 6th Main,
Malleswaram, Bengaluru 560003, Karnataka; Mob : 9449043034
Email: niralibangalore@pragationline.com

Other Branches : Hyderabad, Chennai

Note : Every possible effort has been made to avoid errors or omissions in this book. In spite this, errors may have crept in. Any type of error or mistake so noted, and shall be brought to our notice, shall be taken care of in the next edition. It is notified that neither the publisher, nor the author or book seller shall be responsible for any damage or loss of action to any one of any kind, in any manner, therefrom. The reader must cross check all the facts and contents with original Government notification or publications.

niralipune@pragationline.com | www.pragationline.com

Also find us on f www.facebook.com/niralibooks

Preface ...

We take an opportunity to present this book entitled as "**Network and Information Security**" to the students of Sixth Semester (Third Year Diploma in Computer Engineering and Information Technology Group). The object of this book is to present the subject matter in a most concise and simple manner. The book is written strictly according to the Revised Syllabus (I-Scheme) prepared by Maharashtra State Board of Technical Education (MSBTE).

This book contains five constructive chapters.

- First chapter gives an introduction to computer and information security.
- Second chapter focuses on concepts of user authentication and access control.
- Third chapter covers cryptography.
- Fourth chapter introduces firewall and intrusion detection system.
- Network security, cyber laws and compliance standards are covered in Fifth chapter.

A special words of thank to Shri. Dineshbhai Furia, Mr. Jignesh Furia for showing full faith in us to write this text book. We also thank to entire staff of M/s Nirali Prakashan for their excellent co-operation.

We welcome constructive suggestions from our colleagues and students.

Authors

■■■

Syllabus ...

1. Introduction to Computer and Information Security

1.1 Foundations of Computer Security: Definition and Need of Computer Security, Security Basics: Confidentiality, Integrity, Availability, Accountability, Non-Repudiation and Reliability.

1.2 Risk and Threat Analysis: Assets, Vulnerability, Threats, Risks, Counter Measures.

1.3 Threat to Security: Viruses, Phases of Viruses, Types of Virus, Dealing with Viruses, Worms, Trojan Horse, Intruders, Insiders.

1.4 Type of Attacks: Active and Passive Attacks, Denial of Service, DDOS, Backdoors and Trapdoors, Sniffing, Spoofing, Man in the Middle, Replay, TCP/IP Hacking, Encryption Attacks.

1.5 Operating System Security: Operating System Updates HotFix, Patch, Service Pack.

1.6 Information, Need and Importance of Information, Information Classification, Criteria for Information Classification, Security, Need of Security, Basics Principles of Information Security.

2. User Authentication and Access Control

2.1 Identification and Authentication: User Name and Password, Guessing Password, Password Attacks - Piggybacking, Shoulder Surfing, Dumpster Diving.

2.2 Biometrics: Finger Prints, Hand Prints, Retina, Patterns, Voice Patterns, Signature and Writing Patterns, Keystrokes.

2.3 Access Controls: Definition, Authentication Mechanism, Principle - Authentication, Authorization, Audit, Policies: DAC, MAC, RBAC.

3. Cryptography

3.1 Introduction: Plain Text, Cipher Text, Cryptography, Cryptanalysis, Cryptology, Encryption, Decryption.

3.2 Substitution Techniques: Caesar's Cipher, Modified Caesar's Cipher, Transposition Techniques: Simple Columnar Transposition.

3.3 Steganography: Procedure.

3.4 Symmetric and Asymmetric Cryptography: Introduction to Symmetric Encryption, DES (Data Encryption Standard) Algorithm, Asymmetric Key Cryptography: Digital Signature.

4. Firewall and Intrusion Detection System

4.1 Firewall: Need of Firewall, Types of Firewall - Packet Filters, Stateful Packet Filters, Application Gateways, Circuit Gateways.

4.2 Firewall Policies, Configuration, Limitations, DMZ.

4.3 Intrusion Detection System: Vulnerability Assessment, Misuse Detection, Anomaly Detection, Network - Based IDS, Host-Based IDS, Honeypots.

5. Network Security, Cyber Laws and Compliance Standards

5.1 Kerberos: Working, AS, TGS, SS.

5.2 IP Security - Overview, Protocols - AH, ESP, Modes - Transport and Tunnel.

5.3 Email Security - SMTP, PEM, PGP.

5.4 Public Key Infrastructure (PKI): Introduction, Certificates, Certificate Authority, Registration Authority, X.509/PKIX Certificate Format.

5.5 Cyber Crime: Introduction, Hacking, Digital Forgery, Cyber Stalking/Harassment, Cyber Pornography, Identity Theft and Terrorism, Cyber Terrorism, Cyber Defamation.

5 6 Cyber Laws: Introduction, Need, Categories: Crime Against Individual, Government, Property.

5.7 Compliance Standards: Implementing and Information Security Management System, ISO 27001, ISO 20000, BS 25999, PCI DSS, ITIL Framework, COBIT Framework.

■■■

Contents ...

■■■

1...

Introduction to Computer and Information Security

Chapter Outcomes...

- Explain the importance of the given component of computer security.
- Explain the characteristics of the given type of threat.
- Explain the given type of attacks related with security.
- Describe the features of given type of update of operating system.
- Classify information.
- Explain principles of information security.

Learning Objectives...

- To understand Basic Concepts in Computer Security and Information Security
- To learn Risk and Threat Analysis
- To study Concepts in Operating System Security
- To understand Threats in Security
- To learn Types of Attacks in Security
- To learn Information (Classification, Criteria) and Principles of Information Security

1.0 INTRODUCTION [S-16]

- The term 'security' means protection from danger or unauthorized actions. There are various types of security like project security, personal security, operating system security, information security, national security, operations security, communication security, computer security and so on.
- In a general sense, security means protecting the assets. Security is a state of freedom or protection from a danger, risk or attack.
- With the rapid advances in networked computer technology during the last few decades and the unprecedented growth of the Internet, the public has become increasingly aware of the threats to personal and security through computer crime.
- Identity theft, pirated bank accounts, forgery - the list of electronic crimes is as unlimited as the imaginations of those who use technology in harmful and dangerous ways.
- Information security or computer security is concerned with the control of threats related to the use of information or computer. To achieve this objective, one should develop a secure computing platform so that he/she can restrict the users to perform only particular actions that is permitted to him or her.

- Computer security, is the protection of computer systems and information from harm, theft and unauthorized use. Computer security is the protection of the integrity, availability and confidentiality of information system resources (includes hardware, software, firmware, information/data and so on).
- Information security is the task of guarding information which is processed by a server, stored on a storage device and transmitted over a network like Local Area Network (LAN) or the Internet.
- Information security means protecting information and Information Systems (IS) from unauthorized access, use, disclosure, disruption, modification or destruction.
- An Information System (IS) is a set of interrelated components that collect, process, store and disseminate data and information. An information system provides a feedback mechanism to monitor and control its operations to make sure it continues to meet its goals and objectives.
- Information systems are made up of the major components of hardware, software, data, people, procedures and networks.
- The critical characteristics of information including Confidentiality, Integrity and Availability (CIA), must be protected at all times. This protection is implemented by multiple measures that include policies, education, training and awareness and technology.
- The objective of information system security is to optimize the performance of an organization with respect to the risks to which it is exposed.
- In computer security, a threat is a possible danger that might exploit a vulnerability to breach security and therefore cause possible harm. A threat refers, to anything that has the potential to cause serious harm to a computer system.
- A threat is something that may or may not happen, but has the potential to cause serious damage. Threats can lead to attacks on computer systems, networks and more.
- An attack is any attempt to expose, alter, disable, destroy, steal or gain unauthorized access to or make unauthorized use of an asset.
- Risk is the intersection of assets, threats and vulnerabilities. Risk is defined as, change of injury, damage, or loss. Thus, risk has two elements namely, chance (an element of uncertainty) and potential loss or damage.
- Security measures cannot assure 100% protection against all threats. Therefore risk analysis which is the process of evaluating system vulnerabilities and the threats facing it is an essential part of any risk management program.
- The analysis process identifies the probable consequences or risks associated with the vulnerabilities and provide the basis for establishing a cost-effective security program.
- Risk management is the process of implementing and maintaining counter measures that reduce the effects of risk to an acceptable level.
- The risk analysis process gives management the information it needs to make educated judgments concerning information security. The procedure identifies the existing security controls, calculates vulnerabilities, and evaluates the effect of threats on each area of vulnerability.

1.1 FOUNDATION OF COMPUTER SECURITY [S-16]

- The foundations of computer security include answers to the superficially simple question "What is this all about?" This section gives us detailed knowledge about the concepts of computer security. This section also defines a few of the most important terms of computer security.
- Security is about the protection of assets. The assets of a computer system can be categorized as hardware, software, data and communication lines and networks.
- Security is the technique which makes the accessibility of information/system more reliable. Security means to protect information or computer system from unauthorized user like attackers, hackers who damage to system purposely.

- Cyberspace (computer networks and Internet) is becoming a dangerous place for all organizations and individuals to protect their sensitive data or information. Security is not only to protect information or network, but also allow authorized user to access the system or network.
- Computer security can be viewed as a set of mechanisms that protect computer systems from unauthorized access, theft, damage and disruption of the services they provide.
- Computer security includes protection from both internal and external threats. Internal threats can be flaws in a software program or operating system. External threats are unauthorized access or human error.
- Computer security is the protection of information systems from theft or damage to the hardware, the software and to the information on them, as well as from disruption or misdirection of the services they provide.
- The objective of computer security includes protection of information from theft, corruption, or natural disaster, while allowing the information to remain accessible and productive to its intended users.

Terms related to Computer Security:

1. The term **Computer System Security** means the collective processes and mechanisms by which sensitive and valuable information and services are protected from publication, tampering or collapse by unauthorized activities or untrustworthy individuals and unplanned events respectively. Example, a security system protects our house, warning the neighbors or the police, if an unauthorized intruder tries to get in. We speak of a child's "physical security", hoping he or she is safe from any potential harm.
2. **Computer Security and Information Security** is the protection of computers and data that the computers hold. This can be anything from placing passwords on computers to setting up firewalls. Information security deals with protection of information.
3. **Data Security** means ensuring the data which is kept safe from corruption and access to it is suitably controlled. Thus, data security helps to ensure privacy. Data security refers to the protective measures which ensure that data or computer is kept safe from modification or corruption. It also prevents unauthorised access to data or computer. Thus, data security helps to provide privacy to the data. Thus, data security and privacy help the organisation to prevent data breaches, ensure the integrity of data and protect the important information from disclosure.
4. In the field of networking, the **network security** comprises of the provisions and policies adopted by the network administrator to prevent and monitor unauthorized access, misuse, modification, or denial of the computer network and network-accessible resources. Network security means protection of data on the network during transmission. It consists of different policies and provisions adopted by the administrator. It involves the authorisation and access control of the network. Network administrator is responsible for the proper implementation of access control and authentication to provide the security.

1.1.1 Definition of Computer Security [S-16, 17, 18, 19, W-16]

- Internet is most required thing in today's life. The Internet has changed our lives. Unfortunately, this huge network and its associated technologies will leads to the increasing number of security threats.
- Awareness of standard cyber security practices is the most effective way to protect our self from these threats and attacks.
- Computer security includes the protection, prevention and detection of unauthorized use of computer systems as well as data stored in the computer.
- "The protection afforded to an automated information system in order to attain the applicable objectives of preserving the integrity, availability and confidentiality of information system resources" like hardware, software. **OR**

- Computer security is, defined as, "the protection of computing systems and the data/information that system will access".

OR

- Computer security deals with the prevention and detection of unauthorized actions by users of a computer system.

1.1.2 Need of Computer Security [S-17, 18, W-17]

- The growth of computers and Information Technology (IT) has been explosive. Never before an entirely new technology has been propagated around the world with such speed and with so great a penetration of virtually every human activity.
- Today, the use of computer with internet is increasing rapidly. At the same time security challenges are also increasing. A number of software tools are available which help the attackers to attack easily without much knowledge of computer field.
- Therefore, today's information security is an emerging field which helps to protect the computer from various attacks and also provides the awareness about security among the common people. Information security supports to protect the information from unauthorised persons.
- Information security not only confined to computer security but it includes the security of data or information in different forms.
- We use computer for various applications so it is very important to protect our computer so that unauthorised person cannot access the system and modify or delete or read the data.
- Computer security is the process of preventing and detecting unauthorized use of the computer system. Computer security needed for information security (securing information from unauthorized access, modification and deletion).
- Computer security is important because it keeps information protected. Computer security is needed in many areas such as:
  1. **To Preserve Company/Organizations Assets:** Company assets such as information of organization kept in the computer networks, which is useful as the physical assets of the company.
  2. **To Confirm with Governing Requirements and Moral Responsibilities:** Each organization creates policies and procedures which deal with the security requirements of the organization in question.
  3. **For Competitive Benefit**: Financial services and e-commerce considers network security to be of prime importance.
  4. **Protecting Data/Information that Organization Use and Collect:** Without data an organization losses its records of transaction and ability to deliver a value to its customer. Protecting data at motion and at rest are both critical aspects of information security. The value of data motivates attackers to steal and corrupt the data.
  5. **Enabling the Safe Operation of Application:** A modern organization need to create an environment that safeguards these Applications, specially operating system platform, e-mail, instant messaging application etc.
  6. **Safeguarding Technology Assets in Organization:** To perform effectively, organizations must employ secure infrastructure service which appropriate to the size and the scope of the organization. For example, a small business uses an email service and secure with the personal encryption tool. When an organization grows, it must develop additional security service that uses system of software, encryption methodology and legal agreement that support entire information infrastructure.

1.1.3 Security Basics [S-16, 18]

- Computer security means to protect information or data. In simple words, security is defined as, protecting information system from unintended access.

- It deals with prevention and detection of unauthorized actions by users of a computer. Basic security concepts important to information on the Internet also called as principles of security are confidentiality, integrity, and availability.
- Concepts relating to the people who use the information are accountability, reliability and non-repudiation.

1. Confidentiality:

- Confidentiality is the protection of information or resources. Also, there is a need to keep data/information secret from unauthorized users that want to have access to it, so just the right people can access it.
- It is used as an attempt to prevent the unauthorized disclosure of message contents. When information is read or copied by someone not authorized to do so, the result is known as loss of confidentiality.
- For some types of information confidentiality is a very important attribute. Examples include research data, medical and insurance records, new product specifications, and corporate investment strategies.
- Loss of confidentiality can occur in many ways such as through the intentional release of private company information.

Example in Real Life:

- Consider that there are two people interacting via an email (encrypted) they know the decryption keys of each other and they read the email by entering these keys into the email program.
- If someone else can read these decryption keys when they are entered into the program, then the confidentiality of that email is compromised.
- Consider user A sends message to user B. Other user C gets access to this message which is not desired; hence it leads to loss of confidentiality. When user C access message without permission of A and B, This type of attack is called as Interception.

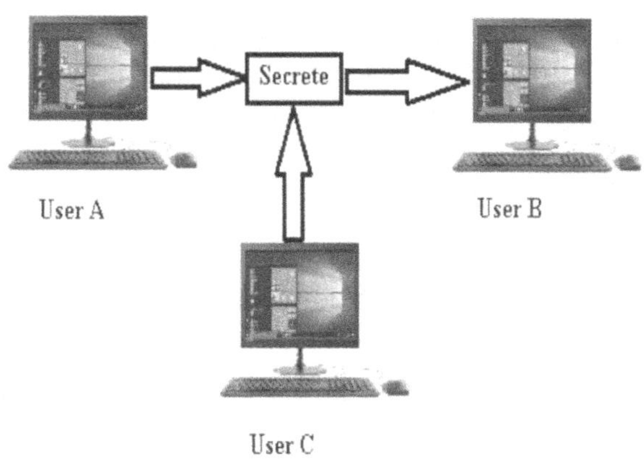

Fig. 1.1: Loss of Confidentiality

2. Integrity: [S-16]

- Integrity refers to the trustworthiness of data or resources, in terms of preventing improper or unauthorized change/modification.
- It means unauthorized person are not allowed to make modifications to data. It means ensuring that information remains unaltered. Only authorized person can edit or change information.
- It includes two variations of integrity as "data integrity" - that data have not been changed inappropriately, whether by accidentally harmful action.
- It also includes "origin" or "source integrity"- that the data actually came from the person or entity we think it did, rather than an unauthorized person.

- Information can be corrupted when it is present on an insecure network. When information is modified in unexpected ways, the result is known as loss of integrity. This means that unauthorized changes are made to information whether by human error.

Example in Real Life:

- Consider online payment system in which user A want to send 100 USD to user B, but information is modified without permission of user A.
- User C can make changes in information by sending 1000 USD to user B. So information is modified hence integrity is loosed.

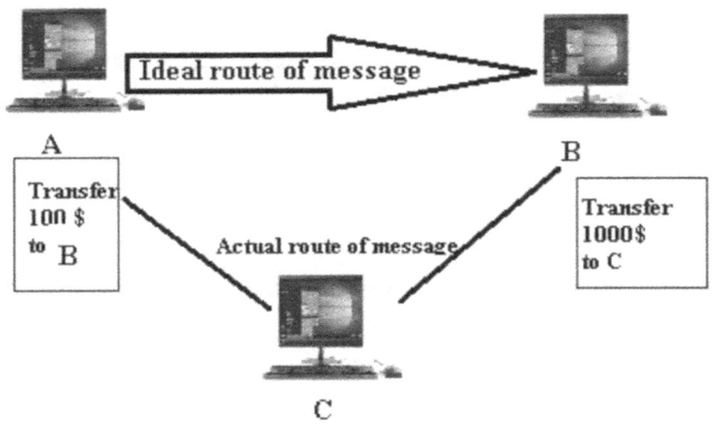

Fig. 1.2: Loss of Integrity

3. **Availability:**

- Availability refers to the ability to access data of a resource when it is needed to authorized person/users. Only authorized individual can create or change information.
- The concept of availability ensures the reliable and timely access to data or by the authorised person. Availability guarantees that the systems are up and running when they are needed.
- Information can be erased or become unavailable, resulting in loss of availability. This means that people who are authorized to get information cannot get what they need.
- To make information available to those who need it and who can be trusted with it, organizations use authentication and authorization.

Example in Real Life:

- Consider hacker has hacked web server of a bank and put it down. We as an authenticated user want to perform an e-banking transfer but it is difficult to access it, the undone transfer is a money lost for the bank.
- Consider user A is authorized user and he wants to access data from server computer B. Due to the intentional actions of unauthorized user C, an authorized user A cannot be able to access server computer B. This would breach the concept of availability, hence such type of attack is called as Interruption.

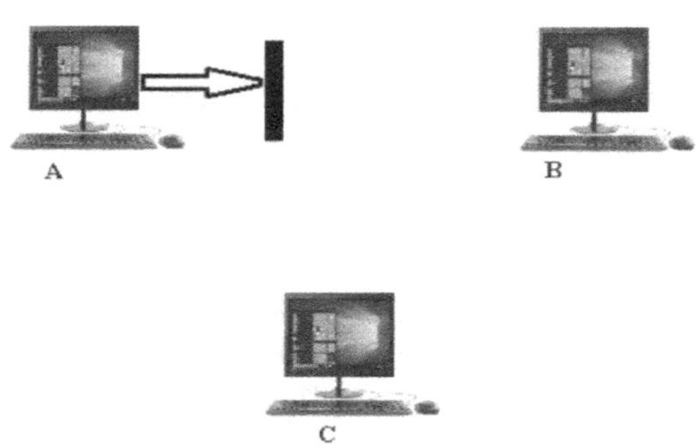

Fig. 1.3: Loss of Availability

4. **Non-Repudiation:**

- Security is strong when the means of authentication cannot later be contradicted the user cannot later deny that he or she performed the activity. This is known as non-repudiation.
- There are some situations where a user sends a message and later on he refuses that she/he had sent that message. Principle of non-repudiation defeats such possibilities of denying something, having done it.

Example:

- Consider user A sends fund transfer request to bank B using internet. After bank performs the fund transfer as per user A's requirement.
- A could claim that she/he never sent the fund transfer instruction to the bank. Thus A repudiates her fund transfer instruction.

Fig. 1.4: Non Repudiation

5. **Accountability:**

- Accountability is an essential part of an information security plan. It means that every individual who works with an information system should have specific responsibilities for information assurance.
- The tasks for which an individual is responsible are part of the overall information security plan and can be readily measurable by a person who has managerial responsibility for information assurance.

Example:

- Consider policy statement in any organization that all employees must avoid installing outside software on a company-owned information infrastructure.
- The person in charge of information security should perform periodic checks to be certain that the policy is being followed. Individuals must be aware of what is expected of them and guide continual improvement.

6. **Reliability:**

- Reliability is an attribute of any computer-related component (software, hardware or a network) that consistently performs according to its specifications. Reliability is the property of leading to consistent intended behavior and results.
- Reliability is also defined as the property of trustworthiness. Data are frequently considered reliable when they are exact and precise, and when they can be reproduced.
- It has been long considered one of three related attributes that must be considered when making, buying, or using a computer product or component.
- Reliability, availability, and serviceability considered to be important aspects to design into any system. If we say product is Reliable then that product is totally free from technical errors. Vendors frequently express a product's reliability quotient as a percentage.
- For example, IBM's z/OS (an operating system for their S/390 server series), has a reputation for reliability because it evolved from a long line of earlier MVS and OS/390 operating system versions.

1.2 RISK AND THREAT ANALYSIS

- A risk is any event or action that could cause a loss or damage to computer hardware, software data/information or processing capability.
- Threat analysis is the analysis of probability of occurrences and consequences of damaging actions/ events to a system. Threat analysis identifies possible threats in computer security process.
- In this section we will study risk and threat analysis.

1.2.1 Assets [S-17, 18, 19]

- In information security, computer security and network security, an asset is any data, device, or other component of the environment that supports information-related activities.
- Assets generally include hardware (e.g. servers and switches), software (e.g. mission critical applications and support systems) and confidential information.
- Assets should be protected from illicit access, use, disclosure, alteration, destruction and/or theft, resulting in loss to the organization.
- A system resources or assets of a computer system can be categorized as follows:
  1. **Hardware** including computer systems and other data processing, data storage and data communications devices.
  2. **Software** including the operating system, system utilities and applications.
  3. **Data** including files and databases, as well as security related data, such as password files.
  4. **Communications Facilities and Networks,** Local and Wide Area Network (LAN and WAN) communication links, bridges, routers, and so on.

Threats and Assets in Computer Security:

1. Hardware:

- A major threat to computer system hardware is the threat to availability. Hardware is the most vulnerable to attack and the least susceptible to automated controls.
- Threat include accidental and deliberate damage to equipment as well as theft. The proliferation of personal computers and workstation and the widespread use of LANs increase the potential for losses in this area.
- Theft of CD-ROM and DVDs can lead to loss of confidentiality. Physical and administrative security measure are needed to deal with these threats.

2. Software:

- Software includes the operating system, utilities and application programs. A key threat to software is an attack on availability.
- Software, especially application software, is often easy to delete. Software can also be altered or damaged to render it useless. Careful software configuration management, which includes making backups of the most recent reversion of software can maintain high availability.
- Computer viruses and related attacks fall into software category. A last problem is protection against software piracy. Although certain counter measures are available by and large problem of unauthorized copying of software has not been solved.

3. Communication Lines and Networks:

- Network security attacks can he classified as passive attacks and active attacks.
- A passive attack attempts to learn or make use of information from the system but does not affect system resources. An active attack attempts to alter system resources or affect their operation.

4. Data:

- Security concerns with respect to data are broad, encompassing availability, secrecy and integrity. In the case of availability, the concern is with the destruction of data files, which can occur either accidentally or maliciously.
- The obvious concern with secrecy is the unauthorized reading of data files or databases and this area has been the subject of perhaps more research and effort than any other area of computer security.

1.2.2 Vulnerability [S-18, 19]

- Vulnerability is a flaw in a system's design, implementation or operation and management that could be exploited to violate the system's security policy.

- A security vulnerability is a weakness/flaw (e.g., a flaw or a hole) in an application, product, or asset that makes it infeasible to prevent an attacker from gaining privileges on the organizations system, compromising data on it, modifying its operation, or assuming non-granted trust.
- Vulnerability is a security weakness in a computer system that permits unauthorized access. For example, an Internet browser could have a vulnerability that crashes the browser or allows someone to read or copy files from our computer when we visit their site.
- A vulnerability is a weakness which can be exploited by a threat actor, such as an attacker, to perform unauthorized actions within a computer system.
- A threat actor or malicious actor is a person or entity that is responsible for an event or incident that impacts or has the potential to impact the safety or security of another entity.
- To exploit vulnerability, an attacker must have at least one applicable tool or technique that can connect to a system weakness.
- In the context of security, concern is with the vulnerabilities of system resources lists the following general categories of vulnerabilities of a computer system or network asset:
  1. It can be **corrupted**, so that it does the wrong thing or gives wrong answers. For example, stored data values may differ from what they should be because they have been improperly modified.
  2. It can become **leaky**. For example, someone who should not have access to some or all of the information available through the network obtains such access.
  3. It can become **unavailable** or **very slow**. That is, using the system or network becomes impossible or impractical.
- These three general types of vulnerability correspond to the concepts of integrity, confidentiality, and availability.

1.2.3 Threats

- A threat is a potential violation of security. The violation need not actually occur for there to be a threat.
- The fact that the violation might occur means that those actions that could cause it to occur must be guarded against, (or prepared for). Those actions are called attacks. Those who execute such actions, or cause them to be executed, are called attackers.
- The three security services are confidentiality, integrity and availability – counter threats to the security of a system.
- A threat is a potential for violation of security which exists when there is a circumstance, capability, action, or event that could breach security and cause harm. That is a threat is a possible danger that might exploit a vulnerability.
- Corresponding to the various types of vulnerabilities to a system resource are threats that are capable of exploiting those vulnerabilities. A threat represents a potential security harm to an asset.
- An attack is a threat that is carried out (threat action) and if successful leads to an undesirable violation of security or threat consequence. The agent carrying out the attack is referred to as an attacker or threat agent.
- We can distinguish two type of attacks:
  - **Active Attack:** An attempts to alter/change/modify system resources or affect their operation.
  - **Passive Attack:** An attempts to learn or make use of information from the system that not affect system resources.
- We can also classify attacks based on the origin of the attack. They are:
  1. **Inside Attack:** Initiated by an entity inside the security perimeter (an "insider"). The inside is authorized to access system resources but uses them in a way not approved by those who granted the authorization.

2. **Outside Attack:** Initiated from outside the perimeter, by an unauthorized or illegitimate user of the system (an "outsider"). On the Internet, potential outside attackers range from amateur pranksters to organized criminals, international terrorists, and hostile governments.

1.2.4 Risk [S-16, 17, 18, 19, W-18]

- Risk is the possibility of something adverse happening. Risks is any event or action that could cause a loss of or damage to computer hardware, software, data, information, or processing capability.
- Risk is an expectation of loss expressed as the probability that a particular threat will exploit a particular vulnerability with a particular harmful result.
- A computer security risk is anything that can negatively affect confidentiality, integrity or availability of data.
- Examples of computer security risks would be misconfigured software, unpatched operating systems, and unsafe habits that cause vulnerabilities.
- Risk analysis is important in any organization. We can define risk as follows:

  Risk $=$ Assets $\times$ Threats $\times$ Vulnerabilities

- In above definition:
  - **Assets:** It is a resource, process or product and so on, something that is important for organization.
  - **Threats:** Person or thing likely to cause damage or danger. For example, Fire, earthquake, attack on website by human
  - **Vulnerability:** It is the absence or weakness of safeguards.
  - **Safeguard**: Protection mechanism to reduce the risk.
  - **Exposure:** It is loss due to the risk.

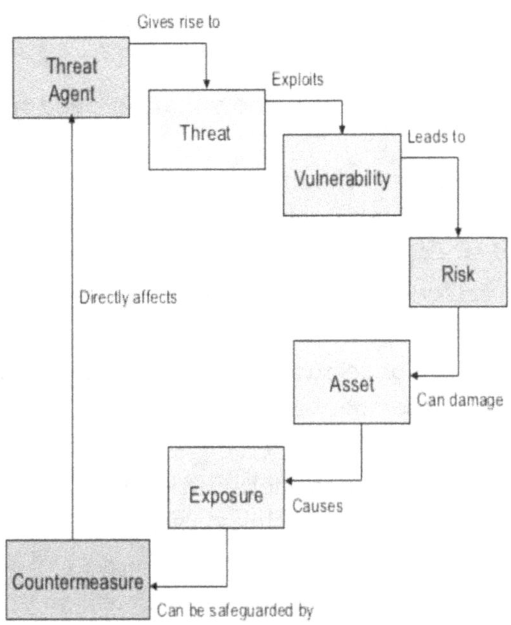

Fig. 1.5: Risk and Threat Analysis

1.2.5 Risk Analysis (Risk Management)

- Risk is potential of losing something of value. Risk analysis is the process of examining a system and its operational context to determine possible exposures and the possible harm they can cause.
- A security risk analysis is a procedure for estimating the risk to computer related assets and loss because of manifested threats.
- A security risk analysis defines the current environment and makes recommended corrective actions if the residual risk is unacceptable. Risk analysis is a vital part of any ongoing security and risk management program.

- Risk analysis refers to the review of risks associated with the particular action or event. The risk analysis is applied to information technology, projects, security issues and any other event where risks may be analysed based on a quantitative and qualitative basis.
- Risk Analysis includes following three main stages:
  1. Assets evaluation
  2. Analysis of threats and vulnerabilities
  3. Selection of safeguard.
- Risk can be calculated by Risk Analysis (RA) and it is the identification and estimation of risks.
- There are two fundamental types/approaches of risk analysis namely, Quantitative Risk Analysis and Qualitative Risk Analysis.

1. Quantitative Risk Analysis: [W-16]

- A process for assigning a numeric value to the probability of loss based on known risks, on financial values of the assets and on probability of threats.
- The objective of qualitative risk analysis is to assess and evaluate the characteristics of individually identified risk and then prioritize them based on the agreed-upon characteristics.
- It is used to determine potential direct and indirect costs to the company based on values assigned to company assets and their exposure to risk.
- For example, the cost of replacing an asset, the cost of lost productivity, or the cost of diminished brand reputation.

2. Qualitative Risk Analysis: [W-16]

- It is a collaborative process of assigning relative values to assets, assessing their risk exposure, and estimating the cost of controlling the risk.
- It differs from quantitative risk analysis in that it utilizes relative measures and approximate costs rather than precise valuation and cost determination.
- In qualitative risk analysis:
  (i) Assets can be rated based on criticality - very important, important, not-important etc.
  (ii) Vulnerabilities can be rated based on how it is fixed - fixed soon, should be fixed, fix if suitable etc.
  (iii) Threats can be rated based on scale of likely - likely, unlikely, very likely etc.

Benefits of Risk Analysis:

- Risk analysis can help an organization to improve their security in many ways. These are:
  1. Concerning financial and organizational impacts, it identifies, rate and compares the overall impact of risks related to the organization.
  2. It helps to identify gaps in information security and determine the next steps to eliminate the risks of security.
  3. It can also enhance the communication and decision-making processes related to information security.
  4. It improves security policies and procedures as well as develop cost-effective methods for implementing information security policies and procedures.
  5. It increases employee awareness about risks and security measures during the risk analysis process and understands the financial impacts of potential security risks.

Risk Management: [S-16]

- Risk management is the process of identification, analysis and either acceptance or mitigation of uncertainty in investment decision-making.
- Risk management is the process for identifying, assessing and prioritizing the risk of different kinds.

- Risk management is the keystone to an effective performance as well as for targeted, proactive solutions to potentials threats and incidents. Risk management is the ongoing process of identifying risk and implementing plans to address them
- Inadequate risk management can result in severe consequences for companies as well as individuals.

Examples of Risk Management:

1. **Fire:** Damage cause to a system due to fire in the premises where information is preserve.
2. **Flood:** Datacenter/Information hub gets affected due to flood. Recession that began in 2008 was largely caused by the loose credit risk management of financial firms.

Components of Risk Management:

- Risk management is an essential part of any project plan and project implementation. Without a thorough knowledge of possible risks, a project cannot be authorized.
- There are always risks at stake which could no doubt benefit the project, but could incur huge monetary losses. The most effective steps in a risk management are Risk Assessment and Risk Control.

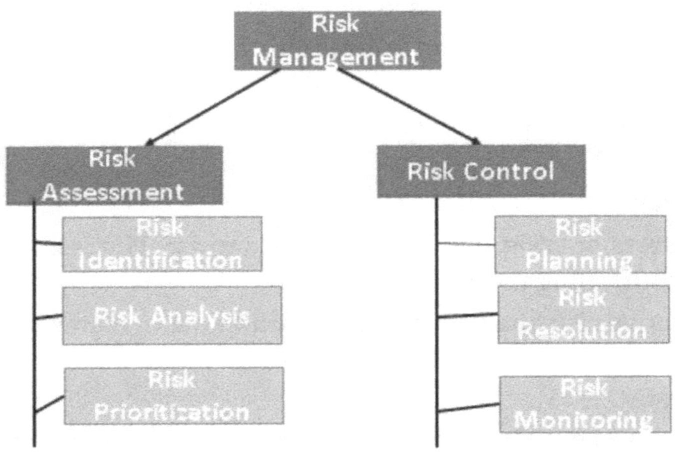

Fig. 1.6: Components of Risk Management

1. **Risk Assessment:**

- This process involves identifying and analyzing program areas and critical technical. Process risks to increase the cost, performance, and schedule objectives:
  (i) Risk Identification is the first step in the proactive risk management process. It is the process of examining the program areas and each critical technical process to identify and document the associated risk .
  (ii) Risk analysis is the process of defining and analyzing the dangers to individuals, businesses and government agencies posed by potential natural and human-caused adverse events. Risk Prioritization is the assigning priorities to different risk.
  (iii) For IT professionals it is necessary to identify the information assets of an organization - people, procedure, data and information, software, hardware, networking components etc. then classify and prioritize them.

2. **Risk Control:** [S-16]

- It is the processes of selecting and applying controls to decrease the risk of an organization's information system. There are following four strategies that can be used to control the risk.
  (i) Avoidance: Apply safeguards that eliminate or reduce residual risk.
  (ii) Transference: Transfer the risk to other assets, other processes or other organizations.
  (iii) Mitigation: Reduce the impact should the vulnerability be exploited..
  (iv) Acceptance: Understand the consequences and accept the risk without control or mitigation

- Risk control includes following steps:

  Step 1 : Risk Planning - deciding sequence of different risk to resolve.

  Step 2 : Selecting appropriate strategy.

  Step 3 : Risk monitoring - checking whether selected strategy for to handle risk is working or not.

1.2.6 Countermeasures [S-18]

- Security countermeasures are the controls used to protect the confidentiality, integrity, and availability of data and information systems.
- According to the Glossary by InfosecToday, the meaning of countermeasure is, 'the deployment of a set of security services to protect against a security threat'.
- Countermeasure is an action, device, procedure or technique that reduces a threat, a vulnerability or an attack by eliminating or preventing it, by minimizing the harm it can cause, or by discovering and reporting it so that corrective action can be taken.
- A threat is a potential for violation of security, which exists when there is a circumstance, capability, action, or event that could breach security and cause harm i.e., a threat is a possible danger enabling the exploitation of a vulnerability.
- A countermeasure is an action or method that is applied to prevent, avert or reduce potential threats to computers, servers, networks, Operating Systems (OS) or information systems (IS). Counter measure tools include anti-virus software and firewalls.
- Protective countermeasures may be in the form of hardware or software. Examples include:
  1. **Routers:** The most common hardware countermeasure is a router that can prevent the IP address of an individual computer from being directly visible on the Internet. A router also mask Internet Protocol (IP) addresses.
  2. **Anti-Virus and Anti-Spyware Applications/Softwares:** Protect against malicious software (malware), including viruses, Trojans and adware.
  3. **Behavioral Techniques:** Applied by users to deter threats, such as suspicious email attachments. Includes regular scanning for viruses and other malware, regular installation of updates and patches for operating systems, staying away from questionable web sites, refraining from opening e-mail messages and attachments from unknown senders and so on.
  4. **Firewalls:** Facilitate authorized network access.
  5. **Intrusion Detection Systems (IDS):** Prevent and/or block unauthorized system access.
  6. **Physical Security (especially in Enterprises):** Prevents hacking and network subterfuge.
  7. **SSL:** Provide security and privacy between clients and servers over the Internet.
  8. **Kerberos:** Kerberos is a network authentication protocol uses secret-key cryptography and facilitates single sign-on.
  9. **Secure Electronic Transmission (SET):** It is a protocol standard to allow users to make secure transactions over the Internet.

1.3 THREAT TO SECURITY [W-16, S-18]

- A computer system threat is that leads to loss or damage of data or physical damage to the hardware and/or infrastructure.
- Knowing how to identify computer security threats is the first step in protecting computer systems. The threats could be intentional, accidental or caused by natural disasters.
- Security threat is defined as, a risk that which can potentially damage computer systems and organization. The cause could be physical such as someone stealing a computer that contains vital data.
- The cause could also be non-physical such as a virus attack. In these tutorial series, we will define a threat as a potential attack from a hacker that can allow them to gain unauthorized access to a computer system.
- Several security threats are a viruses, worms etc.

1.3.1 Viruses [S-16, 17, 19, W-16, 17, 19]

- A computer virus is a type of computer program that, when executed, replicates itself by modifying other computer programs and inserting its own code.
- Virus is malicious software that attaches itself to other software and may damage software functionality when software executes. A computer virus is a self-replicating program that spreads by inserting copies of itself into other executable code.
- A virus is a computer code or program, which is capable of affecting the computer data or information by corrupting or destroying them.
- Computer virus has the tendency to make its copies and spread it across every folder and damage the data of your computer systems.
- Viruses can be triggered by specific events. This virus can cause the following to the computer:
  1. Delete important data from computer.
  2. Avoid detection by redirection of disk data.
  3. Perform tasks by triggering an event with itself. For example, this happens when in an infected computer pop-up tables etc., show up automatically on the screen.
  4. They are common in Windows and Mac OS because these operation systems do not have multiple file permissions and are more spread out.
  5. Access private data such as user id and passwords.
  6. Display annoying messages to the user.
  7. Corrupt data in the computer.
  8. Log the user's keystrokes.
  9. Viruses can be repaired and can be controlled by some good backup procedures.

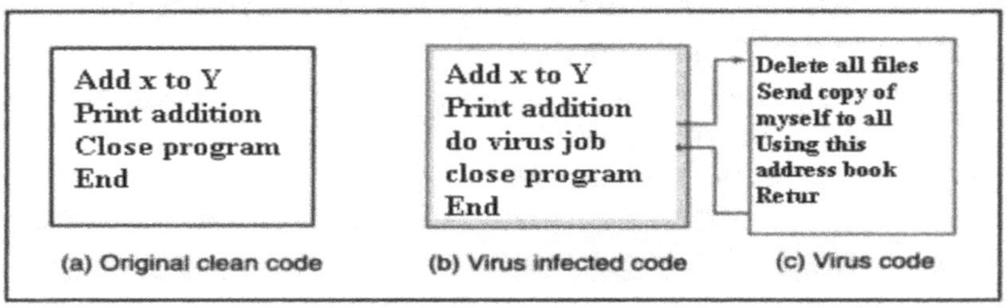

Fig. 1.7: Virus

1.3.1.1 Phases of Viruses [S-17, W-18, 19]

- Fig. 1.8 shows phases in viruses.
- During it lifetime, a virus goes through following four phases:

1. **Dormant Phase:**
   - In this phase virus remains idle
   - Virus gets activated depending on any event or action (for example, a user pressing a key or on a certain date and time etc.).
   - Not all viruses have this stage.
2. **Propagation Phase:**
   - The virus starts propagating, that is multiplying itself.
   - A piece of code copies itself and each copy starts copying more copies hence in Propagating phase.
3. **Triggering Phase:**
   - A Dormant virus moves into this phase when it gets activated, that is, the event it was waiting for gets initialized.
   - The triggering phase can be caused by a variety of system events, including a count of the number of times that this copy of the virus has made copies of itself.

4. **Execution Phase:**
   - In this virus starts executing its function.
   - Function of virus may be destructive (deleting files on disk) or harmless (popping messages on screen).

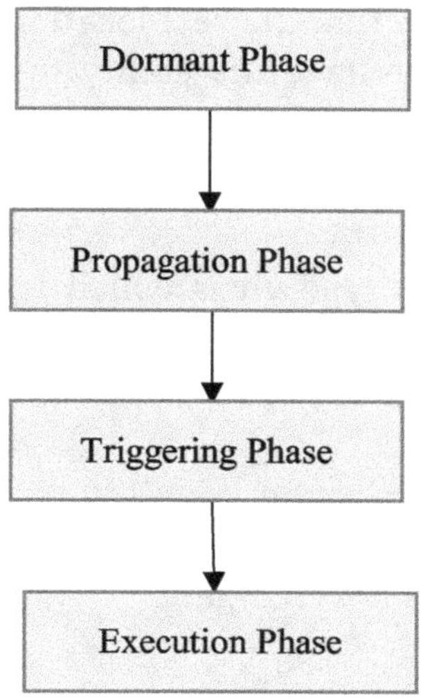

Fig. 1.8: Phases of Virus

1.3.1.2 Types of Viruses [W-16, 17]

- Computer viruses are classified according to their nature of infection and behavior. Different types of computer virus classification are given below:
  1. **File Virus:** This type of virus infects the system by attaching itself to the end of a file. It changes the start of a program so that the control jumps to its code. After the execution of its code, the control returns back to the main program. Its execution is not even noticed. It is also called parasitic virus because it leaves no file intact but also leaves the host functional.
  2. **Boot sector Virus:** It infects the boot sector of the system, executing every time system is booted and before operating system is loaded. It infects other bootable media like floppy disks. These are also known as memory virus as they do not infect file system.
  3. **Macro Virus:** Unlike most virus which are written in low-level language (like C or ALP), these are written in high-level language like Visual Basic. These viruses are triggered when a program capable of executing a macro is run. For example, macro virus can be contained in spreadsheet files.
  4. **Source Code Virus:** It looks for source code and modifies it to include virus and to help spread it.
  5. **Polymorphic Virus:** Polymorphic Viruses have the capability to change their appearance and change their code every time they infect a different system. This helps the Polymorphic Viruses to hide from anti-virus software
  6. **Encrypted Virus:** This viruses are in encrypted form. In order to avoid detection by antivirus, this type of virus exists in encrypted form. It carries a decryption algorithm along with it. So the virus first decrypts and then executes.
  7. **Stealth Virus:** It is a very tricky virus as it changes the code that can be used to detect it. Hence, the detection of virus becomes very difficult. For example, it can change the read system call such that whenever user asks to read a code modified by virus, the original form of code is shown rather than infected code.
  8. **Tunneling Virus:** This virus attempts to bypass detection by antivirus scanner by installing itself in the interrupt handler chain. Interception programs, which remain in the background of an operating system and catch viruses, become disabled during the course of a tunneling virus. Similar viruses install themselves in device drivers.

9. **Multipartite Virus:** This type of virus is able to infect multiple parts of a system including boot sector, memory and files. This makes it difficult to detect and contain.
10. **Armored Virus:** Armored Viruses are type of viruses that are designed and written to make itself difficult to detect or analyze. It uses a variety of techniques to do so like fooling antivirus to believe that it lies somewhere else than its real location or using compression to complicate its code. An Armored Virus may also have the ability to protect itself from antivirus programs, making it more difficult to disinfect.
11. **Multiple Characteristic Viruses:** Multiple Characteristic viruses has different characteristics of viruses and have different capabilities.
12. **Retrovirus:** Retrovirus is another type virus which tries to attack and disable the anti-virus application running on the computer. A retrovirus can be considered anti-antivirus. Some Retroviruses attack the anti-virus application and stop it from running or some other destroys the virus definition database.
13. **Overwrite Virus:** Overwrite virus is the simplest computer virus. It overwrites the code of infected file with its own malicious code. The content of infected file is replaced partially or completely but the size of file does not change.

1.3.2 Dealing with Viruses [S-16]

- There are various ways to deal with virus. Viruses can be repaired and can be controlled by some good backup procedures.
- Preventing viruses is the best option. However, it is almost impossible to prevent them altogether with the world connected to the Internet all the time.
- We have to accept that viruses will attack and would need to find ways to deal with them. Hence, we can attempt to detect, identify and remove viruses. This is shown in Fig. 1.9.
- **Detection** of viruses involves locating the virus, having known that a virus has attacked. Then we need to **identify** the specific virus that has attacked. Finally, we need to **remove** it.
- For this, we need to remove all traces of the virus and restore the affected programs/files to their original states. This is done by anti-virus software.

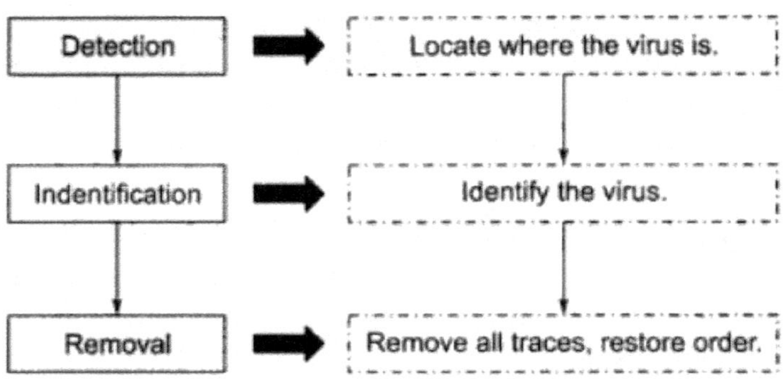

Fig. 1.9: Virus Elimination Steps

1.3.2.1 Indications that System is Infected with a Computer Virus

- A virus is malicious software designed to destroy or damage data files, operating systems and more and it is designed to replicate itself and spread throughout the Internet.
- The following are indications that a computer might be infected by a virus:
  1. The computer takes a long time to start.
  2. The computer experiences frequent crashes, or shutdown and error messages.
  3. The computer behaves inappropriately, such as not responding to clicks or opening files on its own.
  4. The computer's hard drive is acting strangely.

5. E-mail is corrupted.
6. The amount of storage on the computer is reduced.
7. Files and other data on the computer have gone missing.

1.3.2.2 How to Prevent Computer Viruses?

- The following measures can help prevent a virus infection:
  1. Install current anti-virus and anti-spyware software and keep it up to date.
  2. Run daily scans of anti-virus software.
  3. Disable auto run to prevent viruses from propagating to any media connected to the system.
  4. Regularly patch the operating system and applications installed on the computer.
  5. Don't click on web links sent via e-mail.
  6. Don't download files from the Internet or e-mail.
  7. Install a hardware-based firewall.

1.3.2.3 How to Remove a Computer Virus?

- To remove a virus from a computer, do the following:
  1. Enter Safe Mode, (the process for doing so will depend on the version of Windows we are running).
  2. Delete temporary files. While in Safe Mode, use the Disk Cleanup tool to delete Temporary Files.
  3. Download any a real-time virus scanner.
  4. Run the on-demand scanner followed by the real-time scanner. If neither scanner removes the virus, then it might need to be removed manually. This should only be done by an expert who is experienced at using Windows Registry and knows how to view and delete system and program files
  5. Reinstall any files or programs damaged by the virus.

1.3.3 Worms [S-16, W-16, 18]

- A computer worm is self-replicating malware that duplicates itself to spread to uninfected computers.
- A computer worm is a type of malicious software program whose primary function is to infect other computers while remaining active on infected systems.
- A computer worm is self-replicating malware that duplicates itself to spread to uninfected computers.
- Worms often use parts of an operating system that are automatic and invisible to the user. It is common for worms to be noticed only when their uncontrolled replication consumes system resources, slowing or halting other tasks.
- In contrast, a computer worm is stand-alone programming that does not need to copy itself to a host program or require human interaction to spread.
- An attacker may use a worm to accomplish the following tasks:
  1. Install backdoors on the victim's computers.
  2. Worms may also slowdown the network by consuming the bandwidth as they replicate
  3. Install harmful payload code carried within the worm.
- Worm is a self-contained program that spreads to other systems; whereas a virus spreads to programs within the same system.

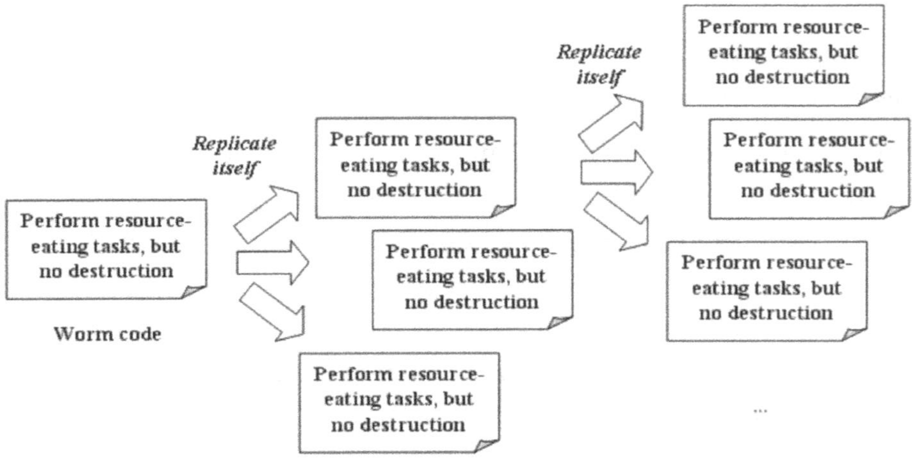

Fig. 1.10: Structure of a Worm

1.3.4 Trojan Horse

- Trojan horse is a program that allows the attack to control the user's computer from a remote location.
- A Trojan horse is a hidden piece of code like virus. A Trojan horse allows an attacker to obtain some confidential information about a computer or a network.
- The program is usually disguised as something that is useful to the user. Once the user has installed the program, it has the ability to install malicious payloads, create backdoors, install other unwanted applications that can be used to compromise the user's computer, etc.
- Following are the activities that the attacker can perform using a Trojan horse:
  1. Damage the user's computer (crashing, blue screen of death, etc.).
  2. Steal sensitive data such as passwords, credit card information, etc.
  3. Modifying users data.
  4. Unauthorized money transfer transactions.
  5. Viewing the users' screenshot.
  6. Downloading browsing history data.
- In a similar fashion a Trojan horse could silently sit in the code for a Login screen by attaching itself to it.
- When the user enters the user id and password, the Trojan horse could capture these details and send this information to the attacker without the knowledge of the user who had entered the id and password.
- The attacker can then merrily use the user id and password to gain access to the system. This is shown in Fig. 1.11.

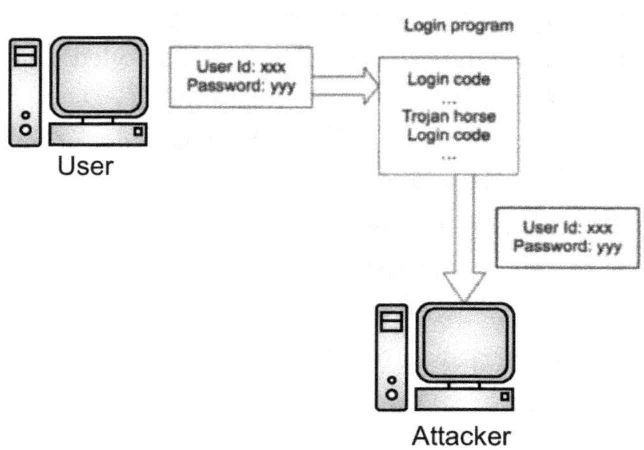

Fig. 1.11: Trojan Horse

Difference between Virus, Worms and Trojan Horse:

Sr. No.	Basis For Comparison	Virus	Worm	Trojan Horse
1.	Meaning	Virus is a malicious software that attaches itself to other software and may damage software functionality when software executes.	A computer worm is self-replicating malware that duplicates itself to spread to uninfected computers.	Trojan horse is a program that allows the attack to control the user's computer from a remote location.
2.	Execution	Depends on the transfer of a file.	Replicates itself without any human action.	Downloaded as software and executed.
3.	Replication occurs	Yes	Yes	No
4.	Remotely controlled	No	Yes	Yes
5.	Rate of spreading	Moderate	Faster	Slow
6.	Infection	Initiates by attaching a virus to an executable file.	Utilizes system or application weaknesses.	Attaches itself to a program and interpret as useful software.
7.	Purpose	Modification of the information.	Halt the CPU and memory.	Steals the user's information

1.3.5 Intruders [S-18, 19, W-16, 19]

- An Intruder is a person who attempts to gain unauthorized access to a system, to damage that system, or to disturb data on that system.
- Intruder attempts to violate security by interfering with system availability, data integrity or data confidentiality.
- An intrusion is defined as the unauthorized use, misuse, or abuse of computer systems by either authorized users or external perpetrators.

1.3.6 Insiders [S-18, 19, W-16, 19]

- Insider is the person who belongs to the said organization and launches security threats and attacks from inside.
- An insider attack is a malicious attack perpetrated on a network or computer system by a person with authorized system access.
- An insider threat is a malicious threat to an organization that comes from people within the organization, such as employees, former employees, contractors or business associates, who have inside information concerning the organization's security practices, data and computer systems.
- The threat may involve fraud, the theft of confidential or commercially valuable information, the theft of intellectual property, or the sabotage of computer systems.
- The insider threat comes in three categories:
  1. **Malicious insiders**, which are people who take advantage of their access to inflict harm on an organization;

2. **Negligent insiders,** which are people who make errors and disregard policies, which place their organizations at risk;
3. **Infiltrators,** who are external actors that obtain authorized access to the credentials without authorization.

1.4 TYPE OF ATTACKS [S-17, W-16, 17, 18]

- An attack is an information security threat that involves an attempt to obtain, alter, destroy, remove, implant or reveal information without authorized access or permission.
- An attack is any attempt to expose, alter, disable, destroy, steal or gain unauthorized access to or make unauthorized use of an asset.
- An attack can be defined as, any kind of malicious activity that attempts to collect, disrupt, deny, degrade, or destroy information system resources or the information itself.
- Security attacks include interruption (i.e., an asset is destroyed or becomes unavailable), interception (this happens when an unauthorized party gains access to an asset), modification, and fabrication (particularly visible when an unauthorized party inserts counterfeit objects such as messages or files).
- Attacks are typically categorized based on the action performed by the attacker. An attack can be passive or active, (See Fig. 1.12).
- Active attack attempts to alter system resources or affect their operation. A passive attack attempts to learn (observing) or make use of information from the system but does not affect system resources (e.g., wiretapping).

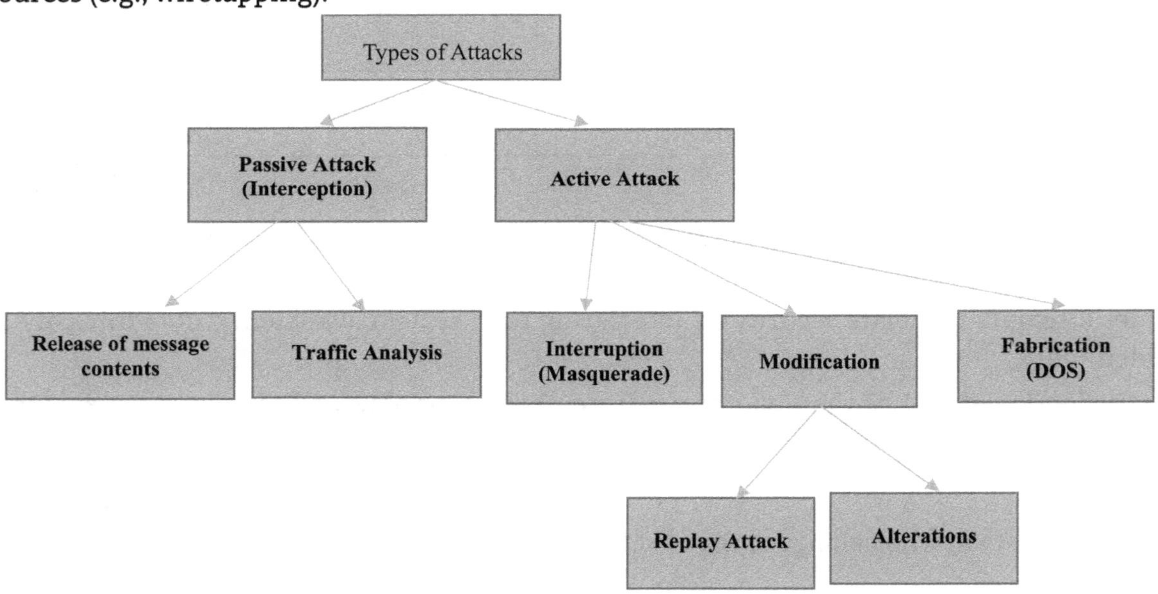

Fig. 1.12: Types of Attack

1.4.1 Passive Attacks [S-17, W-18]

- A passive attack is designed to monitor and record network activity in an attempt to collect information to be used later in an active attack.
- Passive attacks are in the nature of eavesdropping on or monitoring of, transmissions. The goal of the attacker is to obtain information that is being transmitted. This type of attack does not involve modification of data of original message and is often seen as stealing information.
- Passive attacks are harder to detect because attacker does not attempt to perform any modification to the data. Thus, the general approach to deal with passive attacks is to think about prevention, rather than detection or corrective actions.

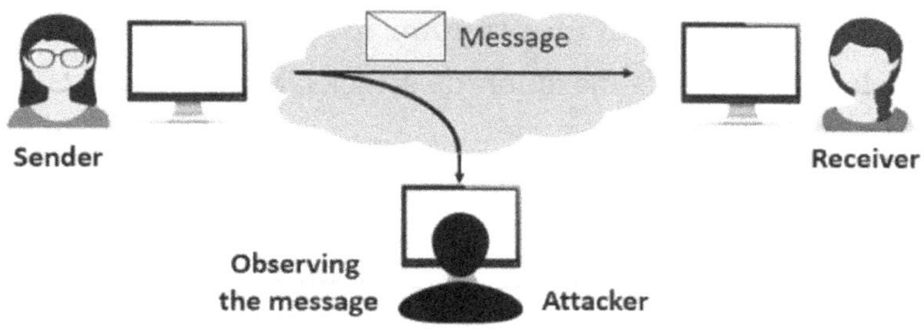

Fig. 1.13: Passive Attack

- This type of attacks is harder to detect. This type of attack can be classified into two types as Release of message contents and Traffic analysis.
  1. **Release of Message Contents**: When we send any confidential email message to our friend we desire that only he/she be able to access it. Otherwise, the contents of message are released against our wishes to someone else. Using certain security procedures we can prevent release of message content.
  2. **Traffic Analysis:** When two persons are communicating to each other using code language so that only communicating person knows the code language to encode and decode the message. Attacker can try to find out the pattern of code language and decode the message such type of attack is called as Traffic analysis attack.
- Passive attacks can be prevented rather than detection and corrective action. For example, actions such as intercepting and eavesdropping on the communication network can be considered as passive attack.

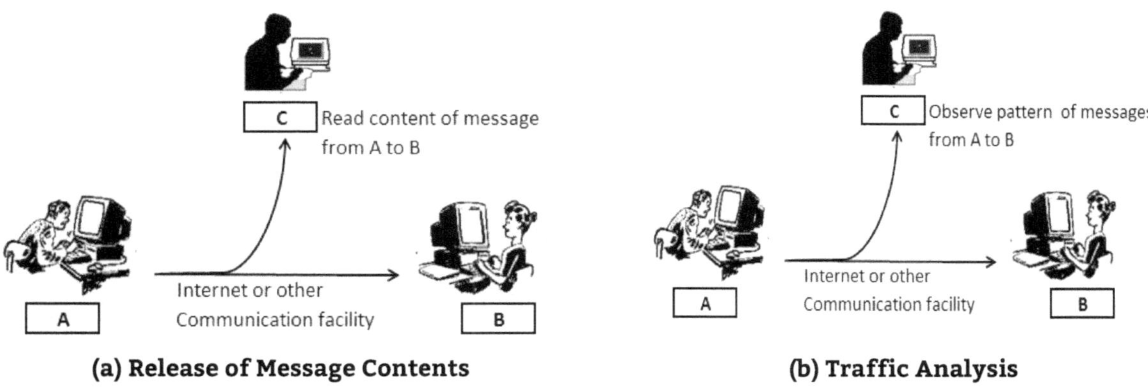

Fig. 1.14

1.4.2 Active Attack **[S-17, W-18]**

- An active attack involves changing the information in some way by conducting some Process on the information.
- Active attacks are the attacks in which the attacker tries to modify the information or creates a false message. Alteration/modification attack involves some change to the original message. Active attacks cannot be prevented easily.

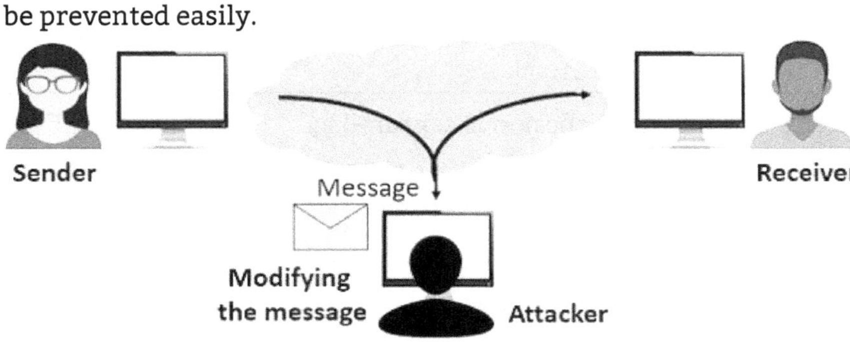

Fig. 1.15: Active Attack

- This type of attacks can be in the form of interruption, modification, fabrication as explained below:
  1. **Interruption attacks** are called as masquerade attacks. Masquerade attacks are caused when an unauthorized user pretends to be other user.
  2. **Modification attacks** can be classified into replay attacks and alteration of messages.
  3. In **replay attacks** user captures a sequence of events and resend them. For example, user P wants to transfer money to user R. Both user P and R have accounts with bank B. User P send message to bank B, requesting for fund transfer. User R could capture this message and send copy of the same to bank Bank B would have no idea that this is unauthorized user and consider it as other request from user P. So that user R would get benefit of this fund transfer. This is called as replay attack.

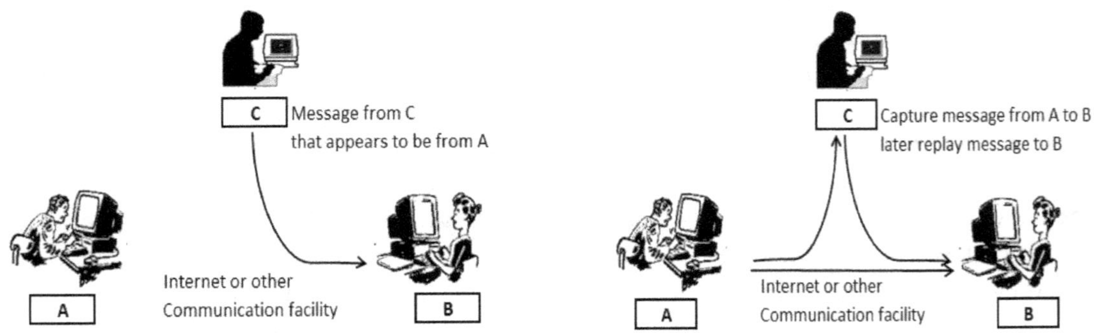

(a) Masquerade **(b) Replay**

Fig. 1.16: Active Attack

Comparison between Active Attack and Passive Attack:

Sr. No.	Basis for Comparison	Active Attack	Passive Attack
1.	Basic	Active attack tries to change the system resources or affect their operation.	Passive attack tries to read or make use of information from the system but does not influence system resources.
2.	Modification in the information	Occurs.	Does not take place.
3.	Harm to the system	Always causes damage to the system.	Do not cause any harm.
4.	Threat to	Integrity and availability.	Confidentiality.
5.	Attack awareness	The entity (victim) gets informed about the attack.	The entity is unaware of the attack.
6.	Task performed by the attacker	The transmission is captured by physically controlling the portion of a link.	Just need to observe the transmission.
7.	Emphasis is on	Detection.	Prevention.
8.	Examples	Masquerade, Replay etc.	Release of message contents, traffic analysis etc.

1.4.3 Denial of Service [W-17, 19]

- A Denial of Service (DoS) attack is a malicious attempt to make a server or a network resource unavailable to users by temporarily interrupting the services of a host connected to the Internet.
- A DoS attack is characterized by using a single computer to launch the attack. DoS attacks typically function by flooding a targeted machine with the useless traffic requests until normal traffic is unable to be processed, resulting in denial-of-service to addition users.
- A DoS is any type of attack where the attackers (hackers) attempt to prevent authentic users from accessing the service.
- In a DoS attack, the attacker usually sends excessive messages asking the network or server to authenticate requests that have invalid return addresses.

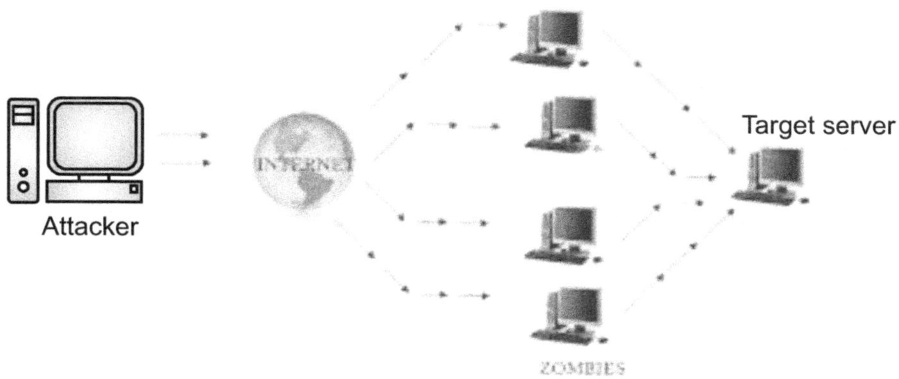

Fig. 1.17: Denial of Service Attack

- A SYN flood is a form of denial-of-service attack in which an attacker sends a succession of SYN requests to a target's system in an attempt to consume enough server resources to make the system unresponsive to legitimate traffic. [W-16]
- Normally when a client attempts to start a TCP connection to a server, the client and server exchange a series of messages which normally runs like this:
  1. The client requests a connection by sending a SYN (synchronize) message to the server.
  2. The server acknowledges this request by sending SYN-ACK back to the client.
  3. The client responds with an ACK, and the connection is established.
- This is called the TCP three-way handshake, and is the foundation for every connection established using the TCP protocol. A SYN flood attack works by not responding to the server with the expected ACK code.
- The malicious client can either simply not send the expected ACK, or by spoofing the source IP address in the SYN, causing the server to send the SYN-ACK to a falsified IP address – which will not send an ACK because it "knows" that it never sent a SYN.

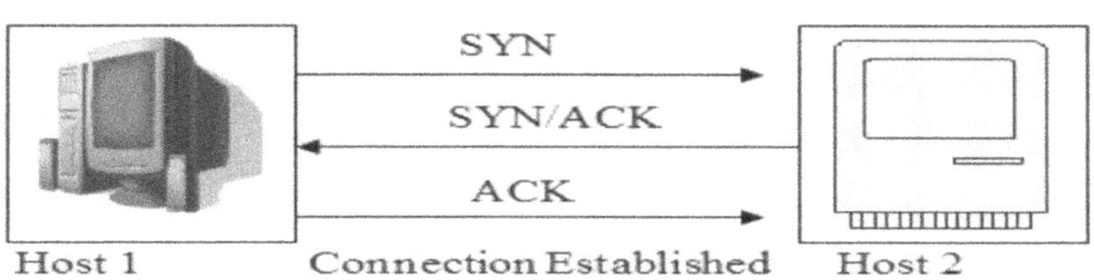

(a) Typical Connection

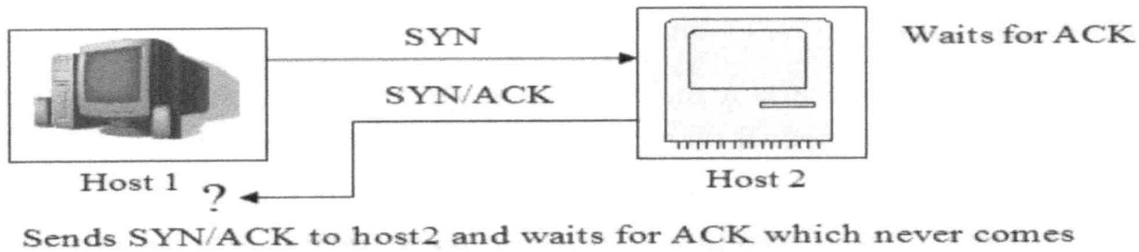

(b) "Denial of Service" Attack

Fig. 1.18

1.4.4 Distributed DoS [S-16, W-17]

- Distributed denial of service attack is the distributed version of DoS. A Distributed Denial of Service (DDoS) attack is a malicious attempt to interrupt normal traffic of a targeted server, service or network by overwhelming the target or its surrounding infrastructure with a flood of Internet traffic.
- DDoS attacks achieve effectiveness by utilizing multiple compromised computer systems as sources of attack traffic.
- A DDoS attack requires an attacker to gain control of a network of online machines in order to carry out an attack.
- Computers and other machines (such as IoT devices) are infected with malware, turning each one into a bot (or zombie). The attacker then has remote control over the group of bots, which is called a botnet.
- Once, a botnet has been established, the attacker is able to direct the machines by sending updated instructions to each bot via a method of remote control.
- When the IP address of a victim is targeted by the botnet, each bot will respond by sending requests to the target, potentially causing the targeted server or network to overflow capacity, resulting in a denial of service to normal traffic.
- Because each bot is a legitimate Internet device, separating the attack traffic from normal traffic can be difficult.
- Distributed denial-of-service attacks target websites and online services. The aim is to overwhelm them with more traffic than the server or network can accommodate.
- The primary way a DDoS is accomplished is through a network of remotely controlled, hacked computers or bots. These are often referred to as "zombie computers." They form what is known as a "botnet" or network of bots.

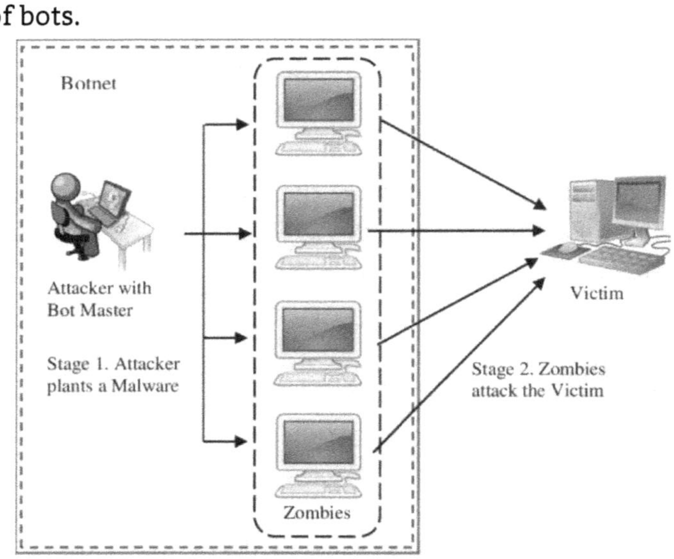

Fig. 1.19: Distributed DDoS

1.4.5 Backdoors [W-17]

- A backdoor is a technique in which a system security mechanism is bypassed undetectably to access a computer or its data.
- The backdoor access method is sometimes written by the programmer who develops a program. A backdoor is also known as a trapdoor.
- A developer may create a backdoor so that an application or operating system can be accessed for troubleshooting. However, attackers often use backdoors that they detect or install themselves as part of an exploit.
- Backdoors can vary widely. For example, Backdoors are put in place by authentic vendors, while others are introduced unintentionally as a result of programming errors.
- Developers sometimes use backdoors during the development process, which are then not removed from production code.
- Backdoors are also commonly put into place through malware. A malware module may act as a backdoor itself, or it can act as a first-line backdoor, which means that it acts as a staging platform for downloading other malware modules that are designed to perform the actual attack.
- Fig. 1.20 shows how a backdoor attack can be used to bypass the security of a network. In this example, the attacker is using a backdoor program to utilize resources or steal information.

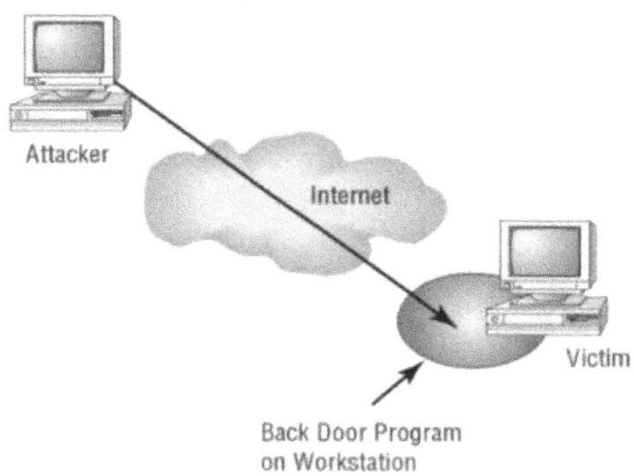

Fig. 1.20: A Backdoor Attack in Progress

- A backdoor attack is usually either an access or modification attack. A number of tools exist to create backdoor attacks on systems. One of the more popular is Back Orifice. Another popular backdoor program is NetBus.

1.4.6 Trapdoors [W-17]

- A trapdoor is a secret entry point into a program that allows someone that is aware of the trapdoor to gain access without going through the usual security access procedures.
- Trapdoors have been used reasonably for many years by programmers to debug and test programs. Trapdoors become threats when they are used by unintended programmers to gain unauthorized access.
- It is difficult to implement operating system controls for trapdoors. Security measures must focus on the program development and software update activities.
- A trapdoors in a computer system is a method of bypassing normal authentication, securing remote access to a computer, obtaining access to plaintext, and so on, while attempting to remain undetected.
- A Trapdoor or Backdoor is a secret means of access to a computer program that bypasses security mechanisms.
- The trapdoors may take the form of installed software. A trapdoor is a security risk when unscrupulous programmers use them to gain unauthorized access.

Example:

- Sort of trapdoors are used as a plot device/ new browser versions to suppress the starvation due to workload on browser

1.4.7 A Man-in-the-Middle Attack [W-16, 18, S-19]

- It is a type of attack where a unauthorized user inserts him/herself into a conversation between two parties, impersonates both parties and gains access to information that the two parties were trying to send to each other.
- A man-in-the-middle attack allows unauthorized actor to interrupt, send and receive data meant for someone else, or not meant to be sent at all, without either outside party knowing until it is too late.
- Man-in-the-middle attacks can be abbreviated in many ways, including MITM, MitM, MiM or MIM.
- A MITM attack exploits the real-time processing of transactions, conversations or transfer of other data.

Example:

- In the following the attacker inserted him/herself in-between the flow of traffic between client and server.
- Now that the attacker has interrupted into the communication between the two endpoints, he/she can insert wrong information and interrupt the data transferred between them.

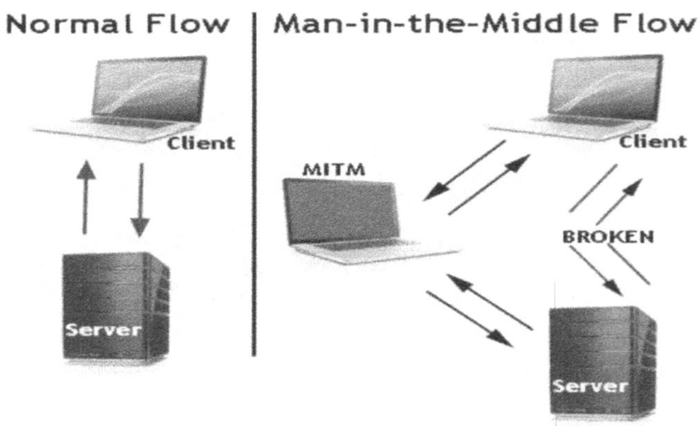

Fig. 1.21: Man-In-The-Middle (MITM) Attack

1.4.8 Spoofing [S-16, 17, 19, W-16, 17, 19]

- Spoofing is the act of disguising a communication from an unknown source as being from a known, trusted source.
- Spoofing can apply to emails, phone calls, and websites, or can be more technical, such as a computer spoofing an IP address, Address Resolution Protocol (ARP) or Domain Name System (DNS) etc.
- Spoofing is a technique used to gain unauthorized access to computers, whereby the attacker sends messages to a computer with an IP address indicating that the message is coming from a trusted host.
- A spoofing attack is when an unauthorized user copies behavior another device or user on a network in order to attacks against network hosts, steal data, spread malware or bypass access controls.
- A spoofing attack is an attempt by someone or something to masquerade as someone else. This type of attack is usually considered an access attack.
- A common spoofing attack that was popular for many years on early Unix and other timesharing systems involved a programmer writing a fake logon program. It would prompt the user for a user ID and password.

- No matter what the user typed, the program would indicate an invalid logon attempt and then transfer control to the real logon program. The spoofing program would write the logon and password into a disk file, which was retrieved later.
- There are several different types of spoofing attacks that unauthorized user can use to accomplish this. Some of the most common methods include IP address spoofing attacks. ARP spoofing attacks and DNS server spoofing attacks.
- The most popular spoofing attacks today are IP spoofing and DNS spoofing. With **IP spoofing**, the goal is to make the data look as if it came from a trusted host when it didn't (thus spoofing the IP address of the sending host). With **DNS spoofing**, the DNS server is given information about a name server that it thinks is legitimate when it isn't. This can send users to a website other than the one they wanted to go to, reroute mail, or do any other type of redirection wherein data from a DNS server is used to determine a destination.
- Fig. 1.22 shows a spoofing attack occurring as part of the logon process on a computer network. The attacker in this situation impersonates the server to the client attempting to log in.
- No matter what the client attempts to do, the impersonating system will fail the login. When this process is finished, the impersonating system disconnects from the client.
- The client then logs in to the legitimate server. In the meantime, the attacker now has a valid user ID and password.

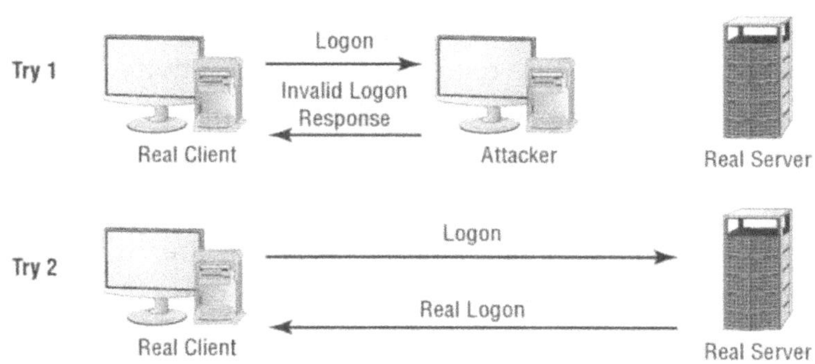

Attacker now has logon and password

Fig. 1.22: A Spoofing Attack During Logon

1.4.9 Sniffing [S-16, 17, 19, W-16, 17]

- Sniffing is a form of traffic monitoring using a sniffer, which is also called a packet analyzer for protocol analyzer.
- A sniffer is a software application that can capture traffic going over the network. Sniffers are commonly used by network administrators to analyze network traffic and troubleshoot problems.
- A sniffer attack (also called a snooping attack or eavesdropping attack) occurs when an attacker uses a sniffer to capture information transmitted over a network. Any data sent over a network in cleartext, including passwords, can be captured and read by the program.
- Sniffing attacks leads to interception of data by capturing network traffic. When data is transmitted across networks, if the data packets are not encrypted, the data within the network packet can be read using a sniffing tools.
- It is a form of "tapping phone wires" and get to know about the conversation. It is also called wiretapping applied to the computer networks.
- A sniffing attack captures and analyzes traffic transmitted over a network. Attackers use protocol analyzers (also called sniffers or packet sniffers) to capture the traffic.
- If the traffic is not encrypted, the attacker can potentially view the information being transmitted, because it's captured in clear text. Although the process can be tedious, a determined attacker can gain a significant amount of data from a sniffing attack.

- Using a sniffer application, an attacker can analyze the network and gain information to eventually cause the network to crash or to become corrupted, or read the communications happening across the network.
- There is so much possibility that if a set of enterprise switch ports is open, then one of their employees can sniff the whole traffic of the network.
- Anyone in the same physical location can plug into the network using Ethernet cable or connect wirelessly to that network and sniff the total traffic.
- In other words, Sniffing allows us to see all sorts of traffic, both protected and unprotected. In the right conditions and with the right protocols in place, an attacking party may be able to gather information that can be used for further attacks or to cause other issues for the network or system owner.
- A sniffer normally turns the NIC of the system to the promiscuous mode so that it listens to all the data transmitted on its segment.
- Promiscuous mode refers to the unique way of Ethernet hardware, in particular, network interface cards (NICs), that allows an NIC to receive all traffic on the network, even if it is not addressed to this NIC.
- By default, a NIC ignores all traffic that is not addressed to it, which is done by comparing the destination address of the Ethernet packet with the hardware address (a.k.a. MAC) of the device.
- While this makes perfect sense for networking, non-promiscuous mode makes it difficult to use network monitoring and analysis software for diagnosing connectivity issues or traffic accounting.
- A sniffer can continuously monitor all the traffic to a computer through the NIC by decoding the information encapsulated in the data packets.
- Sniffing can be either Active or passive in nature.
  1. **Passive Sniffing:** In this the traffic is locked but it is not altered in any way. Passive sniffing allows listening only. It works with Hub devices. On a hub device, the traffic is sent to all the ports. In a network that uses hubs to connect systems, all hosts on the network can see the traffic. Therefore, an attacker can easily capture traffic going through.
  2. **Active Sniffing:** In this the traffic is not only locked and monitored, but it may also be altered in some way as determined by the attack. Active sniffing is used to sniff a switch-based network. It involves injecting Address Resolution Packets (ARP) into a target network to flood on the switch Content Addressable Memory (CAM) table. CAM keeps track of which host is connected to which port.
- Network sniffing involves using sniffer tools that enable real-time monitoring and analysis of data packets flowing over computer networks.
- It can be a hardware device or a separate software program or a combination of both. It is also called as packet sniffing, snoop, network probe, packet analyzer, network analyzer or protocol analyzer.
- A packet sniffer refers to software that captures all network packets. It uses a network adapter card to capture all network packets. These exploit information which is passed in the plain text format.

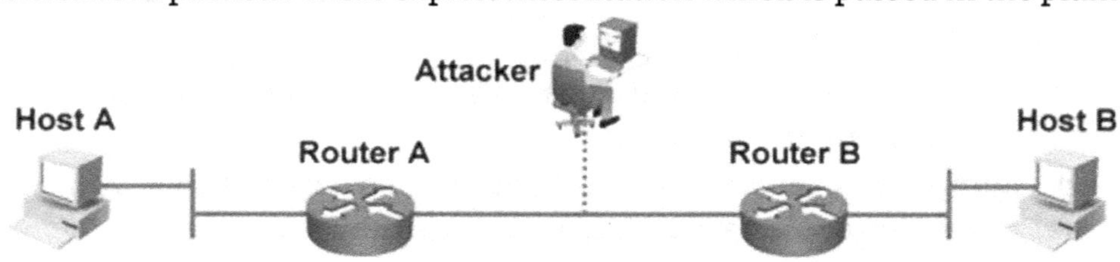

Fig. 1.23: Packet Sniffer Application

- The Packet Sniffer is a tool used by network administrator to sniff each of the "packets" of data travelling over the network, in order to determine the health of network and diagnose network related issues.
- Hence, this tool is called as a Packet Sniffer. Cyber criminals/ hackers use these tools for spying on and stealing data from the network traffic.
- Basically, hackers use Packet Sniffing or Network Sniffers for spying on network user traffic and collecting passwords.
- They use sniffers to eavesdrop on unencrypted data in the data packets to view the information that travels between two entities - client and server, user and web server and communication between two organizations.
- Hackers also use the capture packets for packet injection attacks, man-in-the-middle attacks and also for playing back the data in replay attacks.
- All networks use "packets" to send data. The size of a data file may be quite huge and sending it as a single packet would strain the network and cause congestion. The integrity of the data may also be affected.

1.4.10 TCP/IT Hacking [S-19]

- TCP/IP hacking/hijacking is when an authorized user achieves access to a valid network connection of another user. It is done in order to bypass the password authentication which is normally the start of a session.
- TCP/IP hacking, or session hacking, allows an attacker to reroute data traffic from a network device to a personal computer.
- The attacker can then capture and analyze the data addressed to a target system such as an IP address.
- The attacker then inserts another machine with the same IP address and uses it to gain authorization and access to critical resources and user credentials, such as passwords, and access to critical systems.
- TCP/IP hacking also called active sniffing, involves the attacker gaining access to a host in the network and logically disconnecting it from the network. This can occur due to the TCP three-way handshake.
- The attacker then inserts another machine with the same IP address. This happens quickly and gives the attacker access to the session and to all of the information on the original system. The server will not know this has occurred and will respond as if the client is trusted.

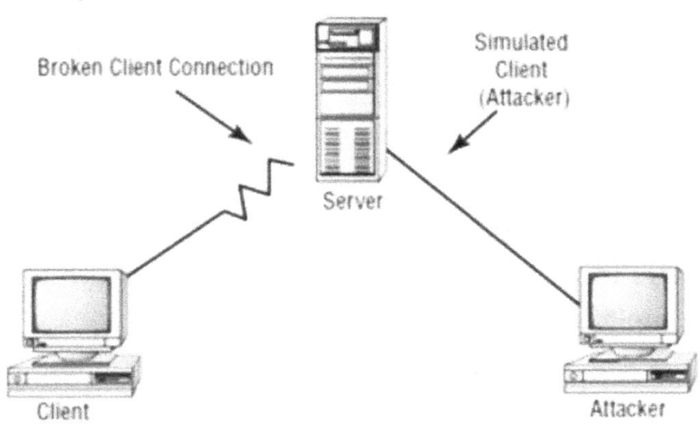

Fig. 1.24

- As with a sequence number attack, there is little you can do to counter the threat. Fortunately, these attacks require fairly sophisticated software and are harder to engineer than a DoS attack such as a TCP SYN attack.

- One of the symptoms of a TCP/IP hacking attack may be the unavailability of a TCP/IP address when the system is started.
- TCP/IP hijacking, or session hijacking, is a problem that has appeared in most TCP/IP-based applications, ranging from simple Telnet sessions to Web-based e-commerce applications.
- In order to hijack a TCP/IP connection, a malicious user must first have the ability to intercept a legitimate user's data, and then insert himself or herself into that session much like a MITM attack.
- A tool known as Hunt is very commonly used to monitor and hijack sessions. It works especially well on basic Telnet or File Transfer Protocol (FTP) sessions.
- A TCP/IP connection is established as shown in Fig. 1.25.

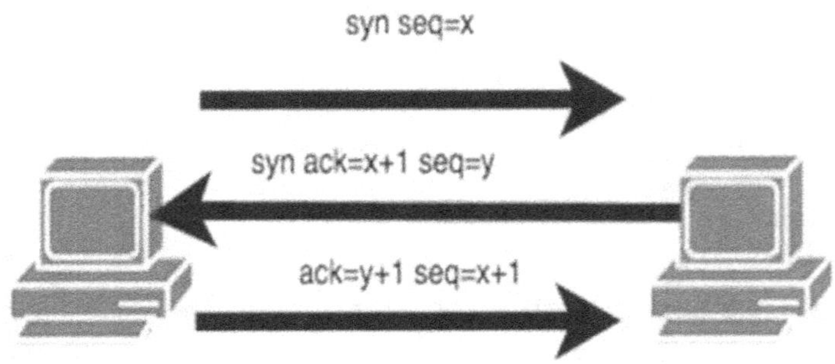

Fig. 1.25

- To hijack this Connection, there are following two Possibilities:
  1. Find the sequence which is a number that increases by 1, but there is no chance to predict it.
  2. The second possibility is to use the Man-in-the-Middle attack which, in simple words, is a type of network sniffing. For sniffing, we use tools like Wireshark or Ethercap etc.

Example:

- An attacker monitors the data transmission over a network and discovers the IP's of two devices that participate in a connection.
- When the hacker discovers the IP of one of the users, he/she can put down the connection of the other user by DoS attack and then resume communication by spoofing the IP of the disconnected user.

1.4.11 Replay Attack

- In replay attacks user captures a sequence of events and resend them. It is also called as playback attack.
- A replay attack is a kind of access or modification attack. In a distributed environment, logon and password information is sent between the client and the authentication system. The attacker can capture the information and replay it again later.
- Replay attacks help attackers to gain access to a network, gain information which would not have been easily accessible or complete a duplicate transaction.
- For example, user P wants to transfer money to user R. Both user P and R have accounts with bank B. User P send message to bank B, requesting for fund transfer.
- User R could capture this message and send copy of the same to bank Bank B would have no idea that this is unauthorized user and consider it as other request from user P. So that user R would get benefit of this fund transfer. This is called as replay attack.

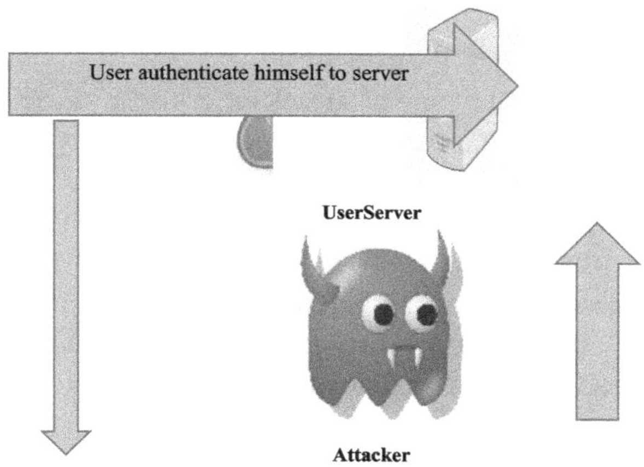

Fig. 1.26: Replay Attack

1.4.12 Encryption Attack

- In case of encryption attack main objective of attacker is to find out plaintext (Original text) from cipher text (Encrypted Text). For this attacker only needs to find out the secret decryption key.
- Hence attacker's main task is find out the secret key used in the encryption. Once the attacker is able to determine the key, the attacked system is considered as broken or compromised.
- Based on the methodology used, attacks on cryptosystems are categorized as follows:
  1. **Cipher text Only Attacks (COA)**: In this the attacker has access to only cipher text. He does not have access to equivalent plaintext. COA is said to be successful when the corresponding plaintext can be determined from a given set of cipher text.
  2. **Known Plaintext Attack (KPA)**: In this the attacker has the plaintext for some parts of the cipher text. The task is to decrypt the rest of the cipher text using this plaintext. This may be done by determining the key or via some other way. The best example of this attack is linear cryptanalysis against block ciphers.
  3. **Chosen Plaintext Attack (CPA)**: In this the attacker has the text of his choice encrypted. So he has the cipher text-plaintext pair of his choice. This simplifies his task of determining the encryption key. An example of this attack is differential cryptanalysis applied against block ciphers as well as hash functions.
  4. **Dictionary Attack**: This attack has many variants, all of which involve compiling a 'dictionary'. In this attacker builds a dictionary of cipher texts and corresponding plaintexts that he has learnt over a period of time. In future, when an attacker gets the cipher text, he refers the dictionary to find the corresponding plaintext.
  5. **Brute Force Attack (BFA)**: In this the attacker tries to determine the key by attempting all possible keys. If the key is 8 bits long, then the number of possible keys is 28 = 256. The attacker knows the cipher text and the algorithm, now he attempts all the 256 keys one by one for decryption. The time to complete the attack would be very high if the key is long
  6. **Side Channel Attack (SCA)**: This type of attack is not against any particular type of encryption system. Instead, it is launched to exploit the weakness in physical implementation of the cryptosystem
  7. **Timing Attacks**: They exploit the fact that different computations take different times to compute on processor. By measuring such timings, it is be possible to know about a particular computation the processor is carrying out. For example, if the encryption takes a longer time, it indicates that the secret key is long.
  8. **Power Analysis Attacks**: These attacks are similar to timing attacks except that the amount of power consumption is used to obtain information about the nature of the underlying computations.

9. **Fault analysis Attacks**: In these attacks, errors are induced in the cryptosystem and the attacker studies the resulting output for useful information.
10. **Man In Middle Attack (MIM)**: It is a type of attack where a unauthorized user inserts him/herself into a conversation between two parties, impersonates both parties and gains access to information that the two parties were trying to send to each other. A man-in-the-middle attack allows unauthorized actor to interrupt, send and receive data meant for someone else, or not meant to be sent at all, without either outside party knowing until it is too late.
11. **Replay Attack:** In this user captures a sequence of events and resend them. It is also called as playback attack. Replay attacks help attackers to gain access to a network, gain information which would not have been easily accessible or complete a duplicate transaction.

1.5 OPERATING SYSTEM SECURITY [W-18]

- Operating system security forms the foundation of the secure operation of computer systems. Operating System security (OS security) is the process of certifying OS integrity, confidentiality and availability.
- OS security refers to specified steps or measures used to protect the OS from threats, viruses, worms, malware or remote hacker intrusions. The ideal goal of operating system security is the development of a secure operating system.
- A secure operating system provides security mechanisms that ensure that the system's security goals are enforced despite the threats faced by the system.
- These security mechanisms are designed to provide such a guarantee in the context of the resource and scheduling mechanisms.
- Security goals define the requirements of secure operation for a system for any processes that it may execute. The security mechanisms must ensure these goals regardless of the possible ways that the system may be misused (i.e., is threatened) by attackers.
- OS security contains all preventive-control methods, which safeguard any computer assets capable of being stolen, edited or deleted if OS security is compromised.
- OS security contains many different techniques and methods which ensure safety from threats and attacks.
- OS security allows different applications and programs to perform required tasks and stop unauthorized interruption.
- OS security may be approached in many ways, including the following:
  1. Performing regular OS patch updates.
  2. Installing updated antivirus engines and softwares.
  3. Scrutinizing all incoming and outgoing network traffic through a firewall.
  4. Creating secure accounts with required privileges only (i.e., user management).
  5. Operating system updates contain new software that helps keep the computer to be updated.
  6. It is always good to keep our OS updated using windows OS updates for its security purpose. Examples of updates include service packs, version upgrades, security updates, drivers, or other types of updates.
- Important and high-priority updates are critical to the security and reliability of the computer. They offer the latest protection against malicious online activities.
- We need to update all of our programs, including Windows, Internet Explorer, Microsoft Office and others. Visit Microsoft Update to scan the computer and see a list of updates, which we can then decide whether to download and install.
- A patch is a program that makes changes to software installed on a computer. Software companies issue patches to fix bugs in their programs, address security problems, or add functionality.

- A patch, sometimes just called a fix, is a small piece of software that is used to correct a problem, usually called a bug, within an operating system or software program. No software program is perfect and so patches are common, even years after a program has been released.
- The more popular a program is, the more likely rare problems occur, and so some of the most popular programs in existence are some of the most patched.
- Service pack is a collection of usually already-released patches is often called a service pack.
- A hotfix is code (sometimes called a patch) that fixes a bug in a product. Users of the products may be notified by e-mail or obtain information about current hotfixes at a software vendor's Web site and download the hotfixes they wish to apply.

1.5.1 Hotfixes

- Hotfixes are sometimes packaged as a set of fixes called a combined hotfix or a service pack. Hotfixes are Microsoft's version of patches. Microsoft bundles hotfixes into service packs for easier installation.
- Hotfixes are used to make repairs to a system during normal operation even though they might require a reboot.
- A hotfix may entail moving data from a bad spot on the disk and remapping the data to a new sector. Doing so prevents data loss and loss of service.
- This type of repair may also involve reallocating a block of memory if, for example, a memory problem occurred. This allows the system to continue normal operations until a permanent repair can be made.
- Microsoft refers to a bug fix as a hotfix. It involves the replacement of files with an updated version.

1.5.2 Service Packs

- A service pack is a comprehensive set of fixes consolidated into a single product.
- A service pack may be used to address a large number of bugs or to introduce new capabilities in an OS. When installed, a service pack usually contains a number of file replacements.
- Make sure we check related websites to verify that the service pack works properly. Sometimes, a manufacturer will release a service pack before it has been thoroughly tested.
- An untested service pack can cause extreme instability in an operating opening system or even worse, render it inoperable.

1.5.3 Patches

- A patch is a temporary (or quick) fix to a program. They may be used to temporarily bypass a set of instructions that have malfunctioned.
- Number of OS manufacturers issue patches that can either be manually applied or applied using a disk file to fix a program.
- When we are working with customer support on a technical problem with an OS or applications product, customer service may have go into the code and make alterations to the binary files that run on the computer system. Double-check each change to prevent catastrophic failures due to improperly entered code.

1.6 INFORMATION [S-16, 18]

- Today's age is an "Information Age", because of advances in computer and communications technology i.e., Information and Communication Technology (ICT).
- In every field of teaching, manager, engineers, accountants etc., these jobs are predominantly based on handling large amount of information.
- Information security is a system consisting of many parts software, hardware, data, people, procedures and networks.

- Information is data that is organized in meaningful fashion. Information is that which informs i.e. that from which data can be derived.
- Information is the data that is:
  1. Accurate and timely.
  2. Specific and organized for purpose.
  3. Presented within a context that gives its meaning.
  4. Can lead to an increase in understanding and decrease in uncertainty.
- Information is a combination of following three parts:
  1. **Data:** It is a collection of all types of information which can be shared and used as per requirement. For example, Personal data.
  2. **Knowledge:** It is based on data that is organized and summarized. It is carried by experienced employee in organization.
  3. **Action:** It is used to pass the required information to a person who needs it with help of Information System (IS).

Concept of Information System (IS):

- An IS is a set of interrelated components that collect process and distribute info to support decision making in organization.
- Information system accept data from environment and manipulate the data to produce information that is used to solve a problem or business need.
- In previous days information's are maintain manually but today's information systems are mostly computerized, software systems. DBMS used to manage the storage and retrieval of the data/information in the system.
- Information system consist of hardware, software, data and application to manage information. Information system usually developed to support specific business functions such as administrative functions, finance, accounting and resource management in every organization.

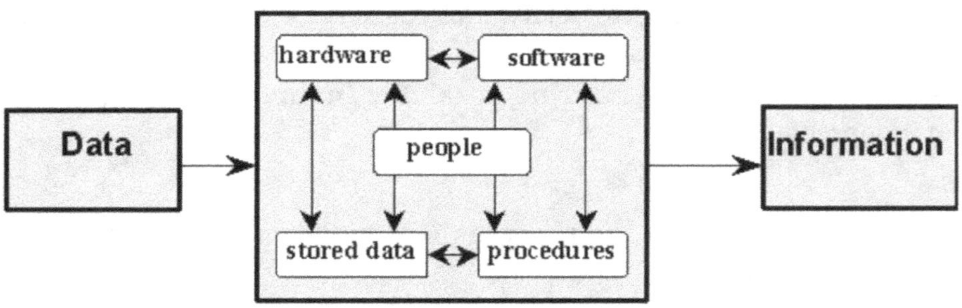

Fig. 1.27: Concept of IS

1.6.1 Need and Importance of Information [S-16, 18]

- Noway's use of computer and communication technology has increased. So we need a system that can manage the information or data. Information is life blood of every organization.
- An Information System (IS) includes hardware, software, data and application etc. to manage information. In organization it is needed to monitor different operations. Also used to document different operations.
- Information is useful or needed for ensuring smooth functioning of all the departments in company/organization.
- Information benefits business world by allowing organizations to work more efficiently and maximize productivity.

- Following table compares data and information:

Sr. No.	Data	Information
1.	Data is used as input for the computer system.	Information is the output of data.
2.	Data is unprocessed facts figures.	Information is processed data.
3.	Data does not depend on information.	Information depends on data.
4.	Data is not specific.	Information is specific.
5.	Data does not carry a meaning.	Information must carry a logical meaning.
6.	Data is the raw material.	Information is the product after processing.

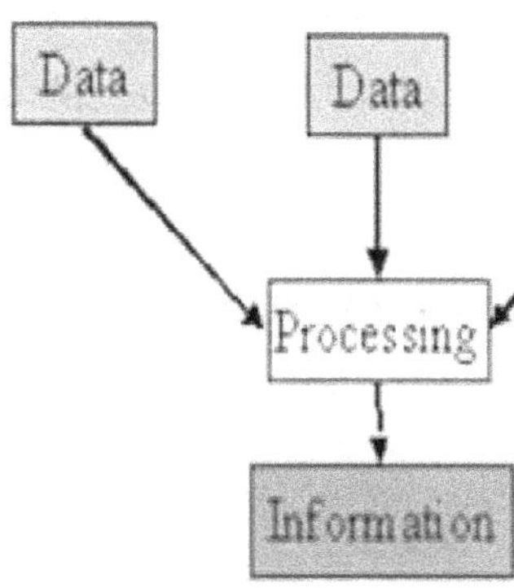

Fig. 1.28: Information is created from Data

1.6.2 Information Classification

- Organization will classify information to provide information security:
  - The main reason for classifying information is that all data or information of organization will not have same level of criticality. Some information may be important and some may not be important.
  - Aim of an organization is to improve Confidentiality, Integrity and Availability (CIA) of information to reduce risk related to information.
  - Information classification is important while securing any trusted system like government sectors.
  - Information classification is used to prevent unauthorized access to a system.
  - Due to privacy laws or any other compliances information may be classified.
  - Due to information classification organization can employ security policies.

Reasons/Advantages of Classification of Information:

1. It helps organizations for security protection.
2. It helps organization to identify info like sensitive info, critical info.
3. It supports CIA (Confidentiality, Integrity, Availability).
4. It will help organization to make decision what type of protection is to be applied to what type of information.
5. It helps to protect intellectual property.
6. Helps to protect personal information.
7. It helps to control private or sensitive information.
8. Helps to protect confidential information from unauthorized access.
9. Protecting information that supports public security and law enforcements.

Classification Levels: **[S-16, W-16]**

1. **Open/Unclassified/Public:**
- Information is not classified and not sensitive.
- Information accessible to both external and internal parties (employee) of organization.
- It does not affect confidentiality.
2. **Internal but Unclassified:**
- Information is accessible to both external parties and internal employees with controlled access rights.
- If information is disclosed it will not create damage to the organization.
3. **Confidential/Sensitive:**
- Information is accessible only to the employee of the organization with strict access rights.
4. **Secret/Highly Sensitive:**
- In this unauthorized access to the information can cause damage to the country's national security.
5. **Top Secret:**
- Highest level of information classification. Example, Info in defense organization.

1.6.3 Criteria for Classification of Information

- Criteria for classification of information are given below:
1. **Value:**
- Value is common criteria for classification.
- Valuable information of organization should be classified. For example, in college student list is classified according to their department.
2. **Age:**
- In this information is classified according to time period. For example, certain information is valid only for certain period so after the period is over that information is not useful.
3. **Useful Life:**
- If validity or deadline of information is over due to changes in information then that information must be declassified. For example, our earlier diploma scheme was E scheme and now current scheme is G. So information is classified accordingly.
4. **Personal Association:**
- Information which is personally associated with particular individual then such information should be classified.
5. **Public:**
- Information is classified on this factor also.
- Public information is not sensitive.
- If it is accessed by unauthorized user it will not affect the security. For example, information given on website of any organization.
6. **Private:**
- Important information of organization can be kept separately.
- Unauthorized user cannot access it. For example, Information related to project going on in organization is kept secret from other organization.

1.6.4 Basic Principles of Information Security

- Security means to protect information or system from unauthorized users like attacker. Security is the practice of protecting information from unauthorized access, use, inspection, recording, destruction.

- Information security is the process of protecting intellectual property of an organization. Protecting any organization following multi layers of security are important:
  1. **Physical Security:** It will protect physical items like RAM, Hard disk, etc.
  2. **Personal Security:** It will protect authorized individual users or groups in organization.
  3. **Operational Security:** It will protect details of particular operation in organization.
  4. **Communication Security:** It will protect communication technology and content of communication.
  5. **Network Security:** It will protect networking component like router, bridge etc.
  6. **Information Security:** It will protect all information assets. Information security is simply the process of keeping information secure (protecting its availability, integrity and privacy). Information security in today's data - centric world in centered in the CIA traidto ensure the safe, storage, flow and utilization of information. The CIA traid refers to the core principles of information security.
- The basic aims/goals of information security are summarized in three principles (also known as Pillars of Information Security) as shown in Fig. 1.29. Fig. 1.30 shows security layers.

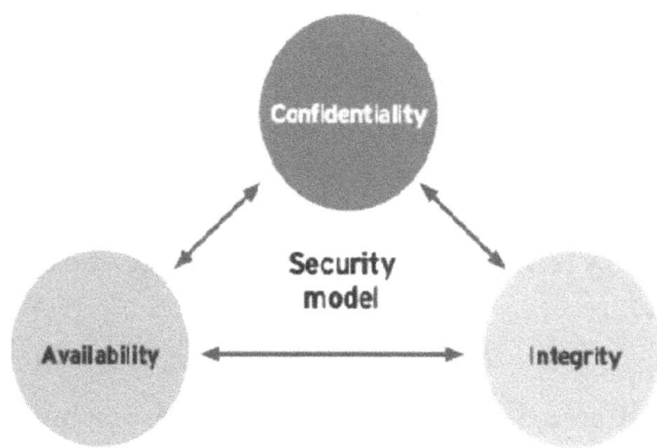

Fig. 1.29: Goals of Security/CIA Model

- Information security is more than just computer security. It also includes wide range of physical security means. For example, protecting assets from natural disasters or thefts.

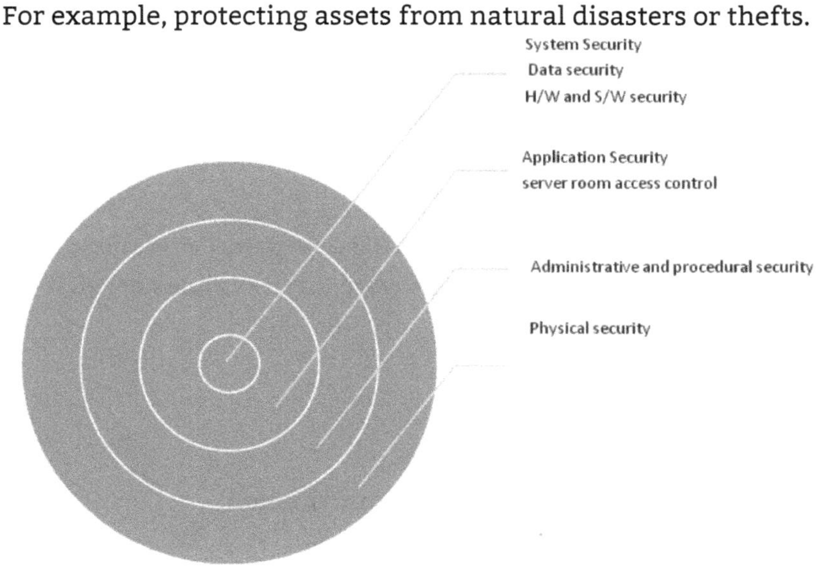

Fig. 1.30: Security Layers

- Principles of information security are:

1. **Confidentiality:** **[S-16]**

- It means making sure that information is only seen by people who have the access rights to see it. Confidentiality refers to limiting information access and disclosure to authorized users "the right people" and preventing access by or disclosure to unauthorized ones "the wrong people."
- Authentication methods like user-IDs and passwords, that uniquely identify data systems' users and control access to data systems resources, underpin the goal of confidentiality.

2. **Integrity:** **[S-16]**

- It means ensuring that information remains unaltered. This means watching out for alterations through malicious action or even simple innocent mistake.
- Integrity refers to the trustworthiness of information resources. Only authorized individual can create or change information.
- It includes the concept of "data integrity" namely, that data have not been changed inappropriately, whether by accident or deliberately malign activity.
- It also includes "origin" or "source integrity" that is, that the data actually came from the person or entity we think it did, rather than an imposter.

3. **Availability:** **[S-16]**

- It implies having access to our information when we need it. Availability refers, unsurprisingly, to the availability of information resources.
- An information system that is not available when we need it is almost as bad as none at all. It may be much worse, depending on how reliant the organization has become on a functioning computer and communications infrastructure.

1.6.5 Need of Security

- The purpose of information security management is to ensure business continuity and reduce business damage by preventing and minimizing the impact of security incidents.
- An information security management system enables information to be shared, ensuring the protection of information and computing assets.
- Information security is needed to protect the system from unauthorized access and modification.
- When computer applications were developed to handle financial and personal data, the need for security exists. People realized that data on computers was extremely important.
- Organizations employed their own mechanism in order to provide basic security mechanism. For example, User id and password for every user.
- As technology improved people realized that the basic security measures were not quite enough. Then internet took the world by storm and there were any examples of what could happen if there was insufficient security built in applications.
- Hence, we need security for:
  1. Protecting resources of organizations.
  2. To avoid business damage.
  3. To avoid unauthorized user to access important information.
  4. To protect personal data.
  5. To protect sensitive information of organization.
  6. Help to protect intellectual property.

Security related Basic Terms:

1. **Digital Signature:** A digital code (generated and authenticated by public key encryption) which is attached to an electronically transmitted document to verify its contents and the sender's identity.
2. **Non-Repudiation:** Non-repudiation is the assurance that someone cannot deny something. Typically, non-repudiation refers to the ability to ensure that a party to a contract or a communication cannot deny the authenticity of their signature on a document or the sending of a message that they originated.
3. **Cryptography:** The art of writing or solving codes.
4. **Encryption:** Encryption is the conversion of data into a form, called a cipher text that cannot be easily understood by unauthorized people.
5. **Cipher:** It is a coded text.
6. **Decryption:** Decryption is the process of converting encrypted data back into its original form, so it can be understood.
7. **Denial of Service:** In computing, a denial-of-service (DoS) or distributed denial-of-service (DDoS) attack is an attempt to make a machine or network resource unavailable to its intended users.
8. **Steganography:** The practice of concealing messages or information within other non-secret text or data.
9. **Spoofing:** Spoofing is the creation of TCP/IP packets using somebody else's IP address

Practice Questions

1. What is computer security?
2. What is information security?
3. Describe foundation of computer security.
4. Describe the details of security basics.
5. Describe need of computer security.
6. Define the terms data security, information security, network security and computer security.
7. Describe the importance of computer security.
8. Describe the term virus and worms with example.
9. Differentiate between viruses and worms.
10. What is virus? Describe the virus spreading mechanism.
11. Explain the term Trojan horse in detail.
12. Describe the term logic bombs.
13. What is threat? Describe all types of Threats.
14. Describe threat, vulnerability and attack as characteristics of computer intrusion.
15. Compare intruders and insiders.
16. What are the main types of computer viruses?
17. Describe the term polymorphic virus.
18. List the triggers of the virus attack.
19. Describe the steps for protection against viruses.
20. Draw the structure of a worm.
21. What is attack? list the types of attack.
22. Describe the term cyber terrorism.

23. What is meant by backdoor attack and trapdoor attack?
24. Describe the terms: (i) Overwriting viruses, (ii) Stealth viruses.
25. Describe the term Denial of Service (DoS) attack with example
26. Describe the term sniffing and spoofing with example.
27. What are different ways of spoofing? Explain.
28. Draw and describe the man-in-the middle attack.
29. Describe the term TCP/IP hijacking.
30. Describe the term malware.
31. List the characteristics of virus.
32. Describe the different phases of viruses.
33. What is data and information?
34. Explain the term information classification.
35. Describe criteria for information classification.
36. Enlist basic principles of information security.
37. Differentiate between data and information.

■■■

2... User Authentication and Access Control

Chapter Outcomes...

- Explain techniques of the given type of attack on passwords.
- Explain mechanism of the given type of biometric.
- Apply the relevant authentication method for the given situation with an example.
- Describe features of the given access control policy.

Learning Objectives...

- To understand Basic Concepts of User Authentication and Access Control
- To learn Biometrics with its Concepts
- To Study Access Control in Security

2.0 INTRODUCTION

- Authentication is any process by which a system verifies the identity of a user who wishes to access the system. Because access control is typically based on the identity of the user who requests access to a resource, authentication is essential to effective security.
- User authentication is the process of verifying whether the identity of a user is genuine prior to granting him access to resources or services in a secured environment.
- User authentication is implemented through credentials which at a minimum consist of a user ID and password.
- We can view access control as the central element of computer security. The principal objectives of computer security are to prevent unauthorized users from gaining access to resources, to prevent legitimate users from accessing resources in an unauthorized manner, and to enable legitimate users to access resources in an authorized manner.
- Biometrics are physical or behavioral human characteristics to that can be used to digitally identify a person to grant access to systems, devices or data.
- Examples of these biometric identifiers are fingerprints, facial patterns, voice or typing cadence. Each of these identifiers is considered unique to the individual, and they may be used in combination to ensure greater accuracy of identification.
- Biometrics authentication (or realistic authentication) is used in computer science as a form of identification and access control.
- Biometric security is a security mechanism used to authenticate and provide access to a facility or system based on the automatic and instant verification of an individual's physical characteristics.

- Authorization (access control) is any mechanism by which a system grants or revokes the right to access some data or perform some action.
- Access control mechanisms determine which operations the user can or cannot do by comparing the user's identity to an Access Control List (ACL).
- Access control refers to a security feature that manages the interaction with a resource. The resource can be either technology or a room containing the technology (physical security).
- Access control is critical to minimizing system vulnerabilities. It restricts not only who or what has access to the resource, but also the type of access that is permitted.

2.1 IDENTIFICATION AND AUTHENTICATION [S-17, 19, W-19]

- Identification means finding out who someone is. Authentication is a mechanism of verifying that identification. Put another way, identification is claiming an identity; authentication is proving it.
- In the physical world, the best analogy would be that any person can claim to be anyone (identification). To prove it (authentication), however, that person needs to provide some evidence, such as a Driver's license, Passport, Pancard and so on.

Identification: "Who are you?"

- The process used to recognize an individual user. It is a way by which individual claims his/her identity to the system.
- This can be accomplished with a username, a process ID, a smart card, or anything else that can uniquely identify a subject.
- Security systems use this identity when determining if user can access an object.

Authentication: "Who you are and how can you prove it?"

- Authentication is the process of determining identity of a user or entity. Authentication is the process of proving an identity and it occurs when subjects provide appropriate credentials to prove their identity.
- Authentication is the process of determining whether someone or something is, in fact, who or what it is declared to be.
- In private and public computer networks (including the Internet), authentication is commonly done through the use of login passwords or pass phrases; knowledge of such is assumed to guarantee that the user is authentic.
- Thus, when we are asked to "authenticate" to a system, it usually means that we enter the username and/or password for that system.
- For example, when a user provides the correct password with a username, the password proves that the user is the owner of the username.
- In short, the authentication provides proof of a claimed identity. Generally there are three methods used in authentication.

Authorization: "What can I do?"

- Authorization is the process of determining which permissions a person or system is supposed to have.
- In multi-user computing systems, a system administrator defines which users are allowed access to the system, as well as the privileges of use for which they are eligible (e.g., access to file directories, hours of access, amount of allocated storage space).
- Authorization can be seen as both the preliminary setting of permissions by a system administrator, and the actual checking of the permission values when a user obtains access.
- Authorization is usually preceded by authentication.

Identification	Who are you?
Authentication	Ok. How can you prove it?
Authorization	What can I do?

2.1.1 User Names and Passwords

- A username is a name that uniquely identifies someone on a computer system. For example, a computer may be setup with multiple accounts, with different usernames for each account.
- A username is almost always paired with a password. A password is a string of characters used to verify the identity of a user during the authentication process.
- This username/password combination is referred to as a login, and is often required for users to log in to computer system.
- Passwords are typically used in conjuncture with a username; they are designed to be known only to the user and allow that user to gain access to a device, application or website.
- The passwords are the most common way to prove the identity when using websites, e-mail accounts and the computer itself, (via User Accounts).
- The use of strong passwords is therefore essential in order to protect the security and identity. Ensure the use strong passwords and do not disclose them to anyone else.

How Password Authentication Works:

- A password is a string of characters. (including letters, digits, or other symbols) used for authenticating a user on a computer system.

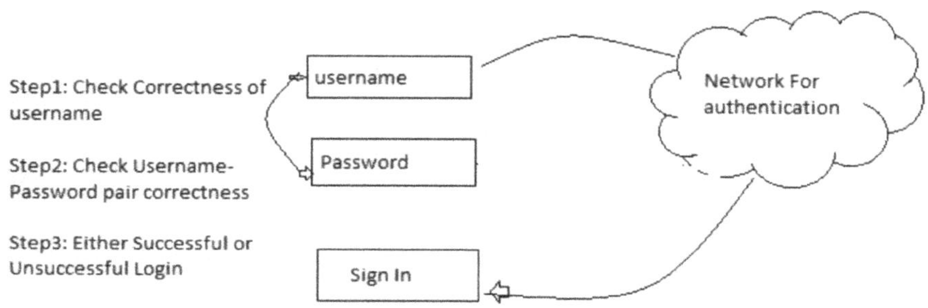

Fig. 2.1

Password Selection Criteria:

- Following are the some guidelines to form a password:
  1. Avoid using dictionary words. These passwords are easy for hackers to figure out using an electronic dictionary.
  2. Don't use personal information. Any part of our name, birthday, Social Security number, or similar information for our loved ones is a bad password choice.
  3. Avoid common sequences, such as numbers or letters in sequential order or repetitive numbers or letters.
  4. If the web site supports it, try to use special characters, such as $, #, and &. Most passwords are case sensitive, so use a mixture of upper case and lower case letters, as well as numbers.
  5. Passwords become harder to crack with each character that we add, so longer passwords are better than shorter ones. Microsoft has an online password strength checker at www.microsoft.com/protect/yourself/password/checker.mspx.
  6. To help we easily remember our password, consider using the first letter from each word in a sentence, a phrase, a poem, or a song title as a password. Be sure to add in numbers and/or special characters.
  7. Create different passwords for different accounts and applications. That way, if one password is breached, our other accounts won't be put at risk too. Do not use the same or variations of the same password for different applications.
  8. Despite admonitions to the contrary, one easy way to remember our passwords is to write them down and keep them in a securely locked place. Never leave them on a Post it note on our monitor, in an address book, in a desk drawer, or under our keyboard or mouse pad (or any other obvious place).

9. If we have already established a password that is not strong, change it. Web sites have a variety of procedures that govern how we can change our password. Look for a link, (such as "my account") somewhere on the site's homepage that goes to an area of the site that allows password and account management.

2.1.2 Guessing a Password

- A password sometimes called a pass-code, is a memorized secret used to confirm the identity of a user.
- Password guessing is the process of attempting to gain access to a system through the systematic guessing of passwords in an attempt to gain a login to a target system.
- Password cracking is the process of recovering passwords from data that have been stored in or transmitted by a computer system.
- Cracking a password may seem like a next to impossible task, but we should surprised how easy it can be. There are dozens of password cracking programs in the market.
- Password cracking is penetrating a system's defences, stealing a file containing valid passwords, decrypting them and using them to gain access to programs, files and data.
- A directory attack is the guessing of a password by repeated trial and error. In a brute-force attack, the attacker simply attempts to guess the password to an account by logically trying every possible combination of characters until the correct password is discovered.
- The hybrid attack combines the dictionary attack and the brute force attack. The hybrid attack would be able to crack this password much faster.

2.1.3 Password Attacks [S-17, 18, 19, W-18]

- Passwords are the most commonly used mechanism to authenticate users to an information system, obtaining passwords is a common and effective attack approach.
- In password attack, an attacker tries to crack the passwords stored in a network account database or a password-protected file.
- The two types of password attacks are:

1. Dictionary Attack:

- A dictionary attack is a technique or method used to breach the computer security of a password-protected machine or server.
- A dictionary attack attempts to defeat an authentication mechanism by systematically entering each word in a dictionary as a password or trying to determine the decryption key of an encrypted message or document.
- This technique uses lists of known passwords, word list substitution and pattern checking to find commonly used passwords, or those that are discoverable with a bit of personal information.
- It is not difficult to find lists of compromised passwords. Hacker can probably unlock 10% to 20% of a password file using just the 10,000 most common passwords. In fact, it has been estimated that about 75% of online adults have used one or more of the 500 most popular passwords.
- After decrypting the password file, a dictionary attack uses text strings and variations thereof to test different combinations.
- For example, many people append numbers to their names or user names, which may be stored in plain text. If a user named Rahul has the password "Rahul123," a dictionary attack will figure out that in seconds. The software simply cycles through every possible combination to identify the ones that work.
- If a little information is known about people in the database, the job is even easier. For example, people frequently use the names of children, addresses, phone numbers, sports teams and birthdays as passwords, either alone or in combination with other characters.

- Since, most people append characters to the end of the password, it's easy for dictionary cracks to cycle through all of those likely possibilities. Social media is an attacker's dream.
- People freely post personal information in their profiles or tweet repeatedly about the sports teams or celebrities they follow. These are natural paths for a dictionary crack to pursue.

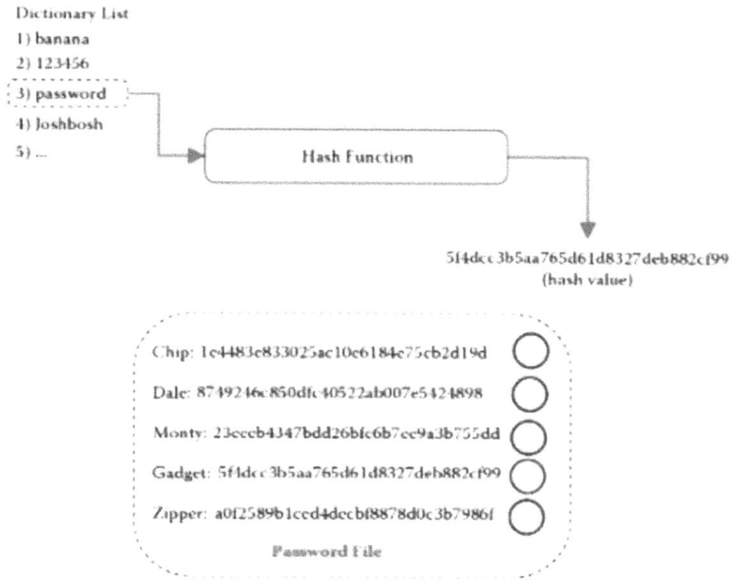

Fig. 2.2: Password Cracking Dictionary Attack

2. Brute Force Attack:

- Brute force attack will try literally every possible combination sequentially until it finds the right combination to authenticate the username trying to be accessed.
- The brute force attack will attempt to use lowercase letters, uppercase letters, numbers, and special characters until it eventually stumbles onto the correct password.
- Brute-force password guessing means using a random approach by trying different passwords and hoping that on work some logic can be applied by trying passwords related to the person's name, job title, hobbies or similar items.
- This is just what it sounds like: a technique to reveal those stubborn passwords that can't be unlocked by a dictionary. Today's multi-core processors and graphics processing units have made brute force attacks more practical than they used to be.
- Machines that can be purchased for less than $1,000 are capable of testing billions of passwords per second. Short passwords are easiest to guess, so attackers typically use brute force attack to unscramble the five and six character passwords that didn't yield to the dictionary approach, a process that might only take a few hours.
- For longer passwords, brute force and dictionary techniques may be combined to narrow the realm of possible combinations. Some brute force cracking software also uses rainbow tables, which are lists of known codes that can sometimes be helpful in reverse-engineering encrypted text.
- For example, how vulnerable are password files to brute force attacks? In 2013 the tech news site ArsTechnica gave an editor who had no experience with password cracking a list of 16,000 encrypted passcodes and challenged him to break as many as possible. Within a few hours, he had deciphered nearly half of them. The same list was then given to some skilled hackers, one of whom cracked 90% of the codes in about 20 hours.
- The biggest problem with password protection is that many people don't use strong passwords.
- The laws of mathematics dictate that longer passwords are harder to break than short ones, and passwords that contain random combinations of characters are more secure than those that conform to a known pattern.

- A 13-digit password that mixes alphanumeric characters and punctuation systems is considered impractical to break with today's technology.
- Unfortunately, few people can remember a random 13-digit string of characters, much less multiple strings for different logins. Equally unfortunate from a security perspective is that computers are getting faster and cracking algorithms are getting better.
- Five years ago, an eight-digit password was considered strong enough. Five years from now, 18 digits may be too weak.
- This is where password management software is valuable. Password managers store passwords of any length and can regularly generate new passwords without the user having to bother to remember them.
- They can also be protected by two-factor authentication, which is considered to be almost unbreakable in any context.

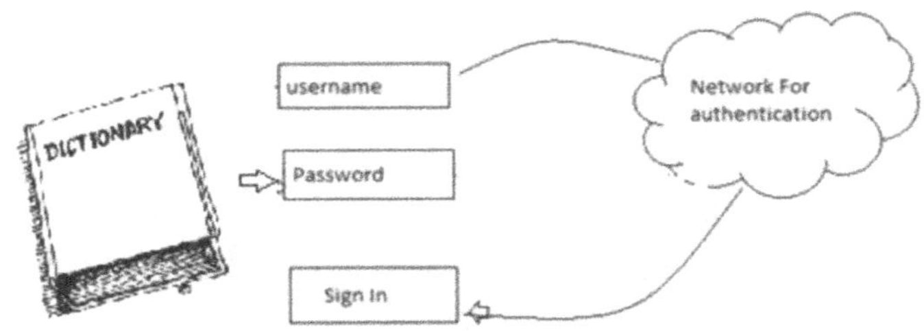

Fig. 2.3

2.1.3.1 Piggybacking **[W-16]**

- Piggybacking refers to gaining access to a wireless Internet connection by bringing the computer within the range of another's wireless connection, and using that service without the subscriber's explicit permission.
- Piggybacking is actually when someone tags along with another person who is authorized to gain entry into a restricted area, or pass something.
- For example, an unauthorized user may hack a communication channel to a computer.
- In fact the attacker gains access to a system via intervals of inactivity in another user's legitimate connection.
- A piggyback attack is specifically where an attacker gains access to a system using another user's connection and periods of inactivity when said user is not using the account.
- The attack is also referred to as a between the line attack, the attacker will exploit network connection weaknesses and force entry into a system using a registered users connection.

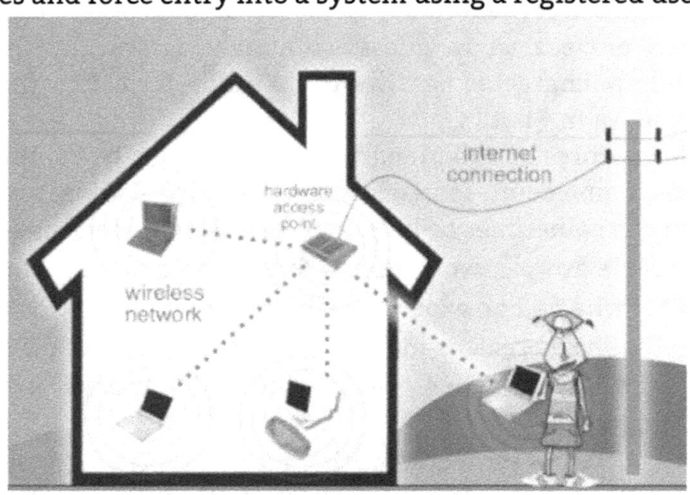

Fig. 2.4: This happens when your network is not secure. One can piggy-back on your internect connection

- Piggybacking refers to a situation where an unauthorized party gains access to some system in connection with an authorized party.

- This can happen in several ways, including piggybacking on public wireless networks and piggybacking into a password-protected system.
- Remember the situation when we tried piggybacking?
  1. May be to gain access of available Wi-Fi network.
  2. May be to gain access to Tata Sky or similar through available signal.
  3. May be to steal electricity from someone else's connection.
- Using the Wi-Fi hotspot of a nearby neighbor who never set up a password for access. Wireless routers out of the box are unsecured with no password, and novice users often leave them as it is. It is not uncommon to find several open Wi-Fi hotspots in an apartment building.

Reasons to Piggybacking:

1. The usual purpose of piggybacking is simply to gain free network access rather than any malicious intent, but it can slow down data transfer for legitimate users of the network.
2. A network that is vulnerable to piggybacking for network access is equally vulnerable when the purpose is data theft, dissemination of viruses, or some other illicit activity.

How to Piggybacking?

1. It is quite simple to access an unsecured wireless network. All we have to do is to get into the range of a Wi-Fi hotspot's signal and select our chosen network from the options presented.
2. If password protected we may guess the passwords using above attacks.
3. Unauthorized network access, even to free Wi-Fi, may be illegal.
4. People have been fined for accessing hotspots from outside businesses, such as coffee shops, that provide free Wi-Fi for customers' use.

How to Protect from Piggybacking?

1. To protect the network from piggybacking, ensure that encryption is enabled for the router.
2. Use Wireless Encryption Protocol (WEP) if that's the only option.
3. If possible use Wireless Protected Access (WPA) or WPA2.
4. Use a strong password for our encryption key, consisting of at least 14 characters and mixing letters and numbers.

2.1.3.2 Shoulder Surfing (Visual Hacking) [W-16]

- Shoulder surfing is a type of social engineering technique used to obtain information such as Personal Identification Numbers (PINs), passwords and other confidential data by looking over the victim's shoulder.

Fig. 2.5

- One way of stealing the password is standing behind an individual and notes the password while he/she is typing it (shoulder surfing).
- Shoulder surfing is a direct observation technique to get passwords, PINs, other sensitive personal information. Shoulder surfing is easily done in crowded places.

- It is comparatively easy to stand next to someone and watch as they fill out a form, enter a PIN number at an ATM machine, or use a calling card at a public pay phone. Do not write passwords in disk or paper so that the Cheater get it easily.
- There are a few ways to prevent the low-tech threat of visual hacking:
  1. Tilt the screen away from the person next to us.
  2. Use a privacy screen on the computing devices.
  3. Create a physical barrier between the screen and prying eyes – using a pillow, the notebook or whatever else we have at the disposal.
  4. Stop working in crowded airplanes, trains, airports, cafes, hotel lobbies and other public spaces.
  5. Work with our back to a wall preventing others from getting behind us and looking over our shoulder.
- There are two types of shoulder-surfing attack:
  1. **Direct Observation Attacks**, in which authentication information is obtained by a person who is directly monitoring the authentication sequence.
  2. **Recording Attacks**, in which the authentication information is obtained by recording the authentication sequence for later analysis to open the device.

2.1.3.3 Dumpster Diving [S-16]

- Dumpster diving refers to the act of literally climbing inside a trash dumpster and searching for information that could be of benefit to the hacker when he or she attacks the computer network.
- "Dumpster diving" means searching trash for useful information. The trash may be in a public dumpster or in a restricted area requiring unauthorized entry.
- Dumpster diving is a technique used to retrieve information that could be used to carry out an attack on a computer network. Dumpster diving is an interesting attack that produces an immense amount of information on an organization, firm, individual, or entity.
- There is a famous saying that most of we might have listened, "one man's trash is another man's treasure". That means what one person considers worthless might be of high value to the other.
- Dumpster diving refers to using various methods to get information about a technology user.
- This is often done to uncover useful information that may help an individual get access to a particular network.
- So, while the term can literally refer to looking through trash, it is used more often in the context of any method (especially physical methods) by which a hacker might look for information about a computer network.

Fig. 2.6

Why Dumpster Diving happens?

1. E-mail address/address.
2. Phone numbers to carry out vishing.

3. Passwords and other social security numbers that we might have written on sticky notes for the convenience.
4. Bank statements/financial statements.
5. Medical records.
6. Important documents.
7. Account login credentials.
8. Business secrets.
9. Marketing secrets.
10. Information of the employee base.
11. Information about the software/tools/technologies that is being used at the company.

Preventive Measures for Dumpster Diving:

1. Destroy any CDs/DVDs containing personal data.
2. In case we no longer need our PC, make sure we have deleted all the data so that it can't be recovered.
3. Use of firewalls can prevent suspicious Internet users from accessing the discarded data.
4. Paper documents should be permanently destroyed.
5. Companies should lock waste bins and should have a safe disposal policy.

- We can take several effective steps to ensure our safety. But the most important step in the process of ensuring safety still remains the same. And it is to spread awareness among our known ones. Perhaps, this is the best thing we can do to mark us safe in this flood of threats.

2.2 BIOMETRICS [S-16, 17, 18, W-16, 17, 18, 19]

- The term "biometrics" is derived from the Greek words "bio" (life) and "metrics" (to measure). Biometrics is the science for determining a Person's Identity (ID) by measuring his/her physiological characteristics.
- Due to rapid increase in cyber crimes it has become extremely important to safeguard confidential data. A biometric system is essentially a pattern recognition system that recognizes person based on a feature vector derived from a specific physiological or behavioral characteristic that a person possesses.
- Biometrics refers to metrics related to human characteristics and traits. Biometrics authentication (or realistic authentication) is used in computer science as a form of identification and access control.
- Biometrics refers to technologies that measure and analyze human body characteristics, such as DNA, fingerprints, eye retinas and irises, voice patterns, facial patterns and hand measurements for authentication purposes.
- Biometric technology can be used for a great number of applications. If security is involved, biometrics can help make operations, transactions and everyday life both safer and more convenient.
- Fig. 2.7 illustrates the two basic modes of a biometric system namely, Verification Mode and Identification Mode.
- The first block (sensor) is the interface between the real world and the system; it has to acquire all the necessary data. Most of the times it is an image acquisition system, but it can change according to the characteristics desired.
- The second block performs all the necessary pre-processing: it has to remove artifacts from the sensor, to enhance the input (e.g. removing background noise), to use some kind of normalization, etc.

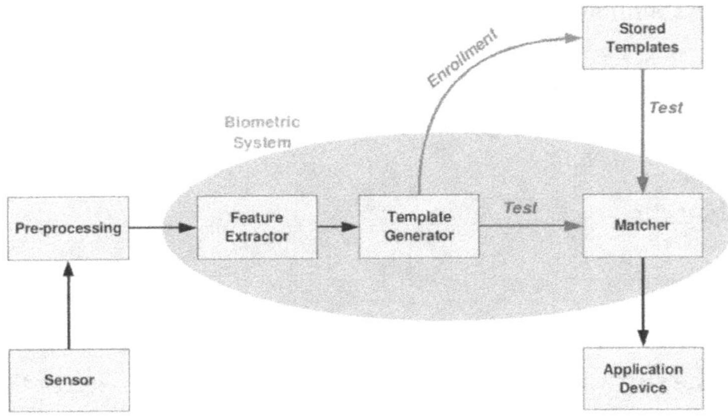

Fig. 2.7: Biometric System

- In the third block necessary features are extracted. This step is an important step as the correct features need to be extracted in the optimal way.

1. In **verification (or authentication) mode** the system performs a one-to-one comparison of a move before advantages captured biometric with a specific template stored in a biometric database in order to verify the individual is the person they claim to be. Three steps are involved in the verification of a person:
   (i) In the first step, reference models for all the users are generated and stored in the model database.
   (ii) In the second step, some samples are matched with reference models to generate the genuine and impostor scores and calculate the threshold.
   (iii) Third step is the testing step. This process may use a smart card, username or ID number (e.g., PIN) to indicate which template should be used for comparison.
2. In **identification mode** the system performs a one-to-many comparison against a biometric database in attempt to establish the identity of an unknown individual.
   (i) The system will succeed in identifying the individual if the comparison of the biometric sample to a template in the database falls within a previously set threshold.
   (ii) Identification mode can be used either for 'positive recognition' (so that the user does not have to provide any information about the template to be used) or for 'negative recognition' of the person "where the system establishes whether the person is who she (implicitly or explicitly) denies to be".
   (iii) The latter function can only be achieved through biometrics since other methods of personal recognition such as passwords, PINs or keys are ineffective.

Advantages of Biometric System:

1. Increase security.
2. Reduce fraud by employing hard-to-forge technologies and materials.
3. Eliminate problems caused by lost IDs or forgotten passwords by using physiological attributes.
4. Reduce password administration costs.
5. Replace hard-to-remember passwords which may be shared or observed.

Disadvantages of Biometric System:

1. For people affected with diabetes, the eyes get affected resulting in differences. Biometrics is an expensive security solution.
2. It is found that with age, the voice of a person differs. Also when the person has flu or throat infection the voice changes or if there are too much noise in the environment this method may not authenticate correctly. Therefore this method of verification is not workable all the time.
3. The finger print of those people working in chemical industries is often affected. Therefore, these companies should not use the finger print mode of authentication.

2.2.1 Types of Biometrics [S-16, 18, W-18, 19]

- Biometric recognition or biometrics refers to the automatic identification of a person based on his/her anatomical (e.g. fingerprint, iris) or behavioral (e.g. signature) characteristics or traits.

2.2.1.1 Eyes - Iris Recognition

- The iris is the colored part of your eye. Iris recognition is an automated method of biometric identification that uses mathematical pattern-recognition techniques on video images of one or both of the irises of an individual's eyes.
- Iris recognition is known for its accuracy and use in high level security systems. Iris recognition involves the system looking at the pattern in one or both of the irises in our eye.

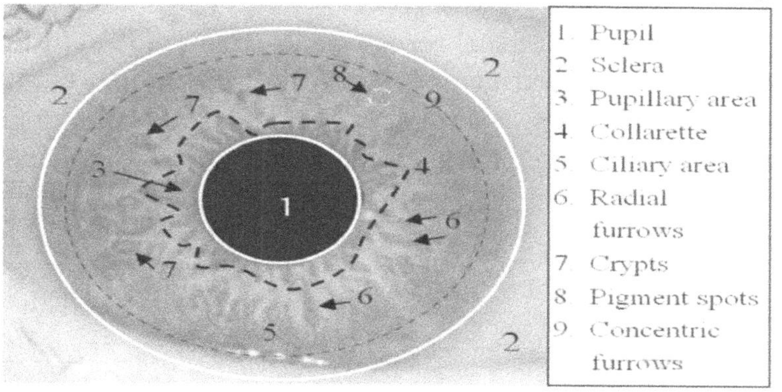

Fig. 2.8

- In this analysis of the iris of the eye is done which is the colored ring of tissue that surrounds the pupil of the eye.
- Based on visible features, i.e. rings, furrows, freckles and the corona. Features and their location are used to form the Iris codes, which is the digital template.
- It is widely considered as the most safe, accurate biometrics technology and capable of performing one-to-many matches at extraordinarily high speeds.

2.2.1.2 Retina Recognition [W-18, S-19]

- The pattern of blood vessels that emanate from the optic nerve and disperse throughout the retina depends on individuals and never changes. No two retinas are the same, even in identical twins.
- Retina recognition technology captures and analyzes the patterns of blood vessels on the thin nerve on the back of the eyeball that processes light entering through the pupil. Retinal patterns are highly distinctive traits.
- Every eye has its own totally unique pattern of blood vessels; even the eyes of identical twins are distinct.
- Although each pattern normally remains stable over a person's lifetime, it can be affected by disease such as glaucoma, diabetes, high blood pressure, and autoimmune deficiency syndrome.
- Retina based recognition is perceived as the most secure method for identification of an identity used to distinguish individuals.

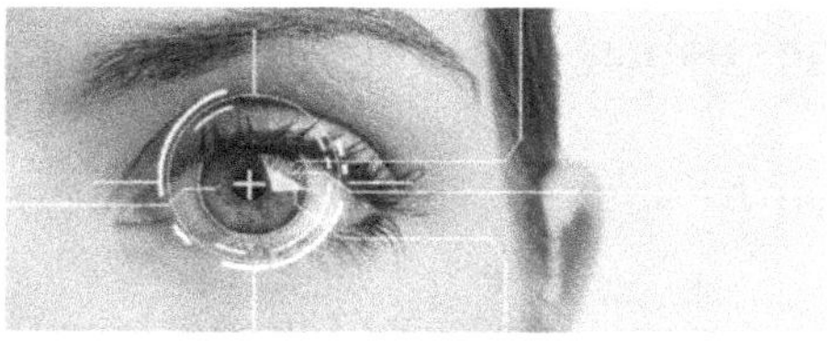

Fig. 2.9

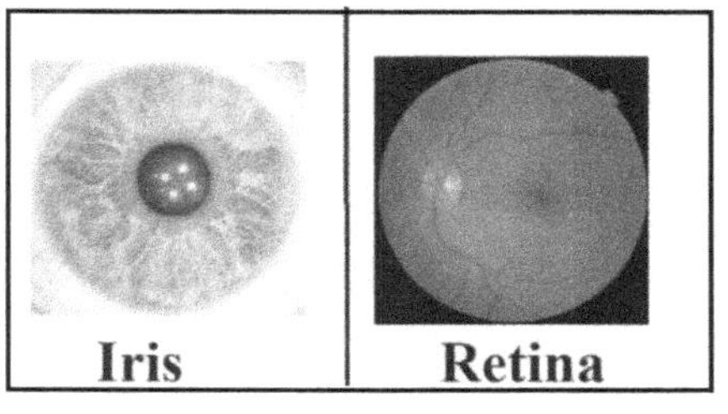

Fig. 2.10

2.2.1.3 Face Recognition

- Facial recognition involves the system recognizing the face by reading characteristics, such as the distance between our eyes, ears and so on.
- Facial images are the most common biometrics characteristics used by humans to make a personal recognition, hence the idea to use this biometrics in technology.
- In this analysis of facial features or patterns for the authentication or recognition of an individual's identity. Most face recognition systems either use Eigen faces or local feature analysis. Uses an image or series of images either from a camera or photograph to recognize a person.
- A facial recognition system is a technology capable of identifying or verifying a person from a digital image or a video frame from a video source.
- There are multiple methods in which facial recognition systems work, but in general, they work by comparing selected facial features from given image with faces within a database.
- It is also described as a Biometric Artificial Intelligence based application that can uniquely identify a person by analysing patterns based on the person's facial textures and shape.

Fig. 2.11

- The principle of facial analysis is of the unique shape, pattern and positioning of facial features.
- It is passive biometrics and does not require a persons cooperation.
- It is highly complex technology and largely software based. Primary advantage is that the biometric system is able to operate "hands-free" and a user's identity is confirmed by simply staring at the screen.

2.2.1.4 Fingerprint Recognition [S-16, 18, 19, W-16, 17]

- Fingerprint identification is one of the oldest indispensable biometric technologies which has drawn an interest in security systems.
- The requirement for reliable personal identification in network society has resulted in a greater interest in biometrics.
- Fingerprint is the most widely used biometric feature because of the well-known distinctiveness (individuality) and persistence properties of fingerprint over time.
- Fingerprint recognition derives a unique template from the attributes of the fingerprint without storing the image itself or even allowing for its reconstruction.
- An extremely useful biometrics technology since fingerprints have been long recognized as a primary and accurate identification method. Uses the ridge endings and bifurcation's on a person's finger to plot points known as Minutiae.
- The number and locations of the minutiae vary from finger to finger in any particular person, and from person to person for any particular finger.
- Fingerprint identification and verification is one of the most significant and reliable identification methods.

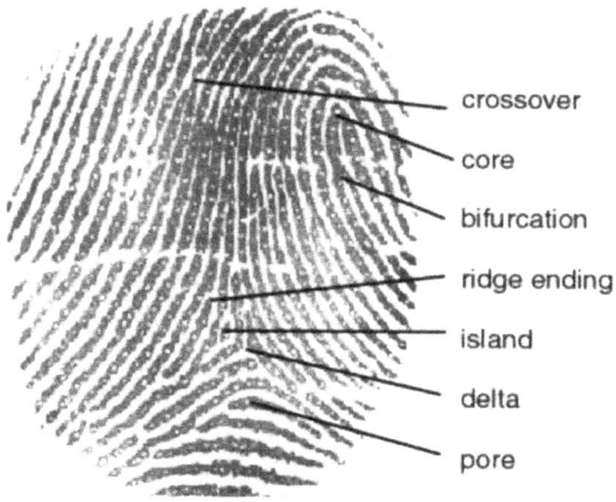

Fig. 2.12

- Fingerprint recognition for identification acquires the initial image through a live scan of the finger (See Fig. 2.12) by v direct contact with a reader device that can also check for validating attributes such as temperature and pulse.
- Fingerprint biometrics has proven to be the best method to implement on devices of different sizes and form factors. Because of it a computer, ultra portables, tablets, smartphones or wearables, fingerprint recognition can be successfully embedded across a range of devices.

2.2.1.5 Hand Geometry Recognition

- Hand geometry is an authentication technology that uses the geometric shape of the hand to identify a user.
- The technique works by measuring and then analyzing the shape and physical features of a user's hand, such as finger length and width and palm width.
- Like fingerprints, this technique also uses a reader. To initiate the device, all users' hands are read and measured and the statistics are stored in a database for future recognition.
- To activate the system the user places the palm of his or her hand on the surface of the reader. Readers usually have features that guide the user's hand on the surface.
- Once on the surface, the hand guided by the guiding features is properly aligned for the reader to read off the hand's attributes.
- The reader is hooked to a computer, usually a server, with an application that provides a live visual feedback of the top view and the side view of the hand.
- Hand features are then taken as the defining feature vector of the user's hand and are then compared with the user features stored in the database.

Fig. 2.13

- In short, hand geometry uses the geometric features of the hand such as the lengths of fingers and the width of the hand to identify an individual.

2.2.1.6 Signature Recognition

- Signature recognition is one of the biometric authentication techniques, where the owner of the signature image is identified.
- Digital signature is a term used to describe a long numeric code that is uniquely assigned to one person, hence the reference to 'signature'.
- The purpose of a digital signature is to be used in encryption systems. A digital signature is issued to an individual by a Certificate Authority (CA).
- An individual's digital signature will normally reside on his/her computer, or can be stored on a card (similar to banking cards). When someone wishes to encrypt an e-document, they will use a password or PIN that in turn allows the digital signature to be used.
- Biometrics signature is a term used for referring to a signature that has been recorded/captured using a variety of input devices such as digitizing tablets, Personal Digital Assistants (PDAs), computer displays or other contact-sensitive technologies.
- Typically, biometrics signatures can also be used to provide and control access security to buildings, networks, computers, documents and databases.
- This method allows real handwritten signatures to be incorporated into e-documents during electronic transactions. Not every technology captures signature information in the same way.
- The authentication of an individual by the analysis of handwriting style, in particular signature. The principle of signature recognition is the movement of the pen during the signing process rather than the static image of the signature. Many aspects of the signature in motion can be studied, such as pen pressure, the sound the pen makes.

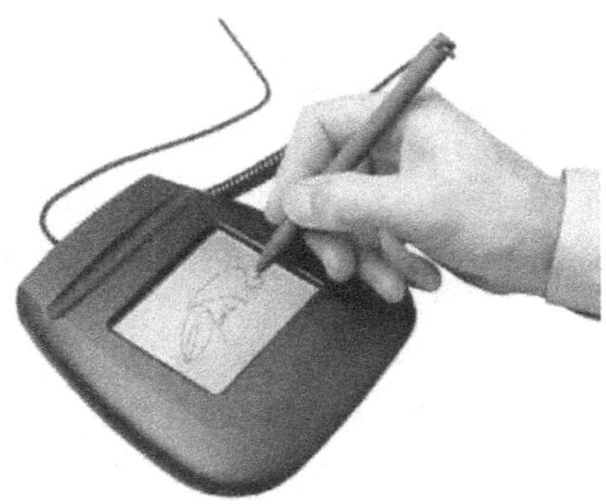

Fig. 2.14

2.2.1.7 Witting Recognition

- Handwriting recognition is the capability of computer to translate or interpret human handwriting characters and display in different ways such as documents, graphics and other devices.
- Furthermore, it is an automated process in computer vision involving the pattern recognition and machine learning techniques for recognition of the human handwriting.
- Typically, there are two different approaches in handwriting recognition namely off-line and on-line. In on-line handwriting recognition, the machine recognizes the writing while the user writes on an electronic interface, such as an electronic pen or a mouse.
- There are two key types of digital handwritten signature authentication, Static and Dynamic. Static is most often a visual comparison between one scanned signature and another scanned signature. Dynamic is becoming more popular as ceremony data is captured along with the X, Y, T and P Coordinates of the signor from the signing device.

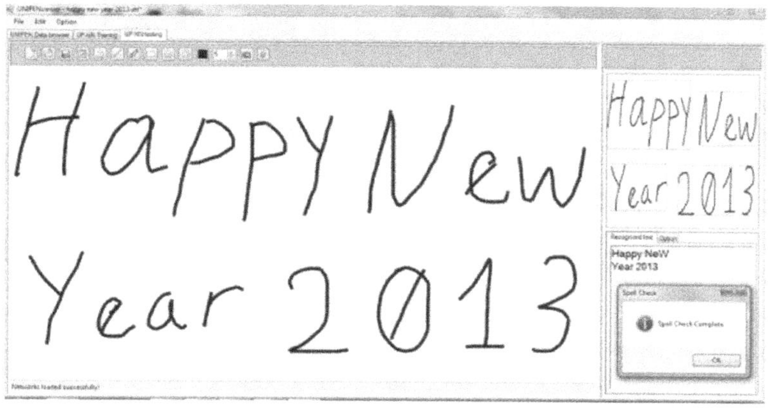

Fig. 2.15: Mouse Drawing Characters Recognition using Multi Networks

- This data can be utilized in a court of law using digital forensic examination tools, and to create a biometric template from which dynamic signatures can be authenticated either at time of signing or post signing, and as triggers in workflow processes.

2.2.1.8 Voice/Speaker Recognition

- Biometrics is the measurement and statistical analysis of a person's physical and behavioural characteristics. For example, voice recognition systems work by measuring the characteristics of a person's speech as air is expelled through their lungs, across the larynx and out through their nose and mouth.
- The speech verification software will compare these characteristics with data already stored on the server and if the two voiceprints are sufficiently similar, the biometric security system will then declare it a match.
- Voice recognition techniques are generally categorized according to two approaches namely, Automatic Speaker Verification (ASV) and Automatic Speaker Identification (ASI).
- ASV uses voice as the authenticating attribute in a two-factor scenario. ASI attempts to use voice to identify who an individual actually is.
- Voice recognition distinguishes an individual by matching particular voice traits against templates stored in a database. Voice systems must be trained to the individual's voice at enrolment time and more than one enrolment session is often necessary.
- Feature extraction typically measures formants or sound characteristics unique to each person's vocal tract. The pattern-matching algorithms used in voice recognition are similar to those used in face recognition.
- Voice recognition is not the same as speech recognition, it is speaker recognition. Voice or speaker recognition is the ability of a machine or program to receive and interpret dictation or to understand and carry out spoken commands.
- Voice recognition has gained prominence and use with the rise of AI and intelligent assistants, such as Amazon's Alexa, Apple's Siri and Microsoft's Cortana.
- Voice recognition systems enable consumers to interact with technology simply by speaking to it, enabling hands-free requests, reminders and other simple tasks.

How Voice Recognition Works?

- Voice recognition software on computers requires that analog audio be converted into digital signals, known as Analog-To-DIGITAL (A/D) Conversion.
- For a computer to decipher a signal, it must have a digital database or vocabulary of words or syllables as well as a speedy means for comparing this data to signals. The speech patterns are stored on the hard drive and loaded into memory when the program is run.

- A comparator checks these stored patterns against the output of the A/D converter an action called pattern recognition.
- In practice, the size of a voice recognition program's effective vocabulary is directly related to the random access memory capacity of the computer in which it is installed.
- A voice recognition program runs many times faster if the entire vocabulary can be loaded into RAM, as compared with searching the hard drive for some of the matches.
- Processing speed is critical, as well because it affects how fast the computer can search the RAM for matches.

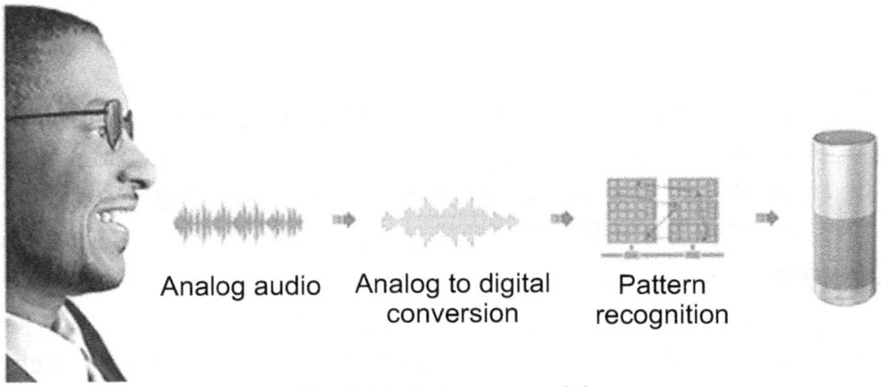

Fig. 2.16: Voice recognition

- Popular and low-cost, but less accurate and sometimes lengthy enrollment.
- Less requirements for users, such that they do not have to go through a separate process for verification.
- Very little hardware is required, and ideally suited to telephone-based system for a remote identification.

2.2.1.9 Keystroke Recognition

- Keystroke dynamics, keystroke biometrics, typing dynamics and lately typing biometrics is the detailed timing information which describes exactly when each key was pressed and when it was released as a person is typing at a computer keyboard.
- To conclude, biometric-based keystroke dynamics scheme provides adequate features to be used to identify the users in different scenarios. It uses the unique characteristics of a person's typing for establishing identity.
- The rhythms which one types at a keyboard are sufficiently distinctive to form the basis of the biometric technology known as keystroke dynamics.
- The behavioral biometric of Keystroke Dynamics uses the manner and rhythm in which an individual types characters on a keyboard or keypad.
- The keystroke rhythms of a user are measured to develop a unique biometric template of the user's typing pattern for future authentication.
- Vibration information may be used to create a pattern for future use in both identification and authentication tasks. Data needed to analyze keystroke dynamics is obtained by keystroke logging.
- Normally, all that is retained when logging a typing session is the sequence of characters corresponding to the order in which keys were pressed and timing information is discarded.
- The keystroke biometric is appealing for following several reasons:
  1. First, it is not intrusive and computer users type frequently for both work and pleasure.
  2. Second, it is inexpensive since the only hardware required is a computer with keyboard.

3. Third, keystrokes continue to be entered for potential subsequent checking after an authentication phase has verified a user's identity, (or possibly been footed) since keystrokes exist as a mere consequence of users using computers.

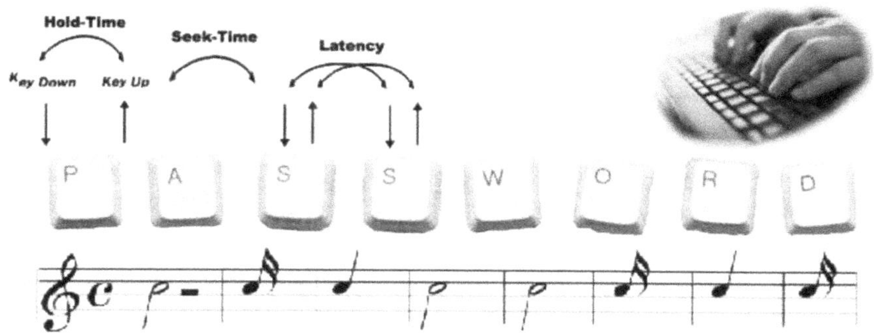

Fig. 2.17

Advantages of Keystroke Dynamics:

1. Keystroke dynamics scheme is a very cost-effective procedure, as it does not require any additional hardware. It require, only the keyboard for it process. This is in addition to only software for keyboard control and for testing and authenticating process.
2. It is easy to setup, process and training is not required to use.
3. It enhance the security of systems.
4. It can be used with and without Internet.
5. Transparency and noninvasiveness.
6. Inimitability.
7. Unremitting observation and validation.

Disadvantages of Keystroke Dynamics:

1. Lower accuracy than physiological biometric schemes.
2. User's vulnerability to exhaustion.
3. Change in typing style from time to time.
4. The typing speed may vary when the user is injured.
5. There are different types of keyboards; hence there is a chance that the typing patterns vary from device to device for the same user.

2.3 ACCESS CONTROL [S-16, 17, W-16, 18]

- Access control is a method of guaranteeing that users are who they say they are and they have the appropriate access to company data.
- Access control, which is an important safeguard in computer security, is used to govern user access to information, resources, services, etc. and to counter malicious attacks.
- Access control's mainly functions are as follows:
  - Prevent illegal entities make accesses to the protected resources in computers.
  - Allow legitimate users to make accesses to protected resources in computers.
  - Prevent legitimate users make unauthorized accesses to protected resources in computers.
- There are two types of access control:
  1. **Physical:** Physical access control limits access to campuses, buildings, rooms and physical IT assets.
  2. **Logical:** Logical access control limits connections to computer networks, system files and data.

Fig. 2.18

2.3.1 Authentication [S-17, 19, W-16, 18]

- Authentication is the process of validating the identity of someone or something. Authentication is the act of proving an assertion, such as the identity of a computer system user.
- Authentication is the process of determining whether someone or something is, in fact, who or what it declares itself to be.
- Authentication technology provides access control for systems by checking to see if a user's credentials match the credentials in a database of authorized users.
- Authentication is important because it enables organizations to keep their networks secure by permitting only authenticated users (or processes) to access its protected resources, which may include computer systems, networks, databases, websites and other network-based applications or services.
- Generally there are three methods used in authentication:
  1. Something – You – Know (e.g. User Id & Password).
  2. Something – You – Have (e.g. Lock & Key).
  3. Something – About – You (e.g. finger print).

2.3.1.1 Authentication Mechanism

- The authentication mechanism consists of three parts that work together to verify the presence of the authenticating characteristics provided by the user. The three parts are the input, the transportation system, and the verifier.
- They are linked with the appropriate technologies. An input component acts as the interface between the user and the authentication system. In a distributed environment this could be a computer keyboard, card reader, video camera, telephone or similar device.
- The captured user, identifying items need to be taken to a place where they are scrutinized, analyzed and accepted or rejected. But in order for these items to reach this point, they have to be transported.
- The transport portion of the system is therefore, responsible for passing data between the input component and the element that can confirm a person's identity.
- In modern day authenticating systems, this information is transported over a network where it can be protected by protocols like Kerberos or sent in plaintext.

Authentication Methods:

- Generally following technologies are used for authentication purpose:
  1. Single sign on.
  2. Remote user access and authentication.

What is Single Sign On?

- Single Sign On (SSO) is the ability for a user to enter the same id and password to logon to multiple applications within an enterprise.
- As passwords are the least secure authentication mechanism, single sign on has now become known as Reduced Sign On (RSO) since more than one type of authentication mechanism is used according to enterprise risk model.
- For example, in an enterprise using SSO software, the user logs on with their id and password. This gains them access to low risk information and multiple applications such as the enterprise portal.
- However, when the user tries to access higher risk applications and information, like a payroll system, the single sign on software requires them to use a stronger form of authentication. This may include digital certificates, security tokens, smart card, biometric or combination.
- Single sign on can also take place between enterprises using federated authentication. For example, a business partner's employee may successfully log on to their enterprise system.
- When they click on a link to our enterprise's application, the business partner's single sign on system will provide a security assertion token to our enterprise using a protocol like SAML, Liberty Alliance, WS Federation or Shibboleth.
- The enterprise's SSO software receives the token, checks it, and then allows the business partner's employee to access our enterprise application without having to sign on. It also works with employees.

Advantages of SSO:

1. Reduced operational cost.
2. Reduced time to access data.
3. Improved user experience, no password lists to carry.
4. Advanced security to systems:
   - Strong authentication.
   - One Time Password devices.
5. Smartcards.
6. Ease burden on developers.
7. Centralized management of users, roles.
8. Fine grained auditing.

Disadvantages of SSO:

1. Single point failure (All system go down is SSO server fails.

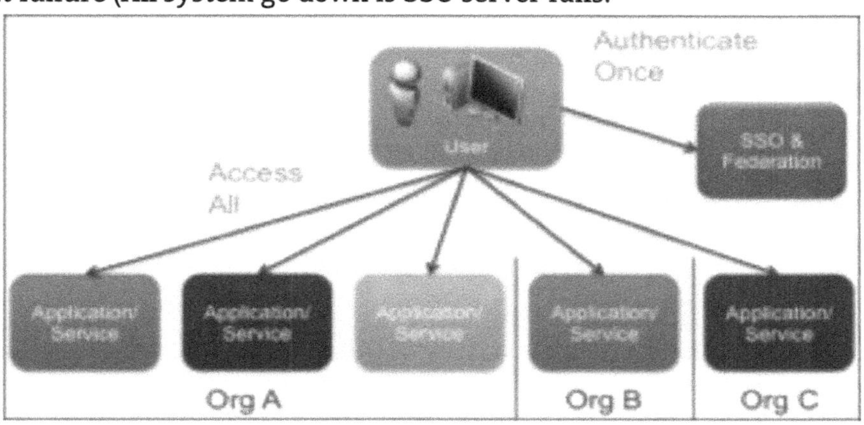

Fig. 2.19

Remote User Access and Authentication:

- When working at remote location from home additional security problems are brought because of insecure networks to create a connections to LAN. Addressing these problem requires additional access control mechanism to protect both LAN and User.

1. **RADIUS:**
   - It stands for Remote Access Dial-In User Service. It is client/server protocol and software. It allows a company to maintain user profiles in a central database that all remote servers can share.
   - RADIUS enables the remote access user to communicate with the central server to authenticate dial-in user and authorize their access to the requested system.
   - It provides better security, allowing a company to set up a policy that can be applied at a single administered network point.
   - Having a central service also means that it's easier to track usage for billing and for keeping network statistics. Authenticating to RADIUS server may require using an ID/password combination etc.

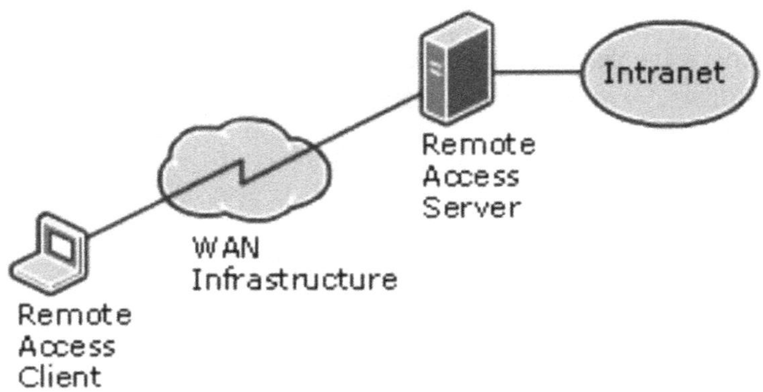

Fig. 2.20: RADIUS

2. **VPN (Virtual Private Network):** **[W-16, 19]**
   - VPN stands for Virtual Private Network. A VPN is a private network that uses a public network (usually the Internet) to connect remote sites or users together.
   - The VPN uses "virtual" connections routed through the Internet from the business's private network to the remote site or employee.
   - With VPN a user connects to the internet via his/her ISP and initiates a connection to the protected network, creating private tunnel between the end points that prevent data modification. By using a VPN, businesses ensure security anyone intercepting the encrypted data can't read it.

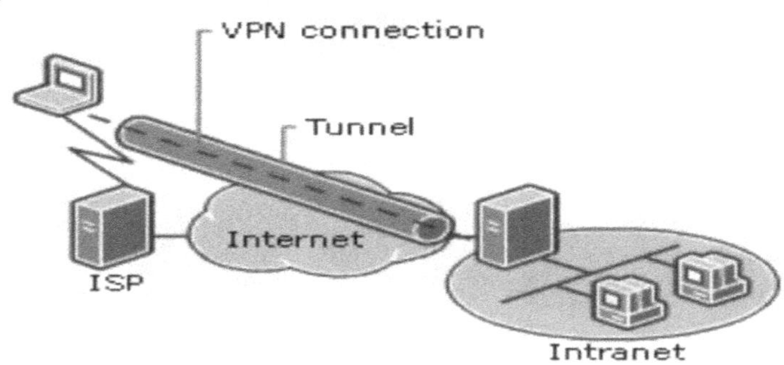

Fig. 2.21: VPN

2.3.2 Authorization **[S-17, 19, W-16, 18]**

- Authorization is the process of determining which permissions a person or system is supposed to have.
- In multi-user computing systems, a system administrator defines which users are allowed access to the system, as well as the privileges of use for which they are eligible (e.g., access to file directories, hours of access, amount of allocated storage space).
- Authorization is a security mechanism used to determine user/client privileges or access levels related to system resources, including computer programs, files, services, data and application features.
- Authorization refers to securing the network by specifying which area of the network, whether it is an application, a device, or a system - a user is allowed to access.
- The authorization level varies from user to user. For example, payroll personnel have access to the payroll systems and engineers have access to design systems, which means that access is based on the need to know.
- This also means that access to system resources and services to users or processes, previously authenticated, is selectively granted.

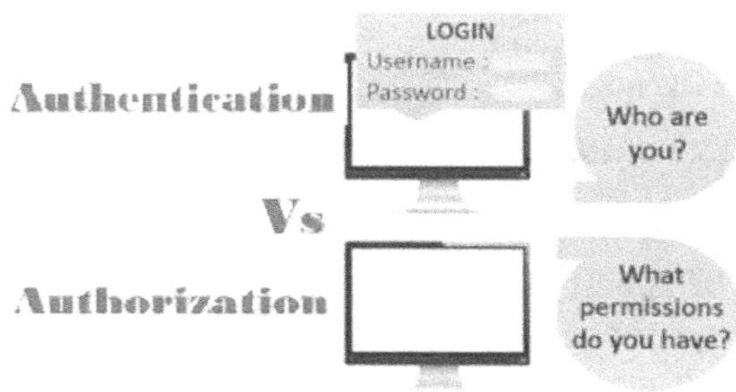

Fig. 2.22

Authorization and Authentication: **[S-17, 19, W-16, 18]**

- The combination of authentication and authorization is called "access control".

Authentication:

- Authentication is used by a server when the server needs to know exactly who is accessing their information or site.
- Authentication is used by a client when the client needs to know that the server is system it claims to be. In authentication, the user or computer has to prove its identity to the server or client.
- Usually, authentication by a server entails the use of a user name and password. Other ways to authenticate can be through cards, retina scans, voice recognition, and fingerprints.
- Authentication by a client usually involves the server giving a certificate to the client in which a trusted third party such as Verisign or Thawte states that the server belongs to the entity (such as a bank) that the client expects it to.
- Authentication does not determine what tasks the individual can do or what files the individual can see. Authentication merely identifies and verifies who the person or system is.

Authorization:

- Authorization is a process by which a server determines if the client has permission to use a resource or access a file.
- Authorization is usually coupled with authentication so that the server has some concept of who the client is that is requesting access.
- The type of authentication required for authorization may vary passwords may be required in some cases but not in others.

- In some cases, there is no authorization; any user may be use a resource or access a file simply by asking for it. Most of the web pages on the Internet require no authentication or authorization.
- Fig. 2.23 shows the authentication and flow of a computer login session. The user is first authenticated as a legitimate user and then authorized as a user for a specific application or database access.

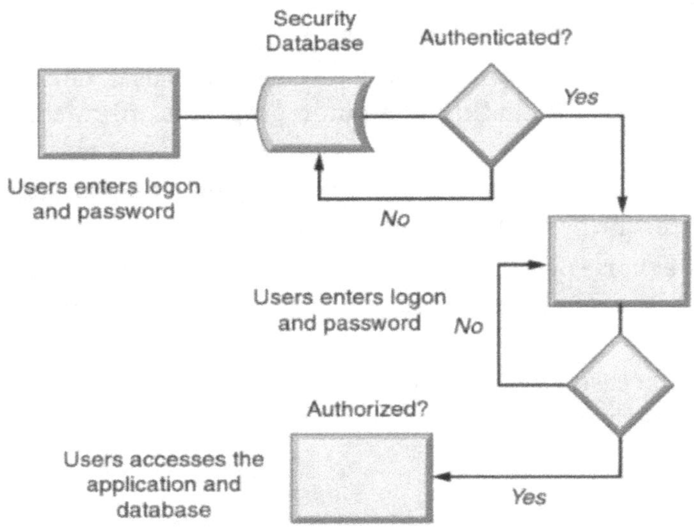

Fig. 2.23: Authentication and Authorization Flow

2.3.3 Authorization Principles

- Authorization is the function of specifying access rights/privileges to resources, which is related to information security and computer security in general and to access control in particular. More formally, "to authorize" is to define an access policy.
- For example, human resources staff are normally authorized to access employee records and this policy is usually formalized as access control rules in a computer system.
- During operation, the system uses the access control rules to decide whether access requests from (authenticated) consumers shall be approved (granted) or disapproved (rejected).
- Resources include individual files or an item's data, computer programs, computer devices and functionality provided by computer applications. Examples of consumers are computer users, computer Software and other Hardware on the computer.
- The prime object of authorization is system security achieved through the controlled access to the system resources.
- The authorization process, together with access control, through the use of authorization data structures, clearly defines who uses what system resources and what resources can and cannot be used.
- The authorization process, therefore, offers undeniable security to the system through the protection of its resources. System resources are protected through principles such as least privilege and separation of duties, which eventually results in increased accountability that leads to increased system security.

1. **Least Privilege:**

- The principle of least privilege requires that the subject be granted authorizations based on its needs. Least privilege principle is itself based on two other principles namely, less rights and less risk.
- The basic idea behind these principles is that security is improved if subjects using system resources are given no more privileges than the minimum they require to perform the tasks that they are intended to perform and in the minimum amount of time required to perform the tasks.

- The least privilege principle has the ability if followed to reduce the risks of unauthorized accesses to the system.

2. Separation of Duties:

- The principle of separation of duties breaks down the process of authorization into basic steps and requires that for every request for authorization from a subject to a system resource, each step be given different privileges.
- It requires that each different key step in a process requires different privileges for different individual subjects.
- This division of labor, not only in the authorization process of one individual request but also between individual subjects, stipulates not only that one subject should never be given a blanket authorization to do all the requested functions but also that no one individual request to an object should be granted blanket access rights to an object.
- This hierarchical or granular authorization distributes responsibilities and creates accountability because no one subject is responsible for large processes where responsibility and accountability may slack.
- For example, authorization to administer a Web server or an e-mail server can be granted to one person without granting him or her administrative rights to other parts of the organization system.

2.3.4 Authentication Principles

- The following principles speak to authenticating that identity.
  1. Identity should be verified as long and as frequently as access to a resource is permitted. If access is ongoing then identity verification should be continuous.
  2. Authentication is about validating whether or not someone is who they claim to be, and about determining whether that person intends to authenticate and is not, for example, being coerced.
  3. In person, human-to-human authentication is the de facto standard in life. When this is not possible and computers must be involved, then computers should provide measures of confidence (or lack thereof) to humans. Those humans should ultimately make authentication decisions, not computers.
  4. Authentication should be trivial for the person legitimately authenticating but hard for an adversary to defeat, much like verifying a key vs. guessing a key in public key cryptography.
  5. The authentication source principle holds that "for each given attribute (piece of identity data), one and only one source is considered to be authentic, i.e., correct."
- In other words, the authentication source principle ensures that one and only one authentic source should be correlated with a specific identity attribute, rendering all other sources for that attribute redundant, and therefore dispensable.

2.3.5 Audits

- Auditing is the process by which unauthorized or abnormal activities are detected on a system Audit simply means to log what access was approved or disapproved so it can be reviewed later.
- Auditing or monitoring, is the process by which subjects are held accountable for their actions while authenticated on a system.
- Auditing is needed to detect malicious actions by subjects, attempted intrusions, and system failures and to reconstruct events provide evidence for prosecution and produce problem reports and analysis.
- Auditing refers to the logging of events that have security significance, such as login/logout, an attempt to perform a privileged action, a modification of an important financial record, etc.

- A related concept is "**monitoring**". But monitoring usually refers to the ongoing examination of the behaviour and health of the system for the purpose of ensuring high availability of the system. Monitoring, of course, can also serve as a security control to detect malicious activities targeting the system.
- Auditing is usually used to support "**accountability**". In information security, accountability refers to making employees directly responsible for actions taken during their daily job assignments.
- To do so, the actions of an individual or a process must be logged in case of a security breach. This requires the tracking of events, whether successful or failed, such as authentications and authorizations, the consumption of network resources, or the changes of important data such as financial records that are initiated by persons or processes.
- A concept related to accountability is "**non-repudiation**", which means an individual or process cannot deny the performance of an action. Of course, audit logs provide the best support for non-repudiation.

2.3.6 Policies [S-18, 19, W-18]

- Policies in security are high level guidelines which determines how accesses are controlled and access decisions are determined.
- Access control is a core security technology to protect sensitive information and critical resources and to counter malicious attacks in computer systems and networks.
- During the past few decades, many access control models have been developed, such as Discretionary Access Control (DAC), Mandatory Access Control (MAC), Role-Based Access Control (RBAC) and so on.
- Access control in computer systems and networks rely on access policies. Access Control (AC) is the selective restriction of access to a place or other resource, while access management describes the process.
- The act of accessing may mean consuming, entering, or using. Permission to access a resource is called authorization.
- Three access control paradigms organize how people gain access are: Role-Based Access Control (RBAC), Discretionary Access Control (DAC) and Mandatory Access Control (MAC).

2.3.6.1 Discretionary Access Control (DAC) [W-16]

- Discretionary Access Control (DAC) is a type of access control system that holds the business owner responsible for deciding which people are allowed in a specific location, physically or digitally.
- DAC is the least restrictive compared to the other systems, as it essentially allows an individual complete control over any objects they own, as well as the programs associated with those objects.

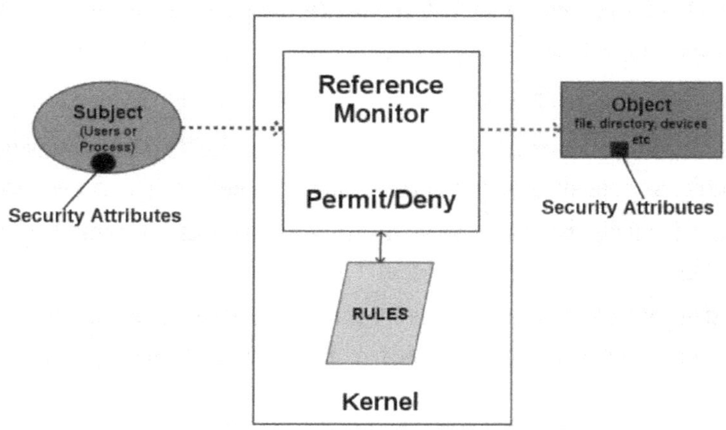

Fig. 2.24: DAC

- The drawback to discretionary access control is the fact that it gives the end user complete control to set security level settings for other users and the permissions given to the end user are inherited into other programs they use which could potentially lead to malware being executed without the end user being aware of it.

2.3.6.2 Mandatory Access Control (MAC) [W-16]

- Mandatory Access Control is more commonly utilized in organizations that require an elevated emphasis on the confidentiality and classification of data (i.e. military institutions).
- MAC doesn't permit owners to have a say in the entities having access in a unit or facility, instead, only the owner and custodian have the management of the access controls.
- MAC will typically classify all end users and provide them with labels which permit them to gain access through security with established security guidelines.

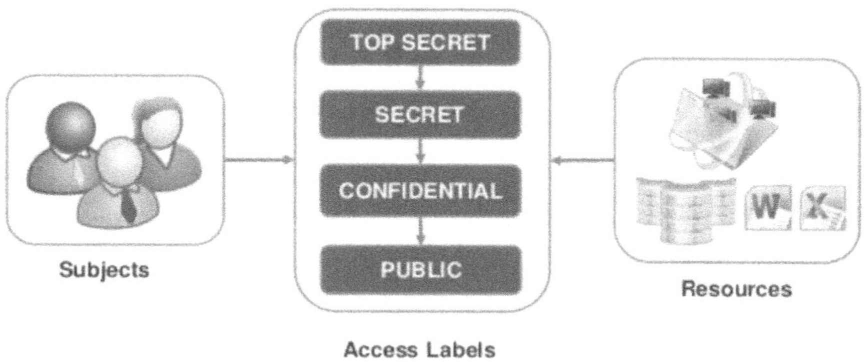

Fig. 2.25: Mandatory Access Control (MAC)

2.3.6.3 Role-Based Access Control (RBAC) [W-16, W-16]

- RBAC is the most demanded in regard to access control systems. Not only is it in high demand among households, RBAC has also become highly sought-after in the business world.
- In RBAC systems, access is assigned by the system administrator and is stringently based on the subject's role within the household or organization and most privileges are based on the limitations defined by their job responsibilities.
- So, rather than assigning an individual as a security manager, the security manager position already has access control permissions assigned to it.
- RBAC makes life much easier because rather than assigning multiple individuals particular access, the system administrator only has to assign access to specific job titles.

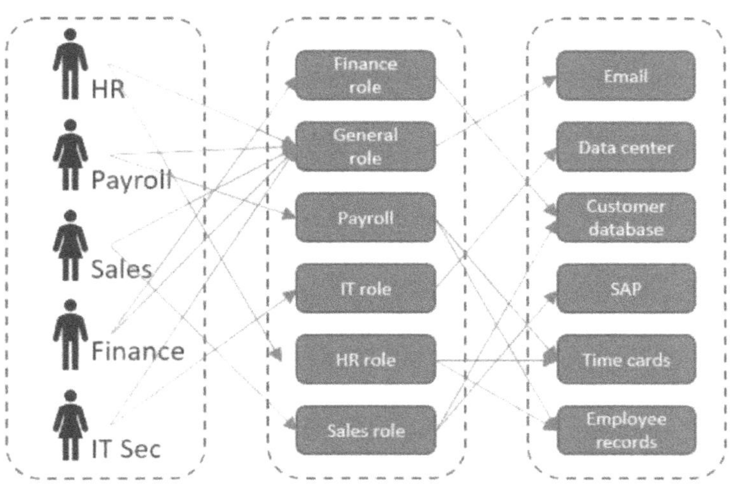

Fig. 2.26: RBAC

Practice Questions

1. What is authentication?
2. What is access control?
3. Describe term identification in detail.
4. What is username and password?
5. Enlist various password attacks.
6. What is password guessing? Give two attacks for it.
7. What is piggy backing? How it works? Explain with example.
8. Describe the terms: (i) Visual hacking, (ii) Dumpster diving.
9. What is biotmetric?
10. Enlist types of biometrics.
11. Define the terms: (i) Authentication, (ii) Automization, (iii) Piggybacking, (iv) Biometric, (v) Access control, (vi) Identification.
12. Enlist authorization principles.
13. What is policy? Enlist its types.
14. Describe the term SSO with its advantages.
15. What is MAC, DAC and RBAC? Compare them.

■■■

3... Cryptography

Chapter Outcomes...

- Encrypt/Decrypt the given text using different substitution techniques.
- Convert plaintext to ciphertext and vice versa using the given transportation technique.
- Convert the given message using steganography.
- Explain the given technique of cryptography using example.

Learning Objectives...

- To understand Concepts in Cryptography
- To study Concept of Steganography
- To learn Symmetric and Asymmetric Cryptography
- To learn Concept of Digital Signature

3.0 INTRODUCTION

- We are living in the information age. We need to keep information about every aspect of our lives. In other words, information is an asset that has a value like any other asset. As an asset, information needs to be secured from attacks.
- To be secured, information needs to be hidden from unauthorized access (confidentiality), protected from unauthorized change (integrity), and avalable to an authorized entity when it is needed (avaliability).
- The art and science of concealing the messages to introduce secrecy in information security is recognized as cryptography.
- The word 'cryptography' was coined by combining two Greek words, 'Krypto' meaning hidden and 'graphene' meaning writing.
- The two types of cryptography are symmetric key encipherment (sometimes called secret key encipherment or secret-key cryptography) and asymmetric key encipherment (sometimes called public key encipherment or public key cryptography).
- The word steganography, with origin in Greek, means "covered writing," in contrast with cryptography, which means "secret writing."
- Cryptography means concealing the contents of a message by enciphering; steganography means concealing the message itself by covering it with something else.
- Steganography is similar but adds another dimension to cryptography. In this method, people not only want to protect the secrecy of an information by concealing it, but they also want to make sure any unauthorized person gets no evidence that the information even exists. For example, invisible watermarking.

3.1 TERMS IN CRYPTOGRAPHY

- Cryptography also called as secret writing which is used to hide the original message. Cryptography is simply the mathematical "scrambling" of data.
- In today's world nothing is secure. Nobody gives the guarantee of 100% security. So, there is a need to protect the computer and data from the attackers.
- Due to rapid increase in the use of Internet, every individual as well as his/her information is having a threat from the attackers. Some information which is beneficial to an individual or a group may be used against them by the attacker.

3.1.1 Plaintext [S-16, 19, W-17]

- A message in its original form is called as plaintext. It is the data to be protected during transmission.
- Plaintext is the message to be encrypted (secret text). Data in readable format called as cleartext.

> Hi Amar
>
> Hope you are doing fine. How about meeting at the train station this Friday at 5 pm?
> Please let me know if it is ok with you.
>
> Regards.
>
> Rohan

Fig. 3.1: Example of a Plaintext Message

3.1.2 Ciphertext [S-16]

- A message in the disguise form is called as ciphertext. It is the encrypted text.
- Ciphertext is the scrambled version of the plaintext produced by the encryption algorithm using a specific the encryption key.

Fig. 3.2: Example of Ciphertext (Encrypted Data)

3.1.3 Cryptography [S-16, 17, 19, W-16, 17, 18, 19]

- Cryptography is art of codifying messages, so that they become unreadable. It is the science of using mathematics to encrypt and decrypt data.
- Cryptography is the art of secret writing. The user can secure his/her message using different techniques of cryptography. He/she can securely store or transmit the message using these techniques.
- Cryptography is the art and science of achieving security by encoding messages to make them non-readable/unreadable.
- Cryptography is a method of storing and transmitting data in a particular form so that only those for whom it is intended can read and process it.
- The art of protecting information by transforming it (encrypting it) into an unreadable format, called cipher text. Only those who possess a secret key can decipher (or decrypt) the message into plain text.

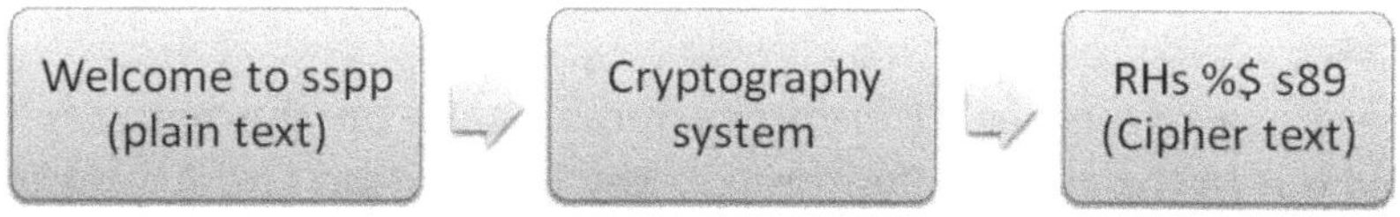

Fig. 3.3: Cryptography System

- Cryptography played an important role in World War II. In the years preceding the war, both the Allies as well as the Germans were investing heavily in building cryptosystems. Many of these systems were based on a combination of mechanical and electronic systems.
- Cryptographic systems or cryptosystems as they are commonly called, convert a plaintext message to a ciphertext message using a cryptographic key.
- The mechanism that applies the key to the message is called a cryptographic algorithm or a cipher. An algorithm for transforming plaintext to ciphertext is called as cipher.
- An algorithm is a step-by-step problem-solving procedure, for solving a problem in a finite number of steps. In the context of encryption, an algorithm is the mathematical formula or set of mathematical rules used to scramble and unscramble data.
- A key is specific string of data used to encrypt the plaintext or decrypt the ciphertext. Key is the secret information in a cryptographic operation.
- Some critical information used in the cipher, known only to sender and receiver is called as key. The process of converting plaintext to ciphertext using a cipher and a key is called as encryption. The process of converting ciphertext back into plaintext using a cipher and a key is called as description.
- Fig. 3.4 shows a sender who wants to transfer some sensitive data to a receiver in such a way that any party intercepting or eavesdropping on the communication channel cannot extract the data.
- The objective of this simple cryptosystem is that at the end of the process, only the sender and the receiver will know the plaintext.

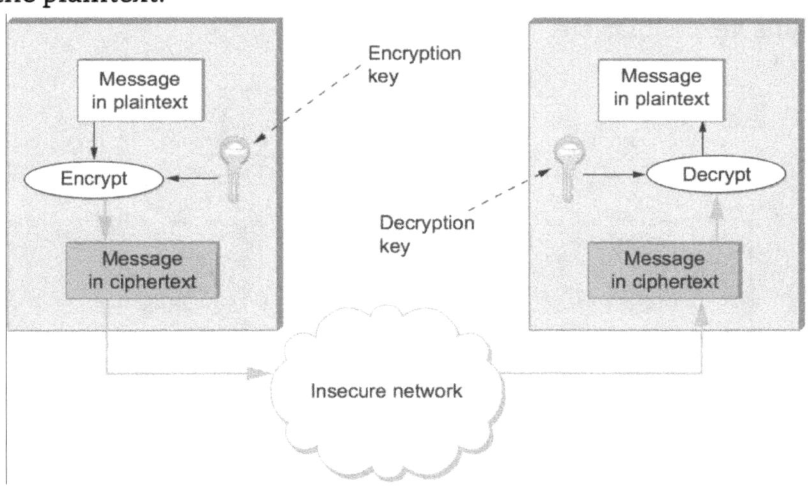

Fig. 3.4

- Encryption algorithm is a cryptographic algorithm that takes plaintext and an encryption key as input and produces a ciphertext.
- Decryption Algorithm is a cryptographic algorithm that takes a ciphertext and a decryption key as input, and outputs a plaintext. The decryption algorithm essentially reverses the encryption algorithm and is thus closely related to it.
- Encryption key is a value that is known to the sender. The sender inputs the encryption key into the encryption algorithm along with the plaintext in order to compute the ciphertext.
- Decryption key is a value that is known to the receiver. The decryption key is related to the encryption key, but is not always identical to it. The receiver inputs the decryption key into the decryption algorithm along with the ciphertext in order to compute the plaintext.

Types of Cryptosystems:

- Fundamentally, there are two types of cryptosystems based on the manner in which encryption-decryption is carried out in the system Symmetric Key Encryption and Asymmetric Key Encryption

Symmetric Key Encryption:

- The encryption process where same keys are used for encrypting and decrypting the information is known as symmetric key encryption.
- The study of symmetric cryptosystems is referred to as symmetric cryptography. Symmetric cryptosystems are also sometimes referred to as secret key cryptosystems.
- A few well-known examples of symmetric key encryption methods are Digital Encryption Standard (DES), Triple-DES (3DES), IDEA, and BLOWFISH.

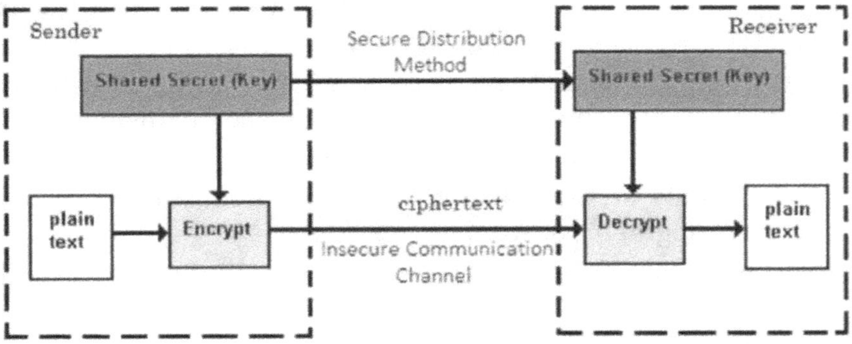

Fig. 3.5: Symmetric Key Encryption

Asymmetric Key Encryption:

- The encryption process where different keys are used for encrypting and decrypting the information is known as Asymmetric Key Encryption.
- Though the keys are different, they are mathematically related and hence, retrieving the plaintext by decrypting ciphertext is feasible.

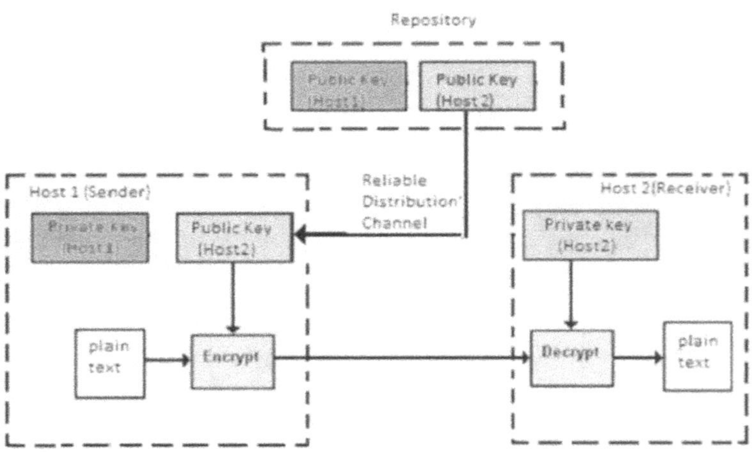

Fig. 3.6: Asymmetric Key Encryption

3.1.4 Cryptanalysis **[S-16, 19, W-16, 17, 18, 19]**

- The study of principles and methods of transforming ciphertext back into plaintext without knowledge of the key is called as cryptanalysis.
- Cryptanalysis is the technique of decoding message from non-readable format back to readable format by trial and error method.
- Cryptanalysis is the art of deciphering the encrypted message/data without knowing the key used for encryption.

3.1.5 Cryptology **[S-19, W-16, 17, 18, 19]**

- It is the combination of cryptography and cryptanalysis.
- The union/combination of cryptography and cryptanalysis is called as cryptology.

3.1.6 Encryption [W-17, S-18]

- It is the process of converting plaintext into ciphertext using key.
- Encryption is a technique of translation of data (plaintext) into a secret code (ciphertext).

Fig. 3.7

3.1.7 Decryption [W-17]

- It is the process of converting cipher text into plain text using key.
- Decryption is a technique of translation of decoded data (ciphertext) into original data (plaintext). A secret key is used for decryption.

Fig. 3.8

Encryption and Decryption:

- Encryption is the process in which a sender converts the original information to another form and sends the resulting unintelligible message out over the network.
- The sender requires an encryption algorithm and a key to transform the plaintext (original message) into a ciphertext (encrypted message), it's also known as enciphering.
- Decryption inverts the encryption process in order to convert the message back to its real form. The receiver uses a decryption algorithm and a key to transform the ciphertext back to original plaintext, it is also known as deciphering.

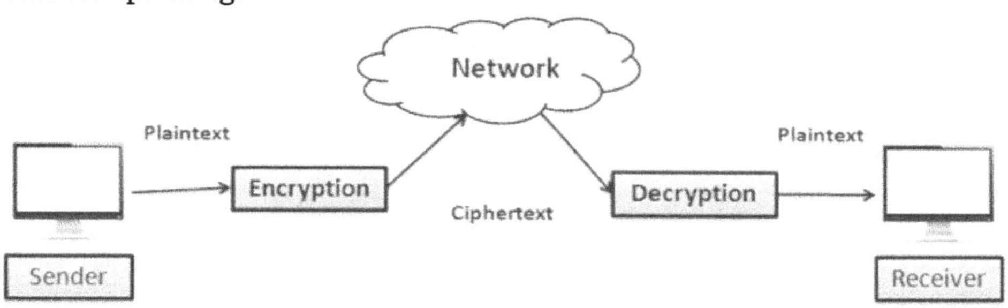

Fig. 3.9

Applications of Cryptography: [W-16]

1. **Secure Communication:** Secure communication is the most straightforward use of cryptography. To prevent eavesdropping – War time communication and business transactions.
2. **Identification and Authentication:** These are the two widely used applications in cryptography. Identification is the process of verifying someone's something's identity.
3. **Secret Sharing:** It allows the trust of a secret to be distributed among a group of people.
4. **Electronic Commerce:** Over the past few years, there has been a growing amount of business conducted over the internet – this form of business is called electronic commerce or e-commerce. For example, encrypted credit card number.
5. **Certification:** Certification is a scheme by which trusted agents such as certifying authorities guarantee for unknown agents, such as users. The trusted agents issue vouchers called certificates which each have some inherent meaning. It was developed to make identification and authentication possible on a large scale.
6. **Key Recovery:** Key recovery is a technology that allows a key to be revealed under certain circumstances without the owner of the key revealing it. For example, accidental erasure, fraudster, terrorism.

7. **Remote Access:** Secure remote access is another important application of cryptography. The basic system of passwords certainly gives a level of security for secure access, but it may not be enough in some cases.
8. **Cell Phone:** It is used in cellular phones as a means of authentication, especially if phone is lost. This prevents people from stealing cellular phone numbers and access codes. Or to prevent eavesdropping of phone calls using voice encryption.
9. **Access Control:** Cryptography is also used to regulate access to satellite and cable T.V. Cable T.V. is set up so people can watch only the channels they pay for.

3.2 SUBSTITUTION TECHNIQUES [S-18, 19]

- It is the very basic technique, which makes use of simple letter substitution to generate ciphertext.
- A substitution technique is a method which replaces (substitutes) each plaintext letter with another alphabetical letter i.e., each of the plaintext letter is substituted (replaced) by another cipher-text letter.

3.2.1 Substitution Cipher

- A substitution technique is the one in which the one in which the letters of plain text are replaced by other letters or by numbers or symbols.
- Substitution Cipher includes Caesar cipher, Play fair cipher and Hill cipher.

3.2.1.1 Caesar Cipher [W-16, 18]

- A cryptographic scheme proposed by Julius Caesar. Caesar cipher is the simplest and well-known substitution encryption technique.
- In cryptography, a Caesar cipher, also known as shift cipher, Caesar's code or Caesar shift. It is one of the simplest and most widely known encryption techniques.
- It involves replacing each letter of alphabet with the letter standing three (3) places down the alphabet.

Replacement Table

Plain	a	b	c	d	e	f	g	h	i	j	k	l	m
Cipher	d	e	f	g	h	i	j	k	l	m	n	o	p
Plain	n	o	p	q	r	s	t	u	v	w	x	y	z
Cipher	q	r	s	t	u	v	w	x	y	z	a	b	c

For example, Plain text = welcome to MIT

Cipher text = zhofrphwrplw

- Caser cipher is a very weak scheme of hiding plain text message. To break caser cipher we do the reverse process.

Algorithm to Break Caser Cipher:

- Read each alphabet in cipher text and search for it in second row of the replacement table.
- Replace that alphabet in cipher text with the corresponding alphabet in same column but in first row of table, (i.e. c replaced by z).
- Repeat process for all alphabets in the cipher message.

For example, Cipher text= PLW VVSS

Plain text= MIT SSPP

3.2.1.2 Modified Version of Casear Cipher

- In this some complications are added in basic Caesar cipher. To make attackers life difficult. In this each alphabet in plain text is replaced by any places down the line of alphabet.
- Not necessary to be third place down the line. i.e. A can be replaced by any other alphabet in (B through Z). Thus for each alphabet we have 25 possibilities of replacement.

For example, plain text= welcome

- Suppose we have decided that replace plain text message with 5 places down the line. So cipher text is Plain text=welcome

  Cipher text=aipgsgi
- Algorithm to break modified version:
  1. Let k=1.
  2. Read each alphabet in cipher text message and replace each alphabet with alphabet with k position down the order.
  3. Increment k by 1.
  4. If k<26 go to step 2 else stop.
  5. Original plain text message is one of the 25 possibilities produced by above steps.

     For example, consider Cipher text = aipgsgi

     Cipher text a i p g s g i

Value of k							
1	b	j	q	h	t	r	j
2	c	k	r	i	u	s	k
3	d	l	s	j	v	t	l
4	e	m	t	k	w	u	m
5	f	n	u	l	x	v	n
6	g	o	v	m	y	w	o
7	h	p	w	n	z	x	p
8	i	q	x	o	a	y	q
9	j	r	y	p	b	z	r
10	k	s	z	q	c	a	s
11	l	t	a	r	d	b	t
12	m	u	b	s	e	c	u
13	n	v	c	t	f	d	v
14	o	w	d	u	g	e	w
15	p	x	e	v	h	f	x
16	q	y	f	w	i	g	y
17	r	z	g	x	j	h	z
18	s	a	h	y	k	i	a
19	t	b	i	z	l	j	b
20	u	c	j	a	m	k	c
21	v	d	k	b	n	l	d
22	w	e	l	c	o	m	e
23	x	f	m	d	p	n	f
24	y	g	n	e	q	o	g
25	z	h	o	f	r	p	h

Fig. 3.10: Attempt to Break Modified Caesar cipher using all Possibilities

- To break modified Caesar cipher above algorithm is used. We can see that cipher text shown in first row of Fig. 3.10 needs maximum 25 different attempts to break according to algorithm. 22nd attempt reveals to break plain text.

3.2.1.3 Monoalphabetic Cipher

- Major weakness of Caesar cipher is predictability. Instead of using uniform scheme for all alphabets in given plain text message it uses random substitution. i.e. A can be replaced by any other alphabet between B to Z. B can be replaced by any other alphabet A or C----Z etc.
- There is no relationship between replacement of B and A. i.e. if we replace A by E then it is not necessary that B is replace with F it can be replaced with any alphabet.
- Monoalphabetic cipher is a substitution cipher in which for a given key, the cipher alphabet for each plain alphabet is fixed throughout the encryption process. For example, if 'A' is encrypted as 'D', for any number of occurrence in that plaintext, 'A' will always get encrypted to 'D'.
- All of the substitution ciphers we have discussed earlier in this chapter are monoalphabetic; these ciphers are highly susceptible to cryptanalysis.

Homophonic Substitution Cipher:

- In this one plaintext alphabet can be mapped to more than one cipher text alphabet. For example, A can be replaced by [D,H,P,R]. B can be replaced by [E, I, Q, S].
- It involves substitution of one plain text character with a cipher text character can be any one of chosen set.

Polygram Substitution Cipher:

- In this rather than replacing one plain text with one cipher text at a time, a block of alphabet is replaced with another block.
- For example, hello replaced with YVQQW. Hell replaced with TXUG with totally different scheme.

Polyalphabetic Substitution Cipher:

- This uses multiple one character key. Each of the key encrypts one plain text character.
- First key encrypts the first plain text character; second key encrypts second plain text character and so on. It uses set of related monoalphabetic substitution rules.
- It uses key that determines which rule is used for which transformation.

3.2.1.4 Play Fair Cipher [S-16, W-16]

- It is based on the use of 5×5 matrix of letter constructed using the keyword.
- Matrix is constructed by filling the letters in keyword from left to right and top to bottom. And then filling the remainder of matrix with the remaining letters in alphabetic order.
- In this scheme, pairs of letters are encrypted, instead of single letters as in the case of simple substitution cipher.
- In playfair cipher, initially a key table is created. The key table is a 5×5 grid of alphabets that acts as the key for encrypting the plaintext.

Rules:

1. Split the plain text as a group of two (2) letters.
2. All letters written in lowercase and without punctuation.
3. If group contain repeated plain text letter then they are separated with filler letter x.
   For example, balloon ba l loon
   balx lo on
4. If a single letter remains at the end to attached with z.
5. If 2 plaintext letters fall in same row of matrix then each letter is replaced by letter to the right.
6. If 2 plaintext letters fall in same column of matrix then each letter is replaced by letter below it.
7. If 2 plaintext letter not in same row or same column then each plain text letter that is present in his row but column occupied by the other letter in plain text letter.

Preparing Matrix:

1. 5 × 5 matrix.

2. Populate with keyword.
   For example, keyword is play fair example.
3. Fill in keyword in matrix by omitting repeated alphabets.

p	l	a	y	f
i	r	e	x	m

4. Populate matrix with alphabets in order again omitting repeated alphabets.

p	l	a	y	f
i	r	e	x	m
b	c	d	g	h
k	n	o	q	S
t	u	v	w	z

Encryption Example:

1. Plain text is MIT POLYTECHNIC,
   Example: Keyboard = play fair example.
   Our matrix will be,

p	l	a	y	f
i	r	e	x	m
b	c	d	g	h
k	n	o	q	S
t	u	v	w	z

2. Split plain text (Rule 3)
   MI TP OL YT EC HN IC
3. By looking in the matrix MI is in the same row so will be replaced by right side letter. (Rule 5) MI →IR.
4. TP is in the same column so will be replace by below letter (Rule 6) TP →PI.
5. OL is in different row different column so will be replaced by the same row alphabet but from the column of another alphabet (Rule 7) OL → NA.
6. YT is replaced by the same (Rule 7) YT → PW.
7. EC replaced with Rule 7 EC → RD.
8. HN replaced with Rule 7 HN → CS.
9. IC replaced with Rule 7 IC → RB.
   Plain text = MIT POLYTECHNIC.
   Cipher text = IR PI NA PW RD CS RB.

Hill Cipher:

- Another interesting multiletter cipher is the Hill cipher, developed by the mathematician Lester Hill in 1929. Hill cipher works on multiple letters at same time.
- The encryption algorithm takes m successive plaintext letters and substitutes for them m ciphertext letters. The substitution is determined by m linear equations in which each character is assigned a numerical value (a = 0, b = 1, ... z = 25).

Encryption Process:

1. First convert the key word into key matrix (2×2) or (3×3). It keyword not provide select any random key matrix.
2. Convert plaintext into diagraph for 2×2 key matrix or trigraph for 3×3 key matrix.
3. Number the plain text alphabets in diagraph or trigraph(A = 0 ...... Z = 25).
4. Multiply two matrices, plain text matrix and key matrix.
5. Perform mod26 of above resultant matrix.
6. Again translate the numbers to alphabets to get cipher text.

Example:

Keyword = HILL

Plaintext = java

- We use 2×2 matrixes:

1. Convert keyword into matrix,

$$\begin{bmatrix} H & I \\ L & L \end{bmatrix} = \begin{bmatrix} 7 & 8 \\ 11 & 11 \end{bmatrix}$$

2. Convert plaintext into diagraph because key matrix is 2×2,

$$\begin{pmatrix} J \\ A \end{pmatrix}\begin{pmatrix} V \\ A \end{pmatrix}$$

3. Replace alphabet with alphabet number,

$$\begin{pmatrix} 9 \\ 0 \end{pmatrix}\begin{pmatrix} 21 \\ 0 \end{pmatrix}$$

4. Perform multiplication with following rules,

$$\begin{pmatrix} a & b \\ c & d \end{pmatrix}\begin{pmatrix} x \\ y \end{pmatrix} = \begin{pmatrix} ax + by \\ cx + dy \end{pmatrix}$$

5. Consider,

$$\begin{pmatrix} 9 \\ 0 \end{pmatrix}\begin{pmatrix} 7 & 8 \\ 11 & 11 \end{pmatrix} = \begin{pmatrix} 7 \times 9 + 8 \times 0 \\ 11 \times 9 + 11 \times 0 \end{pmatrix} = \begin{pmatrix} 63 \\ 99 \end{pmatrix}$$

6. Perform mod 26 of above 26 resultant matrix that is take the remainder after dividing above matrix value by 26,

$$\begin{pmatrix} 63 \\ 99 \end{pmatrix} \text{mod } 26 = \begin{pmatrix} 11 \\ 21 \end{pmatrix}$$

7. Now the translate the number to the alphabet 11= L and 21 = V. So JA = LV.
8. Perform step 4, 5, 6, 7 for plain text VA and you will obtain RX,
9.

$$\begin{pmatrix} 21 \\ 0 \end{pmatrix}\begin{pmatrix} 7 & 8 \\ 11 & 11 \end{pmatrix} = \begin{pmatrix} 21.7 + 0.8 \\ 21.11 + 0.11 \end{pmatrix} = \begin{pmatrix} 147 \\ 231 \end{pmatrix}$$

10.

$$\begin{pmatrix} 147 \\ 231 \end{pmatrix} \text{mod } 26 = \begin{matrix} 17 \\ 23 \end{matrix}$$

11. 17 → R 23 → X
12. Thus, plaintext = java

    cipher text = lvrx

3.2.2 Transposition Techniques [S-17, W-17]

- All the techniques examined so far involve the substitution of a ciphertext symbol for a plaintext symbol. A very different kind of mapping is achieved by performing some sort of permutation on the plaintext letters. This technique is referred to as a transposition cipher.
- One more classical encryption cipher is transposition ciphers. In transposition cipher, the letters are written in a row under the key and then arrange the column as per alphabetical order.
- It is the modified version of substitution technique because this not only substitutes letters but also makes some sort of permutation over the plain text in order to generate cipher text.
- It is another type of cipher where the order of the alphabets in the plaintext is rearranged to create the ciphertext. The actual plaintext alphabets are not replaced.
- Some techniques for Transposition technique includes Rail fence, One time pad (vernam cipher) and Row transposition.
- Transposition technique performs some permutations over the plaintext alphabet.

1. Rail Fence Technique: [S-16, W-16, 19]

- The simplest such cipher is the rail fence technique, in which the plaintext is written down as a sequence of diagonals and then read off as a sequence of rows.

Algorithm:

(i) Write down the plain text message as sequence of diagonals.

(ii) Read the plain text written in step 1 as sequence of rows.

Example: Plain text = come home tomorrow

Arrange plain text as sequence of diagonal as,

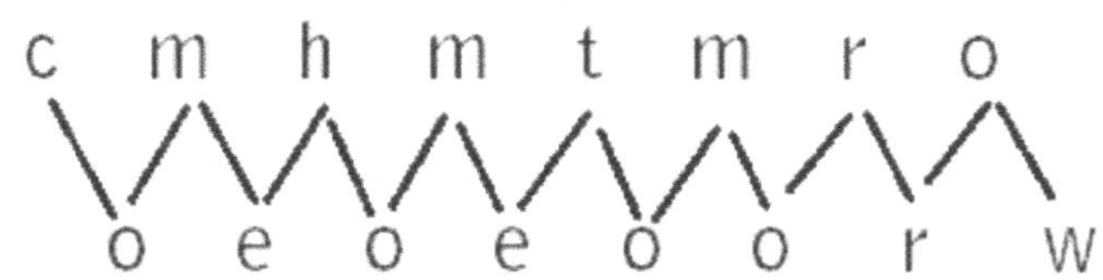

Fig. 3.11

Now read as sequence of row.

Cipher text: cmhmtmrooeoeoorw

2. One Time Pad: [S-16, W-16]

- In 1918, Gilbert Verman developed a cipher called as onetime pad. It is the most secure cryptographic algorithm. In this cipher, the key is a set of random numbers generated by pseudo-random number generator. This generator is used only once to encrypt a message.
- One time pad and key is used for decryption. Mauborgne developed a method of one time pad. A one time pad is a very simple symmetric cipher. The key is selected randomly so that every time new key is used for encryption.
- Therefore, for the same message next time different ciphertext is generated. So, it is difficult to break this cipher. For decryption, same key is used, so secure key transmission is the problem.

Properties of One Time Pad:

1. The number of possible keys is equal to the number of possible plaintexts.
2. The key is selected at random.
3. Key should be used only once.

- It is also called as vernam cipher. Implemented using random set of non-repeating characters as input cipher text.
- Once, an input cipher text is used for transposition, it is never used again for any other message hence it is called as one time pad.
- Size of input cipher text is equal to the size of plain text.

Algorithm:

1. Number the alphabet in plaintext.
2. Take random input cipher text &number alphabet in it i.e. one time pad .
3. Add each number corresponding to plain text alphabet & one time pad alphabet.
4. If sum produced is greater than 25 then subtract 26 from it.
5. Translate each number of the sum back to the corresponding alphabet it gives output cipher text.

Example:

Consider plaintext = how are you

Input cipher text = NCB TZQ ARX (ONE TIME PAD)

Plaintext	H	O	W	A	R	E	Y	O	U
	7	14	22	0	17	4	24	14	20
One time pad	N	C	B	T	Z	Q	A	R	X
	13	**2**	**1**	**19**	**25**	**16**	**0**	**17**	**23**
After addition	**20**	**16**	**23**	**19**	**42**	**20**	**24**	**31**	**43**
Subtract 26 if >25					-26			-26	-26
Total	**20**	**16**	**23**	**19**	**16**	**20**	**24**	**5**	**17**
Cipher text	V	Q	X	T	Q	V	Y	F	R

Plain text = How are you

Cipher text = VQX TQV YFR

It is suitable only for short message.

3. Row Transposition Cipher: **[W-16]**

- In this rearrangement of character is carried out.
- By writing plaintext row wise & reading cipher text column wise in the order of column specified by key.

Algorithm:

1. Take key.
2. Write the plain text row wise& divided into key length number of columns
3. Arrange the key in alphabetical order so accordingly order the columns
4. Read cipher text column wise
5. To complete the table plain text is padded with X.

Example: Plain text: The simplest possible cipher is,

Key: Given (5 columns)

G	I	V	E	N
t	h	e	s	i
m	p	l	e	s
t	p	o	s	s
i	b	l	e	c
i	p	h	e	r
i	s	x	x	x

Arrange key in alphabetical order,

Key = eginv

E	G	I	N	V
s	t	h	i	e
e	m	p	s	l
s	t	p	s	o
e	i	b	c	l
e	i	p	r	n
x	i	s	x	x

Read column wise

Cipher text = seseextmtiihppbpsisscrxelolnx.

3.2.3 Columnar Transposition [S-16]

- In a columnar transposition, the message is written out in rows of a fixed length, and then read out again column by column, and the columns are chosen in some scrambled order. Both the width of the rows and the permutation of the columns are usually defined by a keyword.
- For example, the word ZEBRAS is of length 6 (so the rows are of length 6), and the permutation is defined by the alphabetical order of the letters in the keyword. In this case, the order would be "6 3 2 4 1 5".
- In a regular columnar transposition cipher, any spare spaces are filled with nulls; in an irregular columnar transposition cipher, the spaces are left blank. Finally, the message is read off in columns, in the order specified by the keyword.
- For example, suppose we use the keyword ZEBRAS and the message "WE ARE DISCOVERED. FLEE AT ONCE". In a regular columnar transposition, we write this into the grid as:

6	3	2	4	1	5
W	E	A	R	E	D
I	S	C	O	V	E
R	E	D	F	L	E
E	A	T	O	N	C
E	Q	K	J	E	U

- Providing five nulls (QKJEU) at the end. The cipher text is then read off as:
  EVLNE ACDTK ESEAQ ROFOJ DEECU WIREE
- In the irregular case, the columns are not completed by nulls:

6	3	2	4	1	5
W	E	A	R	E	D
I	S	C	O	V	E
R	E	D	F	L	E
E	A	T	O	N	C
E					

  This results in the following cipher text:
  EVLNA CDTES EAROF ODEEC WIREE
- To decipher it, the recipient has to work out the column lengths by dividing the message length by the key length. Then he can write the message out in columns again, then re-order the columns by reforming the key word.
- Columnar transposition continued to be used for serious purposes as a component of more complex ciphers at least into the 1950's.

3.3 STEGANOGRAPHY [S-16, 17, 19, W-17, 18, 19]

- It is the technique of hiding one message inside other message.
- An encrypted file may still hide information using steganography, so even if the encrypted file is deciphered, the hidden message is not seen. Special software is needed for steganography.
- The word steganography is of Greek origin and means "concealed writing" from the Greek words steganos meaning "covered or protected", and graphein meaning "to write".
- Steganography is the art and science of writing hidden messages in such a way that no one, apart from the sender and intended recipient, suspects the existence of the message.
- Steganography works by replacing bits of useless or unused data in regular computer files (such as graphics, sound, text, HTML, or even floppy disks) with bits of different, invisible information. This hidden information can be plain text, cipher text, or even images.

- Steganography sometimes is used when encryption is not permitted. Or, more commonly, steganography is used to supplement encryption.
- Cryptography protect contents of message. Steganography protects both message and communicating parties.
- Steganography embeds a secret message in cover message parameterized by stego-key and reading of an embedded secret message is possible only having this key.
- In steganography, an unintended recipient or an intruder is unaware of the fact that observed data contains hidden information.
- In cryptography, an intruder is normally aware that data is being communicated, because they can see the coded/scrambled message.

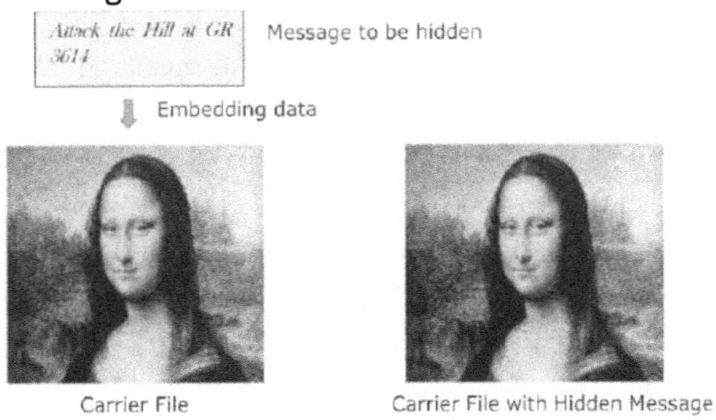

Fig. 3.12

3.3.1 Steganography Process **[W-17, 18]**

- Steganography embeds a secret message in a cover message, this process is usually parameterized by a stego-key, and the detection or reading of an embedded information is possible only having this key.

  Cover media + secret message + stego key = stego medium

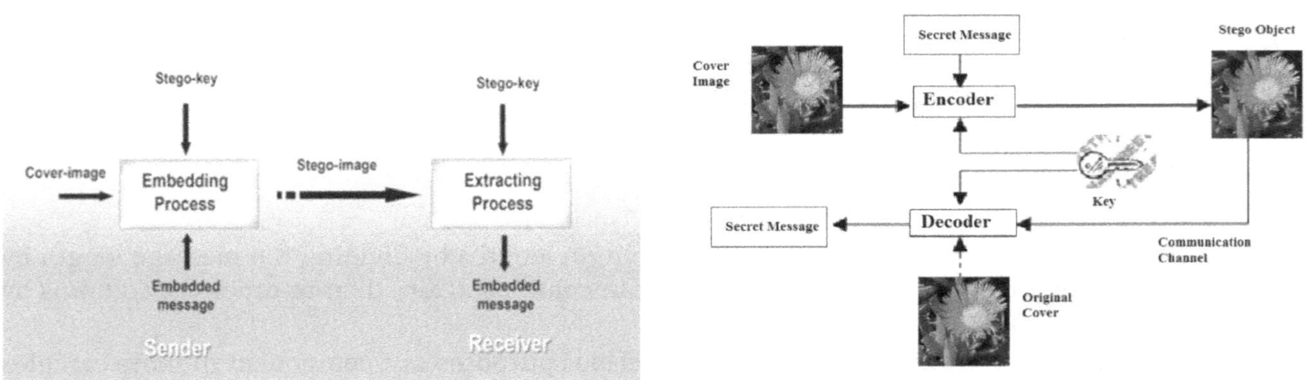

(a) (b)

Fig. 3.13: Process of Steganography

Terminology in Steganography:

1. **Cover Media:** Is the media in which we hide the secret message.
2. **Message (Pay Load)**: Also called as hidden data. It is message which will be hidden in cover or stego media.
3. **Stegomedium (Package, Converted Message):** Medium in which secret message is hidden.
4. **Redundant Bit:** Bit in cover medium that can be modified without compromising that mediums integrity.
5. **Stego Key:** Key used to encode and decode the data.
6. **Stego Function:** Function for encoding and reverse function for decoding.

Thus, secret message is hidden in cover medium without compromising its integrity. By encrypting itusing stego key. Finally, we get stego medium which contain hidden message.

Techniques of Steganography:

1. Character marking, in this selected letters of text are overwritten using pencil.
2. Invisible ink, a number of substances can be used for writing but leave no visible trace until heat or some chemical.
3. Pin punctures, small pin punctures of selected letters are not visible unless paper is held in front of light.
4. Wax tablets in wooden frame.
5. Message below postal stamp.
6. Typewriter ribbon, double typed alphabets.
7. Knitting yarn.

Advantages of Steganography:

1. It can be employed by parties who have something to lose should the fact of their secret communication be discovered.
2. Steganography can protect both the message and communication parties.

Disadvantages of Steganography:

1. Requires lots of overhead to hide few bits of information.
2. Once the system is discovered it becomes virtually worthless.
3. Hiding capacity is less.
4. Quality of the resultant stego image is a major issue.

Applications

1. Used in modern printers.
2. Digital watermarking.
3. Copy write.
4. Convert military operations.
5. To transmit cryptography keys.

3.4 SYMMETRIC AND ASYMMETRIC CRYPTOGRAPHY [S-17]

- Thre are two types of classical encryption techniques:
  1. Symmetric encryption (only one key for encryption and decryption).
  2. Asymmetric encryption (also called public key encryption).
- In symmetric encryption, only one key is required. The same key is used for encryption as well as decryption of the data.
- There are many symmetric encryption algorithms like DES, AES, IDEA, and 3DES.
- In asymmetric encryption, two different keys are required or used. These keys are mathematically related to each other. These keys are called public key and private key.
- The key which is publically available for all are called as public key whereas the key which is known to the owner of the key is called private key. There are many asymmetric encryption algorithms like Diffie-Hellman, RSA and Elliptic Curve Cryptography (ECC).

3.4.1 Symmetric Encryption [S-17, W-18]

- Symmetric key cryptography (or symmetric encryption) is a type of encryption scheme in which the same key is used both to encrypt and decrypt messages. Hence, also called as single key/secret key/shered key technique.
- This key is shared between sender and receiver and known to only sender and receiver and no one else. Symmetric Encryption also called Secret Key Cryptography, uses only one key for both encryption and decryption of a message that is being shared through a communication channel.
- In symmetric encryption the plain text gets encrypted and then converted to the cipher text using an encryption algorithm and a key.

- On reaching the intended receiver, the ciphertext gets converted back to plain text utilizing the same key that was applied for encryption and a decryption algorithm. The key used can be as easy as a secret number or just a string of letters.

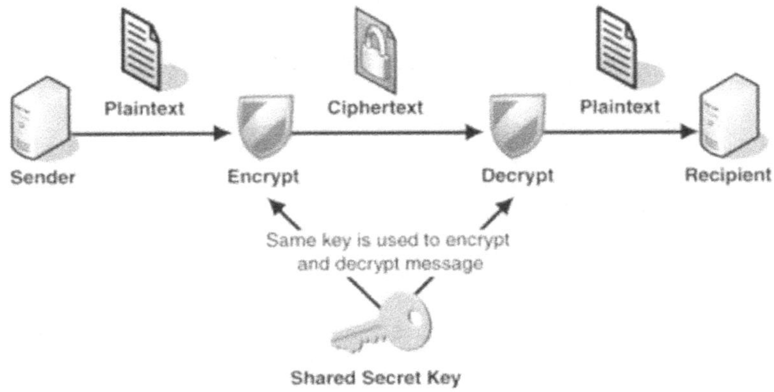

Fig. 3.14: Symmetric Cryptography

Types of Symmetric Cryptography:

1. **Block Cipher:** It is the encryption technique in which 64bit blocks of data is encrypted at a time with encryption algorithm.
2. **Stream Cipher:** It encrypt smaller block of plain text data at time i.e. bit or byte.

Advantages:

1. **Simple:** This type of encryption is easy to carry out. All users have to do is specify and share the secret key and then begin to encrypt and decrypt messages.
2. **Fast:** Symmetric key encryption is much faster than asymmetric key encryption.
3. **Uses Les s Computer Resources:** Single-key encryption does not require a lot of computer resources when compared to public key encryption.
4. **Prevents Widespread Message Security Compromise:** A different secret key is used for communication with every different party. If a key is compromised, only the messages between a particular pair of sender and receiver are affected. Communications with other people are still secure.

Disadvantages:

1. **Need for Secure Communication Channel for Secret Key Exchange:** Sharing the secret key in the beginning is a problem in symmetric key encryption. It has to be exchanged in a way that ensures it remains secret.
2. **Too Many Keys:** A new shared key has to be generated for communication with every different party. This creates a problem with managing and ensuring the security of all these keys.
3. **Origin and Authenticity of Message Cannot be Guaranteed:** Since both sender and receiver use the same key, messages cannot be verified to have come from a particular user. This may be a problem if there is a dispute.

3.4.1.1 Data Encryption Standard (DES) [W-19]

- The Data Encryption Standard (DES) is a symmetric-key block cipher published by the National Institute of Standards and Technology (NIST).
- The Data Encryption Standard (DES) is a symmetric-key algorithm for the encryption of electronic data.
- Although its short key length is of 56 bits, criticized from the beginning, makes it too insecure for most current applications, it was highly influential in the advancement of modern cryptography.
- DES is an implementation of a Feistel Cipher. It uses 16 round Feistel structure. The block size is 64-bit. Though, key length is 64-bit, DES has an effective key length of 56 bits, since 8 of the 64 bits of the key are not used by the encryption algorithm (function as check bits only).

- General structure of DES is depicted in the following illustration in Fig. 3.15. The initial and final permutations are straight Permutation boxes (P-boxes) that are inverses of each other.
- They have no cryptography significance in DES. The heart of this cipher is the DES function, f. The DES function applies a 48-bit key to the rightmost 32 bits to produce a 32-bit output.

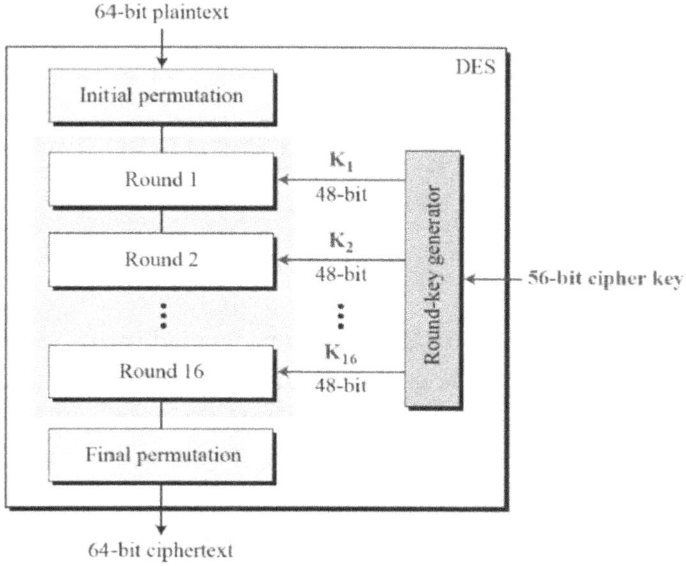

Fig. 3.15: Structure of DES

- The Data Encryption Standard is generally used in the ECB, CBC, or the CFB mode.
- DES is a block cipher. It encrypts data in blocks of size 64 bits each. That is, 64 bits of plain text goes as the input to DES, which produces 64 bits of cipher text.
- DES is based on the two fundamental attributes of cryptography namely, substitution and transposition. The process diagram is shown in Fig. 3.16.

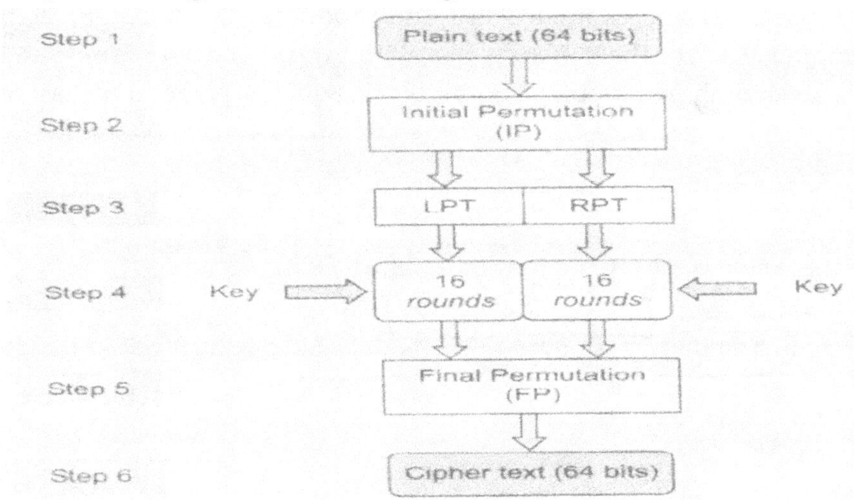

Fig. 3.16

1. Initial Permutation (IP):

- It happens only once. It replaces the first bit of the original plain text block with the 58th bit of the original plain text block, the second bit with the 50th bit of original plain text block and so on.
- The resulting 64-bits permuted text block is divided into two half blocks. Each half block consists of 32 bits.
- The left block called as LPT and right block called as RPT.16 rounds are performed on these two blocks. Details of one round in DES is as shown in Fig. 3.17.

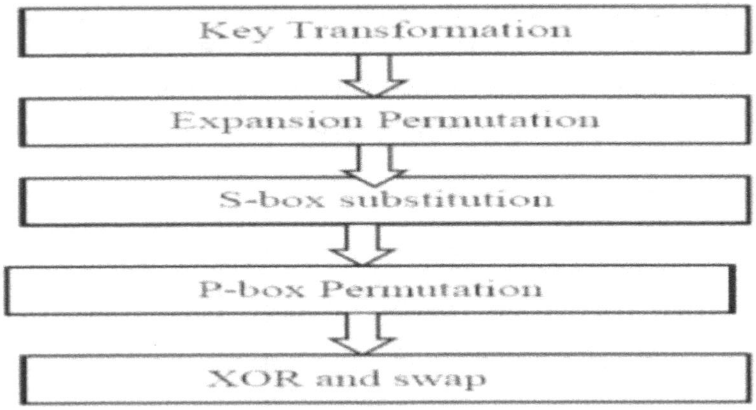

Fig. 3.17

Step 1 : **Key Transformation:** The initial key is transformed into a 56-bit key by discarding every 8th bit of initial key. Thus, for each round, a 56 bit key is available, from this 56-bit key, a different 48-bit sub key is generated during each round using a process called as key transformation Expansion Permutation Key Transformation S-box substitution XOR and swap P-box Permutation.

Step 2 : **Expansion Permutation:** During Expansion permutation the RPT is expanded from 32 bits to 48 bits. The 32-bit RPT is divided into 8 blocks, with each block consisting of 4-bits. Each 4-bits block of the previous step is then expanded to a corresponding 6-bit block, per 4-bit block, 2 more bits are added. They are the repeated 1st and 4th bits of the 4-bit block. The 2nd and 3rd bits are written as they were in the input. The 48 bit key is XORed with the 48-bit RPT and the resulting output is given to the next step.

Step 3 : **S - box Substitution:** It accepts the 48-bits input from the XOR operation involving the compressed key and expanded RPT and produces 32- bit output using the substitution techniques. Each of the 8 S-boxes has a 6-bit input and a 4-bit output. The output of each S-box then combined to form a 32-bit block, which is given to the last stage of a round.

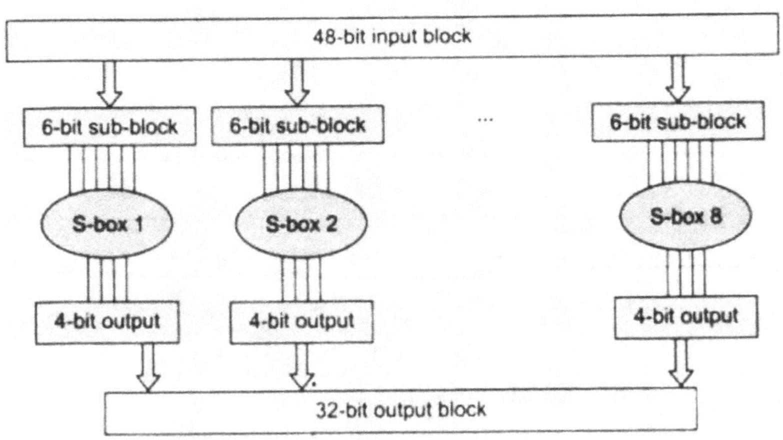

Fig. 3.18

Step 4 : **P - box Permutation:** The output of S-box consists of 32-bits. These 32-bits are permuted using P-box.

Step 5 : **XOR and Swap:** The LPT of the initial 64-bits plain text block is XORed with the output produced by P box permutation. It produces new RPT. The old RPT becomes new LPT, in a process of swapping.

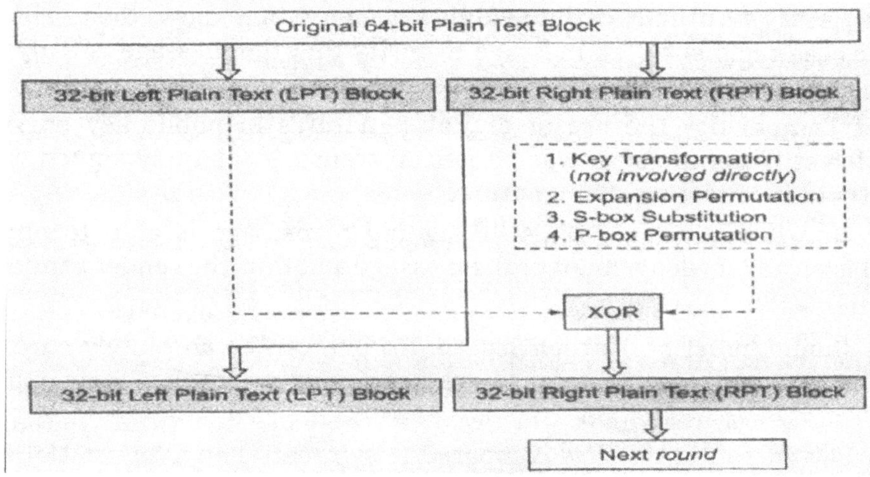

Fig. 3.19

Final Permutation: At the end of 16 rounds, the final permutation is performed. This is simple transposition. For example, the 40th input bit takes the position of 1st output bit and so on.

- The pragmatic approach was not to abandon the DES completely, but to change the manner in which DES is used. This led to the modified schemes of Triple DES (sometimes known as 3DES).
- Triple DES systems are significantly more secure than single DES, but these are clearly a much slower process than encryption using single DES.

3.4.2 Asymmetric Encryption [S-18, 19, W-18]

- Asymmetric Encryption also called as **Public Key Cryptography** and it uses two different keys – a public key used for encryption and a private key used for decryption.
- This encryption technique utilizes a pair of keys (a public key and a private key) for the encryption and decryption processes. The public key is normally used for encryption while the private key is applied for decryption of the message.
- Whereas, the public key can be made freely available to any person who might be interested in sending a message, the private key remains a secret well kept by the receiver of the message.
- A message encrypted using a public key and an algorithm will be decrypted using the same algorithm plus a matching private key that corresponds to the public key used.

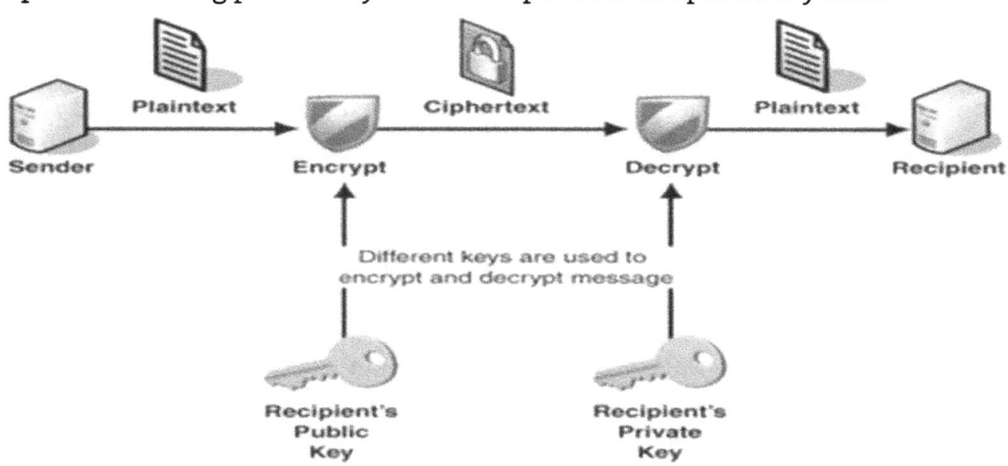

Fig. 3.20: Asymmetric Cryptography Techniques

Advantages:

1. **Convenience:** It solves the problem of distributing the key for encryption. Everyone publishes their public keys and private keys are kept secret.

2. **Provides for Message Authentication:** Public key encryption allows the use of digital signatures which enables the recipient o f a message to verify that the message is truly from a particular sender.
3. **Detection of Tampering:** The use of digital signatures in public key encryption allows the receiver to detect if the message was altered in transit. A digitally signed message cannot be modified without invalidating the signature.
4. **Provide for Non-Repudiation:** Digitally signing a message is akin to physically signing a document. It is an acknowledgement of the message and thus the sender cannot deny it.

Disadvantages:

1. **Public Keys should/must be Authenticated:** No one can be absolutely sure that a public key belongs to the person it specifies and so everyone must verify that their public keys belong to them.
2. **Slow:** Public key encryption is slow compared to symmetric encryption. Not feasible for use in decrypting bulk messages.
3. **Uses more Computer Resources:** It requires a lot more computer supplies compared to single-key encryption.
4. **Loss of Private key may be Irreparable:** The loss of a private key means that all received messages cannot be decrypted.

Comparison between Symmetric Cryptography and Asymmetric Cryptography: **[S-16]**

Sr. No.	Symmetric Cryptography	Asymmetric Key Cryptography
1.	It uses a single key (secret key) for both encryption and decryption of data.	It uses two different keys public key for encryption and private key for decryption.
2.	Both the communicating parties share the same algorithm and the key.	Both the communicating parties should have at least one of the matched pair of keys.
3.	The processes of encryption and decryption are very fast.	The encryption and decryption processes are slower.
4.	Key distribution is a big problem.	Key distribution is not a problem.
5.	The size of encrypted text is usually same or less than the original text.	The size of encrypted text is usually more than the size of the original text.
6.	Based on substitution and permutation of symbols (ch ara cte rs or bits) .	Based on applying mathematical functions to numbers.
7.	It can only be used for confidentiality, i.e., only for encryption and decryption of data.	It can be used for confidentiality of data as well as for integrity and non-repudiation checks (i.e., far digital signatures).
8.	DES and AES are the commonly used symmetric-encryption algorithms.	The most commonly used asymmetric-encryption algorithm is RSA.

3.4.3 Digital Signature **[W-16, 19]**

- It is an electronic signature. It is authentication mechanism used to authenticate identity of the sender. Digital signature was created in response to the rising need to verify information transferred using electronic systems.
- Digital signatures were created in response to the rising need to verify information transferred using electronic systems.
- Digital signatures are the public-key primitives of message authentication. In the physical world, it is common to use handwritten signatures on handwritten or typed messages. They are used to bind signatory to the message.

- Similarly, a digital signature is a technique that binds a person/entity to the digital data. This binding can be independently verified by receiver as well as any third party.
- Digital signature is a cryptographic value that is calculated from the data and a secret key known only by the signer.
- In real world, the receiver of message needs assurance that the message belongs to the sender and he should not be able to repudiate the origination of that message. This requirement is very crucial in business applications, since likelihood of a dispute over exchanged data is very high.
- Digital signature is a digital code, (generated and authenticated by public key encryption) which is attached to an electronically transmitted document to verify its contents and the senders identity.
- Digital signature is based on both hashing function & asymmetric cryptography. Digital signature is easily transportable and cannot be imitated by someone else and can be automatically time stamped.

Why digital signatures are used?

- Digital signature must be a bit pattern with such a information which is unique to the sender. This information helped to prevent forgery and denial.
  - **Authenticity**: The digital signature helps ensure that the signer is who he or she claims to be. This helps prevent others from pretending to be the originator of a particular document, (the equivalent of forgery on a printed document).
  - **Integrity**: The digital signature helps ensure that the content has not been changed or tampered with since it was digitally signed. This helps prevent documents from being intercepted and changed without knowledge of the originator of the document.
  - **Non-Repudiation**: The digital signature helps prove to all parties the origin of the signed content. "Repudiation" refers to the act of a signer's denying any association with the signed content. This helps prove that the originator of the document is the true originator and not someone else, regardless of the claims of the signer. A signer cannot repudiate the signature on that document without repudiating his or her digital key and therefore other documents signed with that key.

Working of Digital Signature (DS):

- It consist of following two processes:
  1. Digital signature creation, (performed by sender).
  2. Digital signature verification, (performed by receiver).
- Digital certificate is a data with digital signature from one trusted Certification Authority, (CA). This data contain:
  1. Who owns the certificate.
  2. Who signs this certificates.
  3. The expiry data.
  4. User name and email address.
- CA (Certification Authority) is trusted agent who certifies public keys for general use. User has to decide which CAs can be trusted.

1. Creation of Digital Signature :

- Signature is created by sender. Message Digest (MD) is extracted from message using hash function. MD is encrypted using private key of sender and we get the digital signature.

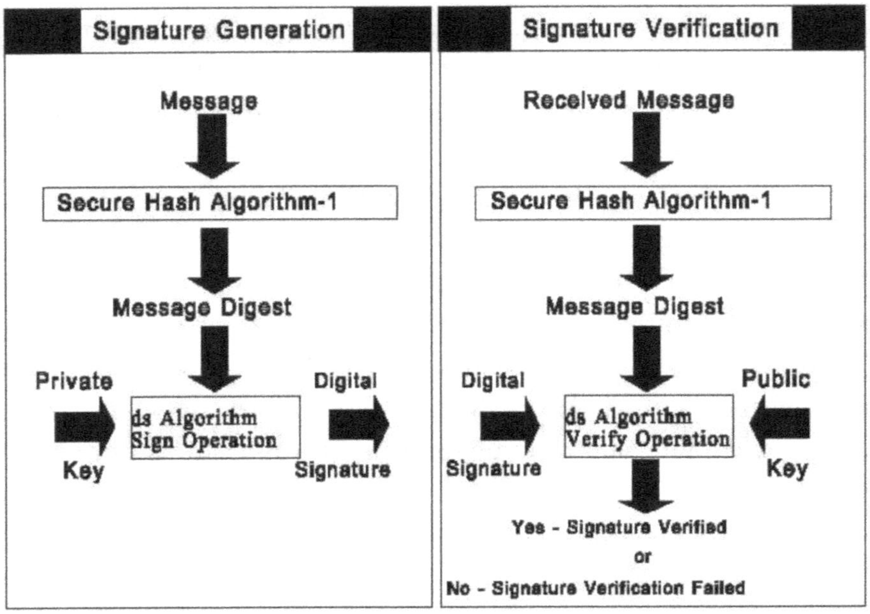

Fig. 3.21

2. **Digital Signature Verification:**

- It is the process of checking the digital signature by reference to the original message and a given public key.
- Hence, determining whether the digital signature was created for the same message using private key that corresponds to the referenced public key.
- Digital signature scheme typically consist of following three algorithms:
  1. **Key Generation Algorithm:** That selects private key uniformly at random from set of possible private keys. The algorithm outputs the private key and corresponding public key.
  2. **Signing Algorithm:** On input of message and private key it produces a signature.
  3. **Signature Verifying:** On input of message, public key and signature, either accepts or rejects the messages claim to authenticity.

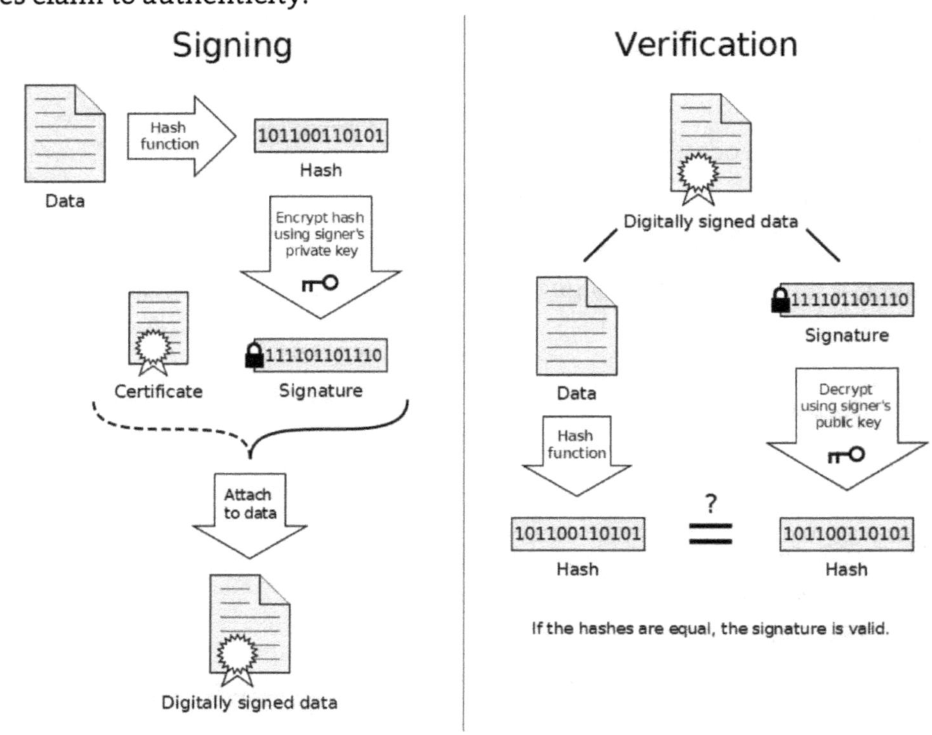

Fig. 3.22: Digital Signature

Example:

- Assume we were going to send the draft of a contract to our lawyer in another town. We want to give our lawyer the assurance that it was unchanged from what we sent and that it is really from us.
    1. We copy and paste the contract into an e-mail note.
    2. Using special software or hash function you obtain message digest of the contract.
    3. We then use private key obtain from public-private key authority to encrypt message digest.
    4. The encrypted message digest becomes digital signature of message. (Digital signature is different each time we send message).
- At the other end our lawyer receives the message.
    1. To make sure it's intact and from we, our lawyer makes hash of the received message.
    2. The lawyer then use public key to decrypt the message digest.
    3. It the hashes match the received message is valid.

Advantages:

1. **Speed:** In business no longer have to wait for paper document to be sent by couriers using DS contracts are easily written completed and signed by all concerned parties in less time.
2. **Cost:** Postal or courier service for paper document is much more expensive as compared using DS.
3. **Security:** Use of DS and electronic document reduces risk of document being intercepted read, destroyed.
4. **Authenticity:** An electronic document signed with DS can stand up in court just as well as any other signed paper document
5. **Non-Republication:** DS identifies you as the signatory & later that cannot be denied.
6. **Tracking:** Digitally signed document can be easily tracked & located in short amount of time.

Disadvantages:

1. The private key must be kept in secure manner.
2. The process of generation & verification of digital signature requires considerable amount of time.
3. Although digital signature provides the authenticity, it does not ensure secrecy of the data.
4. For using the digital signature the user has to obtain private & public key, the receiver has to obtain the digital signature certificate also.

Digital Signature Standards (DSS):

- DSS was developed for performing digital signature. DSS uses digital signature algorithm.
- DSS make use of SHA-1 algorithm for Calculating message digest. Hash function is used to generate MD.
- MD is given input to DSA to generate digital signature. Digital signature sent to the verifier along with the massage.
- Verifier then verifies signature by using sender's public key. Same hash function is used in the verification process.

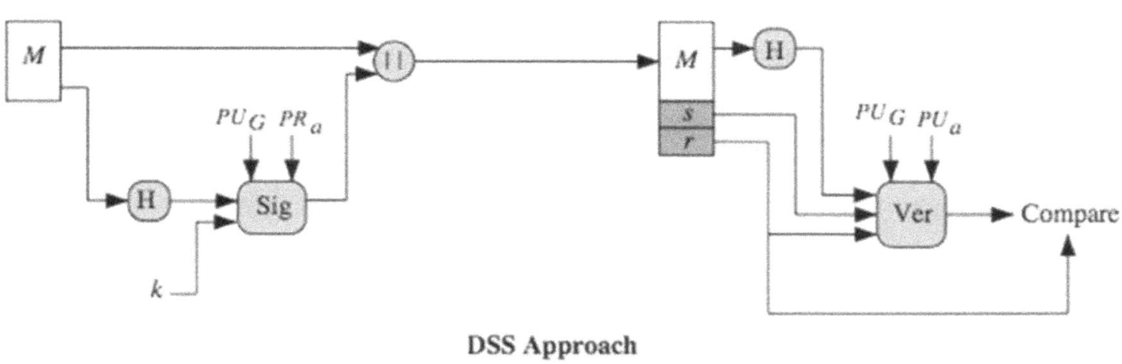

Fig. 3.23: DSS Approach

Where,

M	:	message.	s	:	signature.
H	:	Hash function.	r	:	(g^k mod p)mod q (key pair).
Sig	:	signature.	PUa	:	Public key of sender.
PRa	:	Private key of sender.	Ver	:	Verification function.
PU_G	:	set of global public key.	compare	:	Compare function.

- DSS is a standard and DSA is actual algorithm. DSA provide capability to generate and verify signature.
- Signature generation makes use of private key to generate digital signature. Signature verification makes use of public key which corresponds to, but is not the same as the private key.
- Each user possesses a private and public key pair. Anyone can verify the signature of user by employing that user's public key.

Application of DSS:

1. Electronic mail.
2. Electronic Fund Transfer (EFT).
3. Electronic data interchange.
4. Software distribution.
5. Data storage.

Practice Questions

1. What is cryptography?
2. What is steganography?
3. What is plaintext and ciphertext?
4. What is encryption and decryption?
5. Describe terms: (i) Cryptology, (ii) Cryptanalysis.
6. Enlist application of cryptography.
7. Define the following terms: (i) Cipher, (ii) Key, (iii) Encryption, (iv) Decryption.
8. Explain substitution technique in detail.
9. What is symmetric cryptography? State its advantages and disadvantages.
10. What is asymmetric key cryptography?
11. Describe monoalphasetic ciper with example.
12. What is digital signature? How to create it? Explain with example.
13. With the help of diagram describe process of steganography.
14. Describe transposition technique of cryptography.
15. Differentiate between symmetric and asymmetric cryptography.
16. Explain Caesar's chipher with example.

■■■

4... Firewall and Intrusion Detection System

Chapter Outcomes...

- Compare types of firewall on the given parameters(s).
- Explain function of the given type of firewall configuration.
- Compare various IDS techniques on the given parameters(s).
- Describe features of the given IDS technique.

Learning Objectives...

- To understand Basic Concepts in Firewall
- To study Intrusion Detection System
- To learn various Techniques in Intrusion Detection System (IDS)

4.0 INTRODUCTION

- A firewall is a hardware and/or software which functions in a networked environment to block unauthorized access while permitting authorized communications.
- Firewall is a device and/or a software that stands between a local network and the Internet, and filters traffic that might be harmful.
- A firewall is a network security system that monitors and controls incoming and outgoing network traffic based on predetermined security rules.
- A firewall typically establishes a barrier between a trusted internal network (private) and un-trusted external network (public), such as the Internet.
- In computer networking, trust refers to the ability of an application to perform actions with integrity, to keep confidential information private, and to perform its functions on a continuing basis.
- Intrusion detection is simply trying to detect the signs of a network intruder before damage is done, a service denied or data lost.
- Intrusion detection systems are also as important as the firewall because they help us to detect the type of attack that is being done to our system and then to make a solution to block them.
- An intrusion occurs when an attacker attempts to gain entry or disrupt the normal operations of an Information System (IS), almost always with the intent to do harm.
- Even when such attacks are self propagating, as in the case of viruses and distributed Denial-of-Service (DoS) attacks, they are almost always instigated by an individual whose purpose is to harm an organization. Often, the differences among intrusion types to remain anonymous, while others crave notoriety.
- An Intrusion Detection System (IDS) is a software or hardware device installed on the Network Intrusion Detection System (NIDS) or Host Intrusion Detection System (HIDS) to detect and report intrusion attempts to the network.
- Intrusion detection is an aspect of security whereby a device detects the fingerprint of an attack within the network.

4.1 FIREWALL [S-16, W-19]

- A firewall is a network security device that keeps a track of incoming and outgoing traffic on network and gives permission or blocks data packets based on a set of security rules.
- It's role is to establish a barrier between the internal network and incoming traffic from external sources (such as the internet) in order to block unwanted traffic like viruses and hackers.
- The main purpose of a firewall is to prevent unauthorized access between networks. It is protecting a site's inner network from the Internet.
- All incoming and outgoing data packets the internal network passes through the firewall, which examines each packet and blocks those that do not meet the specified security criteria.
- We can say that firewall is a barrier between Local Area Network (LAN) and the Internet. It allows keeping private resources confidential and reduces the security risks. It controls network traffic, in both directions.
- A firewall's main purpose is to filter traffic and lower the risk that unauthorized packets traveling over the public internet will be able to impact the security of a private network.
- Firewalls consist of wide variety of networked devices and may also be purchased as stand-alone software applications.
- Fig, 4.1 shows a sample firewall between LAN and the internet. The connection between the two is the point of vulnerability. Both hardware and the software can be used at this point to filter network traffic.

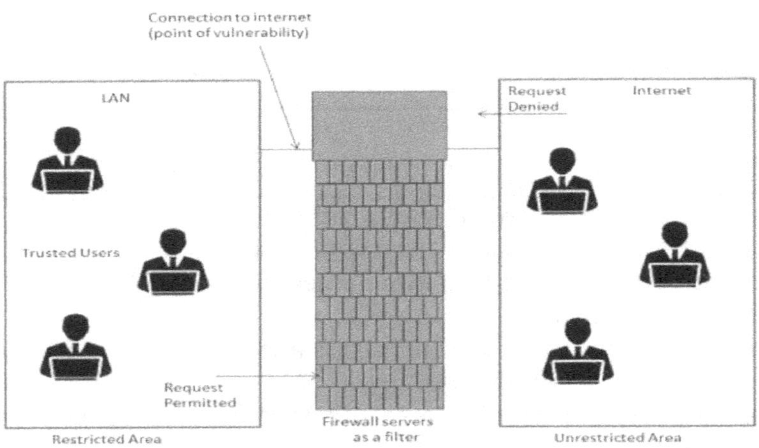

Fig. 4.1

- Firewalls can be implemented in either hardware or software, or a combination of both. Firewalls are frequently used to prevent unauthorized Internet users from accessing private networks connected to the Internet, especially Intranets.
- All messages entering or leaving the Intranet pass through the firewall, which inspects each message and blocks those that do not meet the specified security criteria.

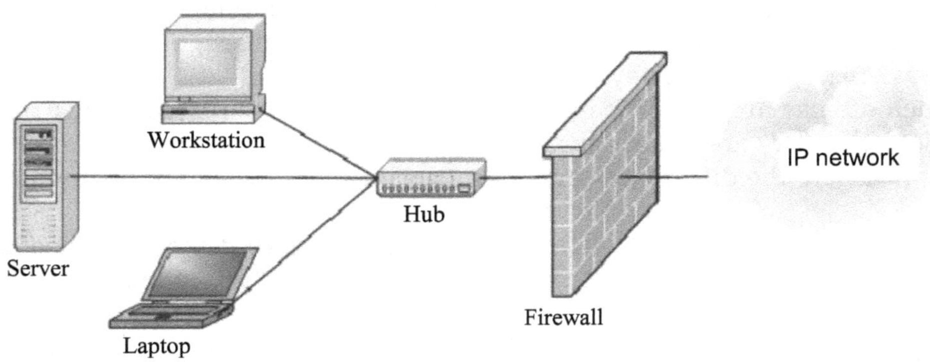

Fig. 4.2: Firewall

- Firewalls are similar to other network devices in that their purpose is to control the flow of traffic. A firewall basically works by examining the IP packets that travel between the server and the client.
- This provides a way to control the information flow for each service by IP address, by port and in each direction.

4.1.1 Need of Firewall [W-17]

- If the computer is connected to the Internet, then it is targeted of various threats from internet such as hackers, keyloggers and Trojans that attacks through unpatched security holes.
- This means that if someone like most people shop and bank online, are vulnerable to identity theft and other malicious attacks.
- A firewall works as a barrier between the computer and internet. When the computer is connected to the Internet, someone can continually sending and receiving information in small units called packets.
- The task of firewall is to filter these packets to check if they meet conditions set by a series of rules, and thereafter allows the data. This way, hackers cannot get access to the information and steal information such as bank account numbers and passwords from us.
- Basic firewalls such as firewall in Windows XP, only keep a track of incoming traffic by default. outgoing traffic, with the credit card information, bank accounts, and social security number is not protected. A good firewall will monitor traffic in both directions i.e. incoming data and the outgoing data.
- Most firewalls also include a feature that continuously updates the list of known good applications and known unwanted applications. Due to this security for personal computer can be achieved.
- So, we need firewall:
  1. To protect the computer from unauthorized remote access.
  2. To block different messages linking to unwanted contents.
  3. To block unwanted contents from the internet that harms to computer.
  4. To prevent illegitimate modification/access to internal data by an outsider attacker.
  5. In order to secure the internal network from unauthorized traffic we need firewall.

4.1.2 Types of Firewall [S-17, 18, 19, W-16, 18]

- Firewall can be categorized into three types depending on the criteria they use for filtering the traffic. The types of firewall include packet filter (Stateless and Stateful), Application-level gateway and Circuit-level gateway.

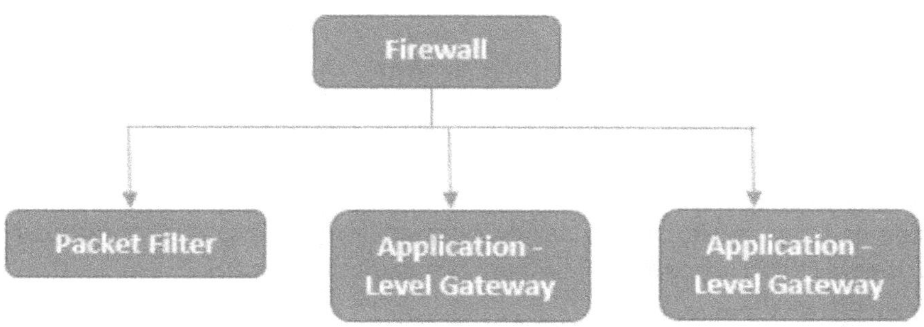

Fig. 4.3: Types of Firewall

4.1.2.1 Packet Filter

- Packet filtering firewalls works at junction points where devices such as routers and switches do their work.
- The internal network is connected to the public network via a router firewall. The firewall examines and filters data packet-by-packet.
- This type of firewall applies set of rules to each packet and based on rule decide whether packet is forwarded or rejected.

- So, packet filtering firewall provide a way to filter IP addresses by either of two basic methods:
    1. Allowing access to known IP addresses
    2. Denying access to IP addresses and ports
- It is also called as screening router or screening filter. These firewalls compare each received packet to a set of recognized criteria -- such as IP addresses allowed, source and destination IP address, protocol, packet type, port number and other aspects of the packet protocol headers.
- Packet filter firewall is shown in Fig. 4.4.
- Conceptually a packet filter can be considered as a router that performs three main actions as shown in Fig. 4.5.

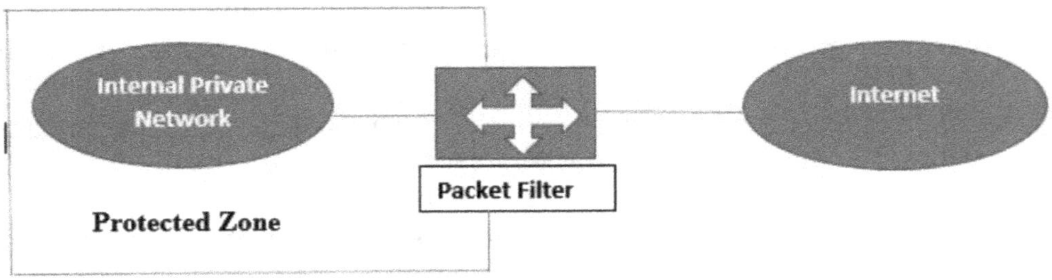

Fig. 4.4: Packet Filter

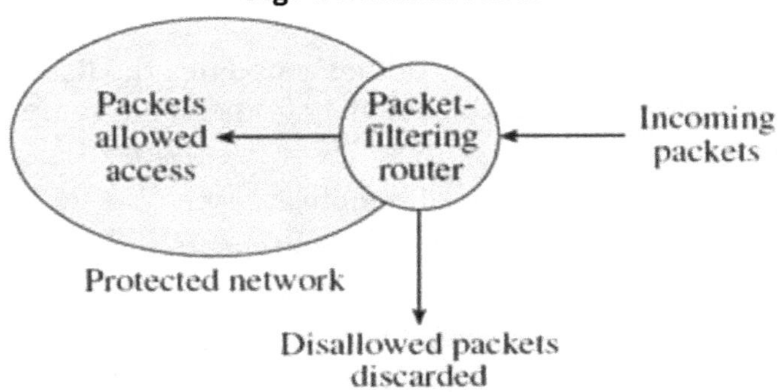

Fig. 4.5: Packet Filter Operation

- Packet filter performs following functions:
    1. Receive each packet as it arrives.
    2. Pass the packet through set of rules based on the contents of the IP and transport header fields of the packet. If there is match with one of the set of rules, decides whether to accept or reject packet based on rule.
    3. If there is no match with any rule then take default action.(default action may be either accept or reject all packets.
- Advanced type of packet filter is called as Dynamic packet filter or stateful packet filter which allows monitoring of packet based on the current state of the network.
- This type of filter has to maintained a list of currently open connections and outgoing packets in order to deal with this rule. Hence it is called as dynamic or stateful.

Advantages of Packet Filter Firewalls:

1. One screening router can help protect an entire network.
2. Packet filtering doesn't require user knowledge or cooperation.
3. Efficient at processing packets.
4. Enable complex security policies through filtering on protocol headers.

Disadvantages of Packet Filter Firewalls:

1. Incapable of filtering at application layer.
2. Can be difficult to securely configure.
3. Some protocols are not well suited to packet filtering.

4. Some policies cannot readily be enforced by normal packet filtering routers.
5. Attacker can break security of packet filter by using IP address spoofing, Source routing attack, Tiny fragment attacks etc.

4.1.2.1.1 Stateful Packet Filtering (Inspection) Firewall

- A packet filter firewall is stateless. It operates on packets on an individual basis and does not store or apply the state information pertaining to the action taken on packets processed earlier.
- Stateful firewalls examine each packet with regards to their overall placement in the packet series belonging to a specific connection.
- A stateful firewall maintains records of all connections passing through it and will be able to determine whether a packet is part of any existing connection or a new connection.
- A stateful firewall is a network firewall that tracks the operating state and characteristics of network connections traversing it.
- Stateful packet firewalls, (performs Stateful Packet Inspection) are able to determine the connection state of packet, unlike Packet filtering firewall, which makes it more efficient. It keeps track of the state of networks connection travelling across it, such as TCP streams.
- A stateful inspection packet filter tightens up the rules for TCP traffic by creating a directory of outbound TCP connections. There is an entry for each currently established connection.
- The stateful packet firewall will now allow incoming traffic to high-numbered ports only for those packets that fit the profile of one of the entries in this directory.
- So the filtering decisions would not only be based on defined rules, but also on packet's history in the state table. Fig. 4.6 shows concept of stateful inspection.

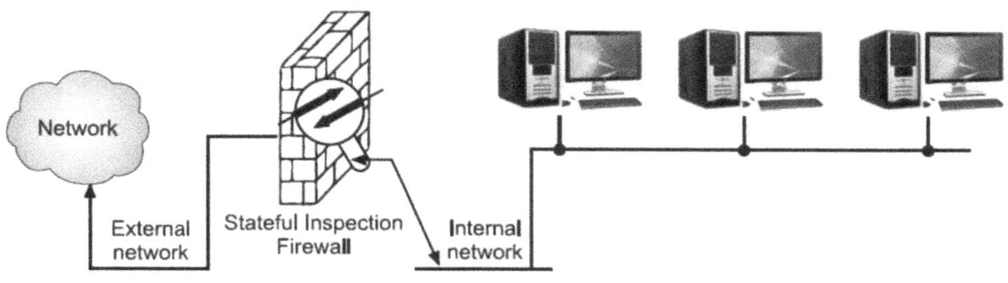

Fig. 4.6: State Inspection Firewall

Advantages:

1. The connection table greatly reduces the chance that a packet will be spoofed to appear as it were part of an existing connection.
2. It has the ability to look into the data of certain packet types.

Disadvantages:

1. It does not protect the internal hosts to the same degree as an application layer firewall.
2. It does not act as proxy or setup a separate connection on behalf of the source.

4.1.2.2 Application-Level Gateway

- It is a proxy firewall which provides network security. An application-level gateway acts as a relay node for the application-level traffic.
- It is also called as proxy server. It functions as a proxy server, preventing any direct connection between a authorized server or client and an unauthorized host.
- The application gateway resides on the client as well as server firewall. It provides high-level secure network system communication.
- For example, when a client requests access to server resources such as files, Web pages and databases, the client first connects with the proxy server, which then establishes a connection with the main server.
- The proxies are application specific. They can filter packets at the application layer of the OSI model.

- Concept of application level gateway is shown in Fig. 4.7.

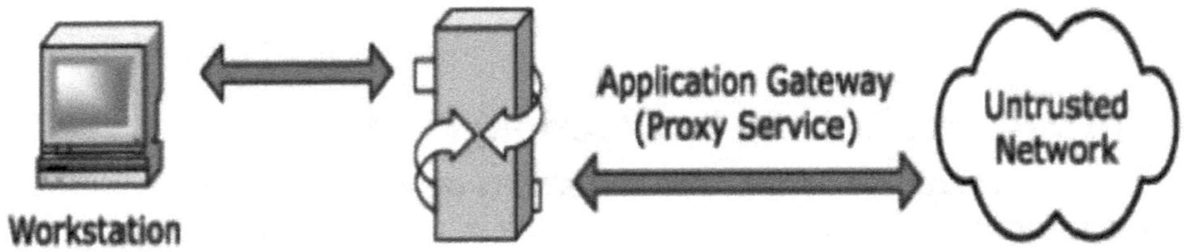

Fig. 4.7: Application Level Gateway

Working of Application Gateway:

- An internal user can communicate the application gateway using a TCP/IP application such as HTTP or TELNET.
- Application gateway ask user regarding remote host with which user wants to make connection for actual communication.
- It also ask user for ID and password which is required to access the services of application gateway. User gives this information to application gateway.
- Application gateway can access remote host in behalf of user and passes the packets from user to remote host. Application gateway acts like proxy of actual end user and deliver packets from user to remote host and vice versa.
- An application gateway is a proxy server that provides access control at the application layer. It acts as an application-layer gateway between the protected network and the untrusted network.
- Because it operates at the application layer, it is able to examine traffic in detail and, therefore, is considered the most secure type of firewall.
- The user contacts the gateway using a TCP/IP application, such as Telnet or FTP and the gateway asks the user for the name of the remote host to be accessed.

Advantages of Application Gateway:

1. More secure than Packet filter firewall.
2. It works as a key point in security of a network.
3. Do not allow direct communication between endpoints.
4. Reduce overhead of examining packets by using rules instead it simply detects whether the user is allowed to work with TCP/IP application or not.

Disadvantages of Application Gateway:

1. Overhead in terms of connection.
2. It requires more processing power and has become potential to become a bottleneck of the network.
3. Require additional client configuration.

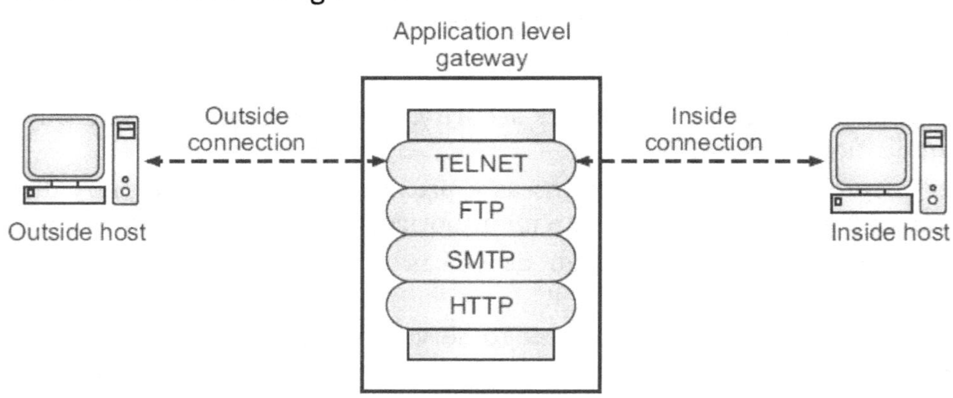

Fig. 4.8: Application Level Gateway

4.1.2.3 Circuit-Level Gateway

- The circuit-level gateway is an intermediate solution between the packet filter and the application gateway. A circuit-level gateway is a type of firewall.
- Circuit-level gateways work at the session layer of the OSI model. Information passed to a remote computer through a circuit-level gateway appears to have originated from the gateway.
- It is variation of application gateway which performs more functions as compared to application gateway.
- Circuit level gateway creates new connection between itself and the remote host. User has no knowledge regarding this connection. User thinks that there is direct connection between itself and remote host.
- Circuit level gateway changes the IP the source IP address in the packets from the end users I address to its own. So, the IP address of the computer of internal users are hidden from the outside world. SOCKS server is an example of the real-life implementation of circuit gateway.

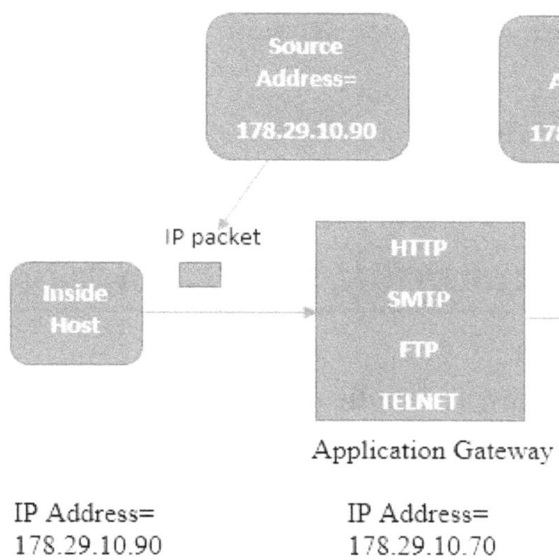

Fig. 4.9: Circuit Level Gateway

- Circuit-level gateway monitor TCP handshaking between packets to determine whether a requested session is legitimate.
- A circuit level gateway is a proxy server that validates TCP and UDP sessions before allowing a connection or circuit through the firewall.
- It is actively involved in the connection establishment and does not allow packets to be forwarded until the necessary access control rules have been satisfied.
- A circuit level gateway does not permit an end-to-end TCP connection; rather, the gateway sets up two TCP connections, one between itself and a TCP user on an inner host and one between itself and a TCP user on an outside host.
- Once, the two connections are established, the gateway typically relays TCP segments from one connection to the other without examining the contents. The security function consists of determining which connections will be allowed.
- A circuit-level gateway is not as secure as an application gateway because it validates TCP and UDP sessions without full knowledge of the applications that use these transport services.
- Moreover, once a session has been established, any application can run across that connection. This behavior exposes the protected network to attacks from intruders.

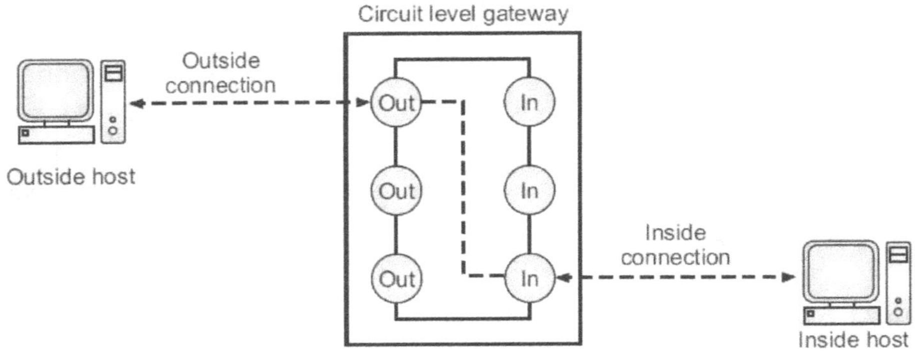

Fig. 4.10: Circuit Level Gateway

Advantages of Circuit Level Gateway:

1. Relatively inexpensive.
2. More efficient processing traffic than application level gateway.
3. Provides privacy for data passing in/out of private network.

Disadvantages of Circuit Level Gateway:

1. Protect circuits rather than individual packets.
2. Require modification to network protocol stack.
3. Incapable of content filtering.

4.2 FIREWALL POLICIES, CONFIGURATION, LIMITATIONS, DMZ

4.2.1 Firewall Policies [W-19]

- A firewall policy indicates how firewalls should handle network traffic for specific IP addresses and several address ranges, protocols, applications and content types (e.g. active content) based on the organization's information security policies.
- Before a firewall policy is created, some form of risk analysis should be performed to develop a list of the types of traffic needed by the organization and categorize how they must be secure including which types of traffic can traverse a firewall under what circumstances.
- This risk analysis should be based on an evaluation of threats, vulnerabilities, and counter measures to overcome vulnerabilities and the impact if systems or data are compromised.
- Firewall policy should be documented in the system security plan and maintained and updated frequently as classes of new attacks or vulnerabilities arise, or as the organization's needs regarding network applications change.
- The policy should also include specific guidance on how to address changes to the rule set. Generally, firewalls should block all inbound and outbound traffic that has not been permitted by the firewall policy i.e. traffic that is not needed by the organization.
- Consider the categories of firewall policies based on, IP Addresses and Protocols, Applications, User Identity and Network Activity.

1. **Policies Based on IP Addresses and Protocols:**

- Firewall policies should only allow necessary IP protocols. Examples of commonly used IP protocols, with their IP protocol numbers are ICMP (1), TCP (6), and UDP (17).
- Other IP protocols, such as IPsec components Encapsulating Security Payload (ESP) (50) and Authentication Header (AH) (51) and routing protocols may also need to pass through firewalls.
- These necessary protocols should be restricted whenever possible to the specific hosts and networks within the organization with a need to use them.
- By allowing only necessary protocols, all unnecessary IP protocols are denied by default.

(i) IP Addresses and other IP Characteristics:

- Firewall policies should only permit appropriate source and destination IP addresses to be used. Specific recommendations for IP addresses include:
  - Traffic with invalid source or destination addresses should always be blocked, regardless of the firewall location.
  - Traffic with an invalid source address for incoming traffic or destination address for outgoing traffic should be blocked at the network perimeter. This traffic is often caused by malware, spoofing, denial of service attacks, or misconfigured equipment.
  - Traffic with a private destination address for incoming traffic or source address for outgoing traffic should be blocked at the network perimeter. Perimeter devices can perform address translation services to permit internal hosts with private addresses to communicate through the perimeter, but private addresses should not be passed through the network perimeter.
  - Outbound traffic with invalid source addresses should be blocked.
  - Incoming traffic with a destination address of the firewall itself should be blocked unless the firewall is offering services for incoming traffic that require direct connections.
  - Firewalls at the network perimeter should block all incoming traffic to networks and hosts that should not be accessible from external networks.
  - These firewalls should also block all outgoing traffic from the organization's networks and hosts that should not be permitted to access external networks.
  - Deciding which addresses should be blocked is often one of the most time-consuming aspects of developing firewall IP policies.
  - It is also one of the most error-prone, because the IP address associated with an undesired entity often changes over time.

(ii) IPv6:

- IPv6 is a new version of IP that is increasingly being deployed. For the features that are the same between IPv4 and IPv6, firewalls should work the same.
- Some firewalls cannot handle IPv6 traffic at all, others are able to handle it but have limited abilities to filter IPv6 traffic and still others can filter IPv6 traffic to approximately the same extent as IPv4 traffic.
- Every organization, whether or not it allows IPv6 traffic to enter its internal network, needs a firewall that is capable of filtering this traffic. These firewalls should have the following capabilities:
  - The firewall should be able to use IPv6 addresses in all filtering rules that use IPv4 addresses.
  - The administrative interface should allow administrators to clone IPv4 rules to IPv6 addresses to make administration easier.
  - The firewall needs to be able to filter ICMPv6, as specified in RFC 4890, Recommendations for Filtering ICMPv6 Messages in Firewalls.
  - The firewall should be able to block IPv6-related protocols if they are not required.
  - For firewalls that permit IPv6 use, traffic with invalid source or destination IPv6 addresses should always be blocked
  - Organizations that do not yet use IPv6 should block all native and tunneled IPv6 traffic at their firewalls.

(iii) TCP/UDP:

- Application protocols can use TCP, UDP, or both, depending on the design of the protocol. An application server typically listens on one or more fixed TCP or UDP ports.
- Some applications use a single port, but many applications use multiple ports. Some applications use both TCP and UDP, For example, DNS lookups can occur on UDP port 53 or TCP port 53.

- Application clients typically use any of a wide range of ports. As with other aspects of firewall rulesets, deny by default policies should be used for incoming TCP and UDP traffic.
- Less stringent policies are generally used for outgoing TCP and UDP traffic because most organizations permit their users to access a wide range of external applications located on millions of external hosts.
- In addition to allowing and blocking UDP and TCP traffic, many firewalls are also able to report or block malformed UDP and TCP traffic directed towards the firewall or to hosts protected by the firewall.

(iv) ICMP:

- Attackers can use various ICMP types and codes to perform reconnaissance or manipulate the flow of network traffic.
- ICMP is needed for many useful things, such as getting reasonable performance across the Internet.
- Some firewall policies block all ICMP traffic, but this often leads to problems with diagnostics and performance. Other common policies allow all outgoing ICMP traffic.
- To prevent malicious activity, firewalls at the network perimeter should deny all incoming and outgoing ICMP traffic except for those types and codes specifically permitted by the organization.
- For ICMP in IPv4, ICMP type three messages should not be filtered because they are used for important network diagnostics.
- The ping command is an important network diagnostic, but incoming pings are often blocked by firewall policies to prevent attackers from learning more about the internal topology of the organization's network.
- For ICMP in IPv6, many types of messages must be allowed in specific circumstances to enable various IPv6 features.
- ICMP within an organization's network generally should not be blocked by firewalls that are not at the perimeter of the network, unless security needs outweigh network operational needs.
- Similarly, if an organization has more than one network, ICMP that comes from or goes to other networks within the organization should not be blocked.

(v) IPSec:

- An organization needs to have a policy whether or not to allow IPsec VPNs that start or end inside its network perimeter.
- The ESP and AH protocols are used for IPsec VPNs, and a firewall that blocks these protocols will not allow IPsec VPNs to pass.
- Organizations that allow IPsec VPNs should block ESP and AH except to and from specific addresses on the internal network those addresses belong to IPsec gateways that are allowed to be VPN endpoints.
- Enforcing this policy will require people inside the organization to obtain the appropriate policy approval to open ESP and/or AH access to their IPsec routers.
- This will also reduce the amount of encrypted traffic coming from inside the network that cannot be examined by network security controls.

2. Policies Based on Applications:

- Inbound application firewalls or application proxies take a different approach they let traffic destined for a particular server into the network, but capture that traffic in a server that processes it like a port-based firewall.
- The application-based approach provides an additional layer of security for incoming traffic by validating some of the traffic before it reaches the desired server.

- Inbound application firewall's or proxy's additional security layer can protect the server better than the server can protect itself and can also remove malicious traffic before it reaches the server to help reduce server load.
- In some cases, an application firewall or proxy can remove traffic that the server might not be able to remove on its own because it has greater filtering capabilities.
- An application firewall or proxy also prevents the server from having direct access to the outside network.
- The main **considerations when deciding whether or not to use an inbound application firewall or proxy** are:
  - Is a suitable application firewall available? Or, if appropriate, is a suitable application proxy available?
  - Is the server already sufficiently protected by existing firewalls?
  - Can the main server remove malicious content as effectively as the application firewall or proxy?
  - Is the latency caused by an application proxy acceptable for the application?
  - How easy it is to update the filtering rules on the main server and the application firewall or proxy to handle newly developed threats?
- Application firewalls can introduce problems if they are not highly capable.
- Unless an application firewalls is significantly more robust than the server and easy to keep updated, it is usually best to stay with the application server alone.
- Application firewalls can also introduce problems if they are not fast enough to handle the traffic destined for the server.
- However, it is also important to consider the server's resources if the server does not have sufficient resources to withstand attacks, the application firewall or proxy could be used as a shield.

3. Policies Based on User Identity:

- Traditional packet filtering does not see the identities of the users who are communicating in the traffic traversing the firewall, so firewall technologies without more advanced capabilities cannot have policies that allow or deny access based on those identities.
- However, many other firewall technologies can see these identities and therefore enact policies based on user authentication.
- One of the most common ways to enforce user identity policy at a firewall is by using a VPN.
- Firewalls that enforce policies based on user identity should be able to reflect these policies in their logs.
- That is, it is probably not useful to only log the IP address from which a particular user connected if the user was allowed in by a user-specific policy, it is also important to log the user's identity as well.

4. Policies Based on Network Activity:

- Many firewalls allow the administrator to block established connections after a certain period of inactivity.
- Time-based policies are useful in thwarting attacks caused by a logged-in user walking away from a computer and someone else sitting down and using the established.
- However, these policies can also be bothersome for users who make connections but do not use them frequently.
- For instance, a user might connect to a file server to read a file and then spend a long time editing the file. If the user does not save the file back to the file server before the firewall-mandated timeout, the timeout could cause the changes to the file to be lost.
- A different type of firewall policy based on network activity is one that redirects traffic if the rate of traffic matching the policy rule is too high
- Another policy might be to drop incoming ICMP packets if the rate is too high. Crafting such policies is quite difficult because throttling and redirecting can cause desired traffic to be lost or have difficult-to-diagnose transient failures.

4.2.2 Firewall Configuration

- Firewall configuration is combination of packet filter and application or circuit level gateway. In addition to the use of simple configuration on single system more complex configurations are possible.
- Based on this there are three configurations of firewall:
  1. Screened Host Firewall system, Single-Homed Bastion.
  2. Screened Host Firewall system, Dual-Homed Bastion.
  3. Screened Subnet Firewall System.

Bastion Host:

- A system identified by firewall administrator as critical strong point in the network security.
- Bastion host acts as a platform for application level or circuit level gateway.
- On bastion host only that services are installed which should be considered by network admin.

Three Possible Configurations of Firewall:

1. Screened Host Firewall System, Single-Homed Bastion

- This type of firewall configuration is as shown in Fig. 4.11.

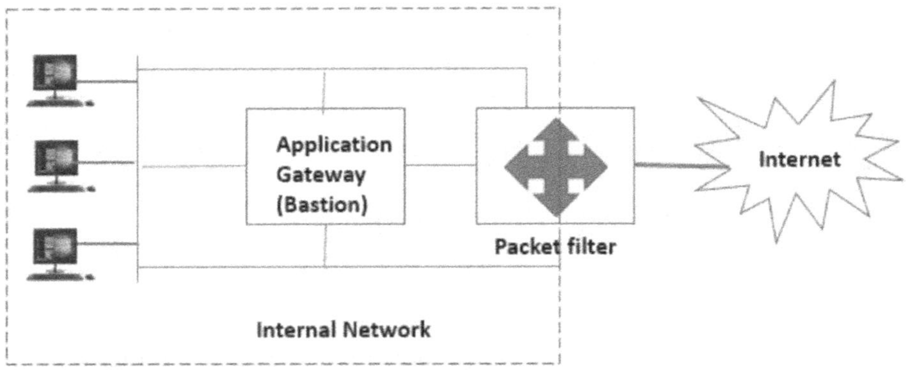

Fig. 4.11: Screened Host Firewall System, Single-Homed Bastion

- In this type of configuration, a firewall consists of two systems:
  (i) Packet Filtering Router:
  - The packet filtering router is configured so that, for traffic from internet only IP packets which is destined for Bastion (Application Gateway) are allowed by examining the destination address field of every incoming IP packet.
  - Similarly, for traffic from internal network only IP packet originated from bastion (Application Gateway) are allowed by examining the source address field of every outgoing IP packet.

  (ii) Bastion host (Application Gateway):
  - Bastion (Application Gateway) performs following two functions namely, Authentication and Proxy function.
  - This type of configuration increases the security of the network by performing checks at both packet and application level.
  - Drawback of this type of configuration is that the internal users are connected to the application gateway as well as to the packet filter.

2. Screened Host Firewall System, Dual-Homed Bastion

- This type of firewall configuration overcomes the drawback of screened host firewall system, single-homed bastion configuration.
- In this type direct connection between the internal host and packet filters are avoided. Here, packet filter is connected only to bastion (application gateway).
- There is separate connection between bastion (application gateway) and internal hosts. Now here if packet filter is attacked only bastion (application gateway) is visible to attacker internal hosts remain protected.

- This type of firewall configuration is as shown in Fig. 4.12.

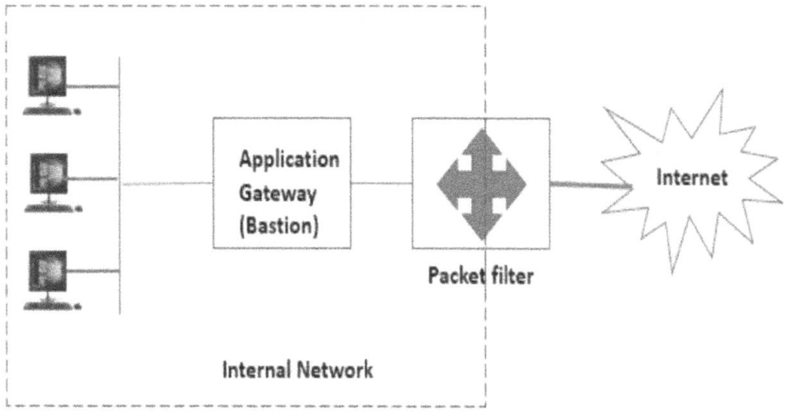

Fig. 4.12: Screened host Firewall System, Dual-Homed Bastion

3. **Screened subnet Firewall system:**

- This type of configuration has highest level of security than all above types of configurations.
- It is improvement over screened host firewall system, dual-homed bastion.
- This type of firewall configuration is as shown in Fig. 4.13.

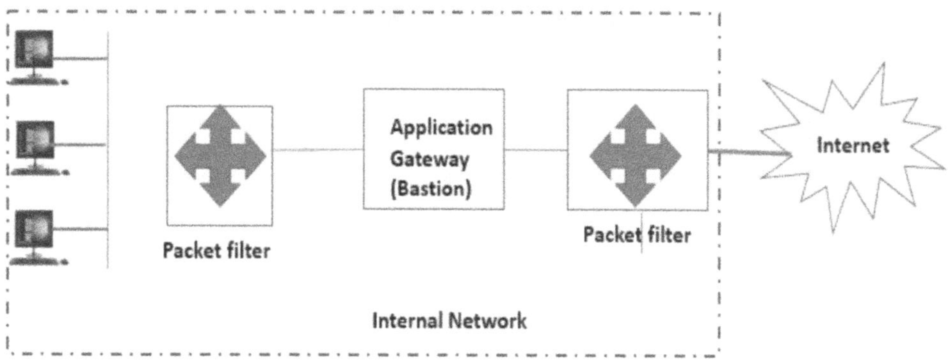

Fig. 4.13

- In these two packet filters are used. One between Internet and bastion (application gateway) and another between internal network and Bastion (Application Gateway). So, this type of firewall configuration has three levels of security.

4.2.3 Limitations of Firewall [W-18]

- A firewall is a crucial component of securing the network and is designed to address the issues of data integrity or traffic authentication and confidentiality of your internal network.
- Network gains these benefits from a firewall by receiving all transmitted traffic through the firewall.
- The importance of including a firewall in our security strategy is apparent; however, firewalls have the following limitations:
  1. Firewalls cannot protect against what has been authorized.
  2. It cannot stop social engineering attacks or an unauthorized user intentionally using their access for unwanted purposes.
  3. Firewalls cannot fix poor administrative practices or poorly designed security policies.
  4. It cannot stop attacks if the traffic does not pass through them.
  5. They are only as effective as the rules they are configured to enforce.
  6. Firewall cannot protect you against malicious insiders.
  7. A firewall cannot protect you against connections that don't go through it.
  8. A firewall cannot protect against completely new threats.
  9. A firewall cannot fully protect against viruses.
  10. A firewall cannot set itself up correctly.
  11. Firewalls cannot deal with the real problem.

4.2.4 Demilitarized Zone (DMZ) [S-17]

- DMZ concept is very common in firewall architecture. Firewalls can be arranged to form a DMZ.
- A DMZ (Demilitarized Zone) is an area of the network that sits between the Internet and the organization's internal network.
- DMZ is a "neutral zone" that keeps external users and the internal network apart, reducing opportunities for unauthorized access.
- Much like in the non-computerized world, a network DMZ, sometimes called a "perimeter network" is a "neutral zone" that attempts to keep external users and the internal network apart.
- When organizations have servers (e.g. Web server's servers) that it needs to make available to the outside world in that case DMZ is needed.
- For this firewall has minimum following three network interfaces:
  1. Interface connects to the internal private network
  2. Interface connects to the external public network
  3. Interface connects to the public servers (which forms a DMZ network)
- In computer networks a DMZ is a computer host or small network inserted as a neutral zone between organizations private network and the outside public network.
- The concept of DMZ is shown in Fig. 4.14.

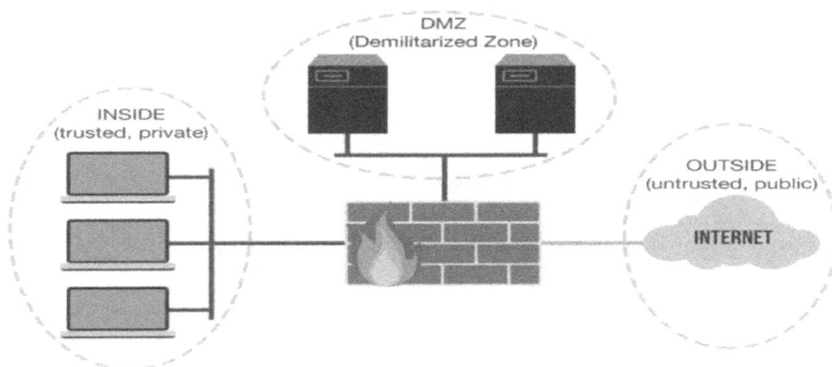

Fig. 4.14: Demilitarized Zone (DMZ) Networks

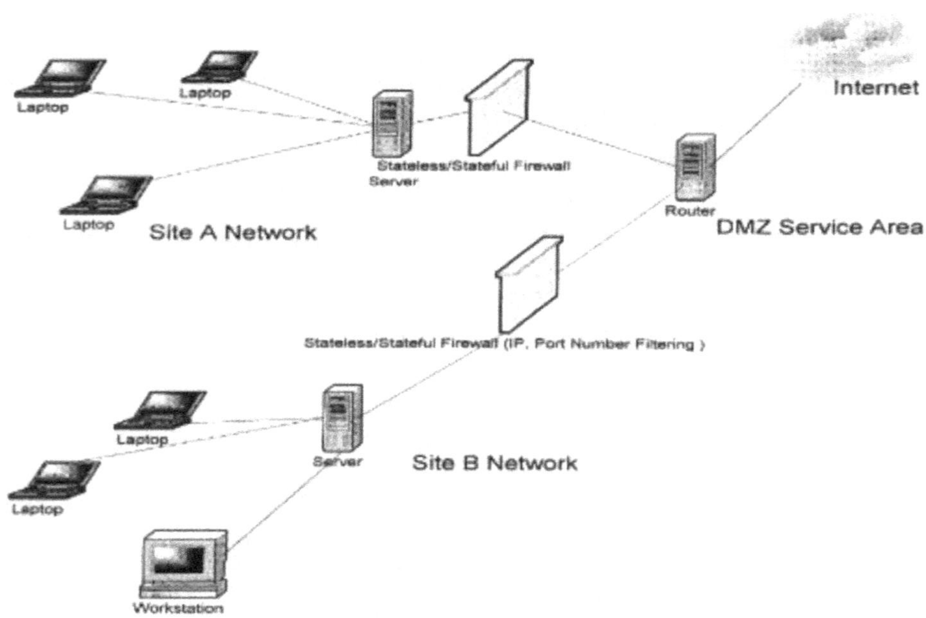

Fig. 4.15: A Packet Filter Firewall with DMZ

- Advantage of such scheme is that the access to any service on the DMZ can be restricted.
- Internal private network is not directly connected to the DMZ so if attacker has hacked DMZ then internal private network remains protected.

4.3 INTRUSION DETECTION SYSTEM [W-16, 17, W-17, 19]

- An Intrusion Detection System (IDS) is a system trying to detect and alert on attempted intrusions into a system or network.
- An IDS is a device or software application that monitors a network or systems for malicious activity or policy violations.
- An IDS is a system that monitors network traffic for suspicious activity and issues alerts when such activity is discovered.
- Intrusion detection systems help computer systems prepare for and deal with different types of attacks. It is a software application that scans a network or a system for harmful activity or policy breaching.
- Any malicious activity is normally reported either to an administrator or collected centrally using a Security Information and Event Management (SIEM) system.
- A SIEM system integrates outputs from multiple sources and uses alarm filtering techniques to differentiate malicious activity from false alarms.
- Intrusion detection systems are also as important in the firewall because they help us to detect the type of attack that is being done to our system and then to make a solution to block them.
- The monitoring part like tracing logs, looking for doubtful signatures and keeping history of the events triggered. They help also the network administrators to check the connection integrity and authenticity that occur.
- Although intrusion detection systems monitor networks for potentially malicious activity, they are also disposed to false alarms. Hence, organizations need to fine-tune their IDS products when they first install them.
- It means properly setting up the intrusion detection systems to recognize what normal traffic on the network looks like as compared to malicious activity.
- Intrusion prevention systems also monitor network packets inbound the system to check the malicious activities involved in it and at once sends the warning notifications.
- Hence, we can say that Intrusion detection systems perform a variety of following functions:
  1. Monitoring and analysis of user and system activity.
  2. Auditing of system configurations and vulnerabilities.
  3. Assessing the integrity of critical system and data files.
  4. Recognition of activity patterns reflecting known attacks.
  5. Statistical analysis for abnormal activity patterns.
  6. Operating system audit trail management, with recognition of user activity reflecting policy violations.

Structure of IDS:

- Fig. 4.16 shows structure of IDS with its components.

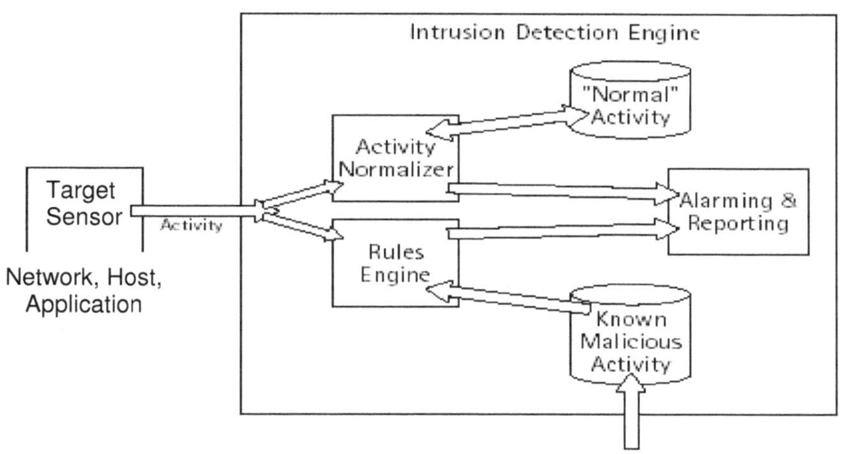

Fig. 4.16: Components of IDS

- Various components of IDS are explained below:
  1. The network, host, application, or target sensor provides data packets, host activity, application activity, or change detections to the rules engine (misuse detector) and the activity normalizer (anomaly detector). The sensor might be a physical network sensor or it might be a program running in a host system collecting application and server logs.
  2. The rules engine searches the data for patterns from the known malicious activity database (signatures).
  3. The activity normalizer performs analysis (usually statistical) of the data, adjusting the baseline as the usage changes over time. The activity normalizer must constantly adjust the baseline of normal activity to reflect the dynamic nature of the monitored computer systems and network.
  4. The known malicious activity database must be constantly updated with the latest patterns of malicious activity.
  5. Both the rules engine and the activity normalizer in turn trigger the alarming and reporting as necessary.
- If all of the above activities are performed in a single system, the breadth of analysis that can occur will be limited by the resources of the single system.
- If multiple systems are used in conjunction for detection, better breadth of analysis is possible, but with a trade-off of increased time for detection, higher cost, and greater complexity.
- Intrusion Detection System is basically classified into two types namely, NIDS and HIDS.

4.3.1 Network Based Intrusion Detection System (NIDS) [W-19]

- Network Intrusion Detection Systems (NIDS) are set up at a planned point within the network to examine traffic from all devices on the network.
- Network-based intrusion detection sensors collect information from the network itself
- Once, an abnormal behavior on network is observed, the alert can be sent to the administrator. NIDS is as shown in Fig. 4.17.

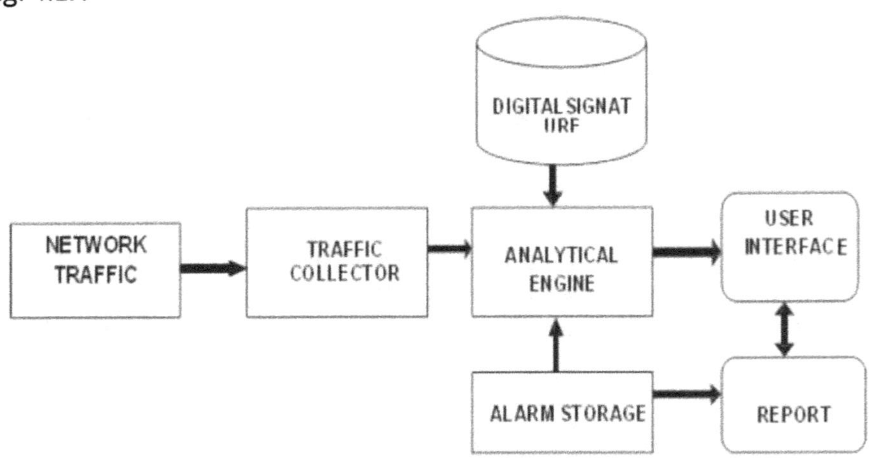

Fig. 4.17: Network Intrusion Detection Systems (NIDS)

- NIDS consist of following components:
  1. **Traffic Collection:** Collects activity as events from IDS to examine. On Host-based IDS, this can be log files, Audit logs or traffic coming to or leaving a system. On network based IDS, this is typically a mechanism for copying traffic of network link.
  2. **Analysis Engine:** Examines collected network traffic and compares it to known patterns of suspicious or malicious activity stored in digital signature. The analysis engine act like a brain of IDS.
  3. **Signature database:** A collection of patterns and definitions of known suspicious or malicious activity.
  4. **User Interface and Reporting:** Interfaces with human element, providing alerts when suitable and giving the user a means to interact with and operate the IDS.
- An example of an NIDS is installing it on the subnet where firewalls are located in order to see if someone is trying crack the firewall.

Advantages of Network-Based Intrusion Detection Systems:

1. The deployment of network-based IDSs is usually easy with minimal effort.
2. Network-based IDSs can be made very secure and is often invisible to most attackers.
3. They can monitor a heterogeneous set of hosts and operating systems simultaneously, due to the fact that standard network protocols (e.g. TCP, UDP and IP) are supported and used by most major operating systems

Disadvantages of Network-Based Intrusion Detection System:

1. Network-based IDSs cannot analyze encrypted information. This problem is increasing as more organizations and attackers use virtual private networks, which normally utilize encrypted information.
2. The processing load in a large or busy network may cause significant difficulties to the analysis engine part of the IDS. This condition (high processing load) can seriously limit an IDS's ability to detect attacks when the network load is above a specific amount of network traffic.
3. The need to analyze packets as fast as possible, force developers to detect fewer attacks. Thus, the detection effectiveness is often compromised for the sake of cost effectiveness.

4.3.2 Host-Based Intrusion Detection Systems (HIDS) [W-18, 19]

- Host-Based Intrusion Detection Systems (HIDS) run on independent hosts or devices on the network.
- A HIDS monitors the incoming and outgoing packets from the device only and will alert the administrator if suspicious or malicious activity is detected.
- It takes a snapshot of existing system files and compares it with the previous snapshot. If the analytical system files were edited or deleted, an alert is sent to the administrator to investigate.
- These frequently use the host system's audit and logging mechanism as a source of information for analysis. This IDS architecture generally uses rule-based engines for analyzing.
- HIDS is looking for certain activities in the log file are:
  - Logins at odd hours.
  - Login authentication failure.
  - Adding new user account.
  - Modification or access of critical system files.
  - Modification or removal of binary files.
  - Starting or stopping processes.
  - Privilege escalation.
  - Use of certain programs.
- Host-based intrusion detection systems (HIDS) is as shown in Fig. 4.18.

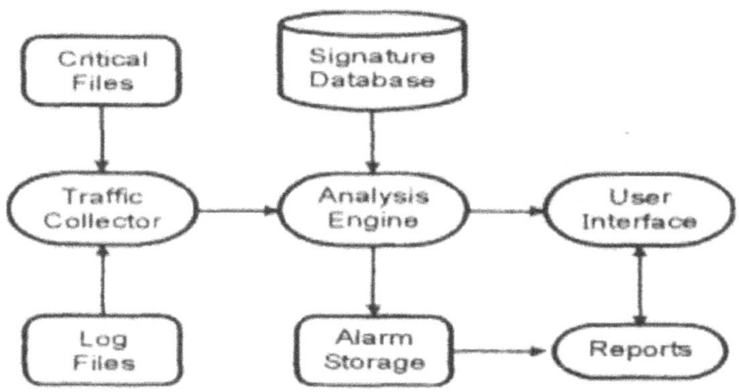

Fig. 4.18: Host-Based Intrusion Detection Systems (HIDS)

- Basic components of HIDS are as follows:

1. Traffic collector:

- This component collects activity or events from the IDS to examine.

On Hostbased IDS, this can be log files, audit logs, or traffic coming to or leaving a specific system

2. Analysis Engine:

- This component examines the collected network traffic and compares it to known patterns of suspicious or malicious activity stored in the signature database.

The analysis engine acts like a brain of the IDS.

3. Signature Database:

- It is a collection of patterns and definitions of known suspicious or malicious activity.

4. User Interface and Reporting:

- This is the component that interfaces with the human element, providing alerts and giving the user a means to interact with and operate the IDS.

- An example of HIDS usage can be seen on mission critical machines, which are not expected to change their layout.
- The host-based IDS looks for signs of intrusion on the local host system.

Advantages:

1. Operating system specific and detailed signatures.
2. Examine data after it has been decrypted.
3. Application specific.
4. Determine whether or not an alarm may impact that specific..

Disadvantages:

1. Should have a process on every system to watch.
2. High cost of ownership and maintenance.
3. Uses local system resources.
4. If logged locally, could be compromised or disable.

4.3.3 Misuse Based Intrusion Detection System

- Misuse detection is an approach to detecting computer attacks. In a misuse detection approach, abnormal system behaviour is defined first, and then all other behaviour is defined as normal.
- It stands against the anomaly detection approach which utilizes the reverse: defining normal system behaviour first and defining all other behaviour as abnormal. With misuse detection, anything not known is normal.
- An example of misuse detection is the use of attack signatures in an intrusion detection system. It works similar to computer antivirus application.
- Misused detection system analyzes the system or network environment and compare the activity against pattern of known intrusive computer and network behavior.
- This pattern must be uploaded over a time to include the latest attack patterns similar to antivirus application. Typical misuse detection system is shown in Fig. 4.19.

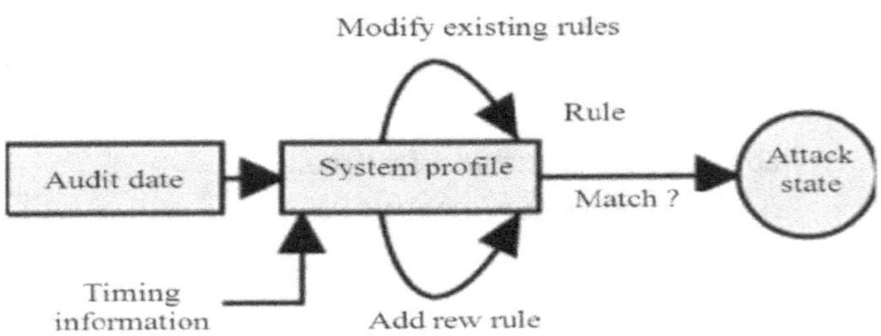

Fig. 4.19: Misuse Detection System

Advantages:

1. It can be used very quickly.
2. Due to pattern matching rate of false positive decreases.
3. Computer administrator can write their own patterns or signatures according to organizations security policy.
4. IDS that follows misuse detection method that needs constant updations to stay ahead of hackers.

Disadvantages:

1. Vulnerable to evasion.
2. Many misuse detectors are designed to use tightly defined patterns or signatures that prevent them from detecting various common attacks.
3. This type of IDS must be constantly updated with attack signature or pattern that represent newly discovered attacks or modified existing attacks.

4.3.4 Anomaly-Based IDS

- It is also called as behavioral based detection method. This system is used for detecting both network and computer intrusions and misuse by monitoring system activity and classifying it as either normal or anomalous.

- Anomaly-based IDS typically work by taking a baseline of the normal traffic and activity taking place on the network.
- They can measure the present state of traffic on the network against this baseline in order to detect patterns that are not present in the traffic normally.
- Such methods can work very well when we are looking to detect new attacks or attacks that have been deliberately assembled to avoid IDS.
- Anomaly-based IDS was introduced to detect the unknown malware attacks as new malware are developed rapidly.
- In anomaly-based IDS there is use of machine learning to create a trustful activity model and anything coming is compared with that model and it is declared suspicious if it is not found in model.
- Machine learning based method has a better generalized property in comparison to signature-based IDS as these models can be trained according to the applications and hardware configurations.
- This model works by establishing accepted rules and nothing exceptional differences. If an IDS looks only at network packet header for differences it is called as protocol anomaly detection.
- This model triggers off when the following event occurs:
  - Unusual user account activity.
  - Excessive file and object access.
  - High CPU utilization.
  - Inappropriate protocol use.
  - Unusual login frequency.
  - High number of sessions.
  - Unusual contents.
- Typical anomaly detection system is shown in Fig. 4.20.

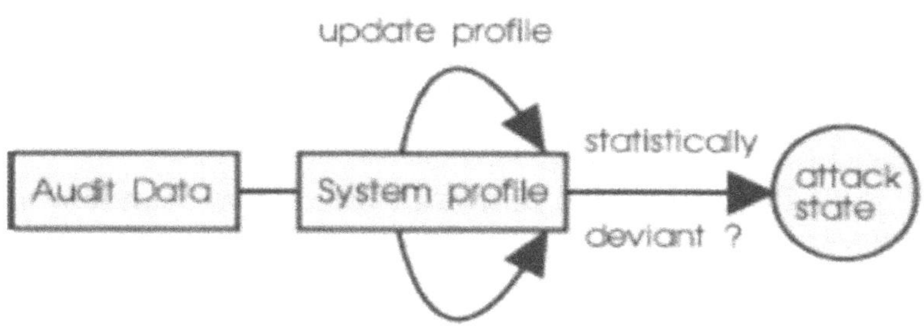

Fig. 4.20: Typical Anomaly Based IDS

Advantages:

1. Analyzes ongoing traffic, activities, transaction and behavior for anomalies.
2. Potential to detect previously unknown type of attack.
3. Catalogs the differences between baseline behavior and ongoing activity.

Disadvantages:

1. Prone to false positive.
2. Heavy processing overhead.
3. Vulnerable to attack while creating time consuming baseline.

4.3.5 Vulnerability Assessment

- Vulnerability assessment products are also known as scanners. Vulnerability assessment products perform rigorous examinations of systems in order to determine weaknesses that might allow security violations.
- They are security management tools that:
  - Conduct exhaustive checks of systems in an attempt to locate exposures to security vulnerabilities.
  - Report the number, nature, and severity of these exposures.
  - Allow a system administrator to determine the security status of a system at a particular time.

- Allow security auditors to determine the effectiveness of an organization's system security administration.
- In some cases, once an incident occurs, allow investigators to determine the way of entry for an attacker.
- Vulnerability assessment products complement intrusion-detection systems, they allow system administrators to be proactive in securing their systems by finding and closing security holes before attackers can use them.
- Intrusion-detection systems are by nature reactive, they monitor for attackers targeting systems in hopes of interrupting the attacks before the system is damaged.

Vulnerability Assessment Approach:

- There are two categories of vulnerability assessment are considered:

1. Network Vulnerability Scanner:

- A network vulnerability scanner operates remotely by examining the network interface on a remote system. It will look for vulnerable services running on that remote machine and report on a possible vulnerability.
- For example, it is well-known that rexd is a weak service, a network vulnerability scanner will attempt to connect to the rexd service on the target system. If the connection succeeds, the scanner will report a rexd vulnerability.
- Since a network vulnerability scanner can be run from a single machine on the network, it can be installed without impacting the configuration management of other machines.
- Frequently, these scanners are used by auditors and security groups because they can provide an "outsider's view" of security holes in a computer or network.

Advantages:

(i) Network vulnerability scanners can report on a variety of target architectures.

(ii) Easy to install.

Disadvantages:

(i) Network vulnerability scanners are almost exclusively signature-based systems. signature-based vulnerability scanner can only detect those vulnerabilities it is programmed to recognize. If a new vulnerability comes into play, as they frequently do, there is a number of opportunities for the attacker to attack.

(ii) Output required skilled interpretation network vulnerability scanners contain a huge amount of vulnerability data. If anyone ever breaks into the scanner system, compromise of most other machines on the network.

2. Host Vulnerability Scanner:

- A host vulnerability scanner differs from a network vulnerability scanner in that it is confined entirely to the local operating system.
- A network vulnerability scanner requires the target machine be accessible from the network in order for it to operate, a host vulnerability scanner does not.
- Host vulnerability scanners are software packages that are installed on particular operating systems.
- Once, the software is installed it can be configured to run at any time of the day or night. Usually the scans performed by this type of tool are scheduled to run at a low priority to reduce the impact of the scan on production work.

Advantages:

(i) Host vulnerability scanners tend to be much more tuned and accurate for a given operating system.

(ii) Host vulnerability scanners do not consume network bandwidth when they run.

(iii) Host vulnerability scanners are less likely to be used against us by a successful intruder.

Disadvantages:

(i) Host vulnerability scanners are, against signature based.

(ii) Installing host vulnerability scanners requires the cooperation of system administrators.

4.3.6 Honeypots [S-18]

- It the technique used to study hacker movement and interested to help better defenses against later attacks usually made up of virtual machines that sits on a network or single client.
- It is a system on internet that is designed to attract and trap people who attempt to find access into others computer system. It includes hacker, cracker and script.
- It is security resource whose value lies in being attacked or compromised. They can provide early warning about new attack and utilization trends and they allow in-depth examination of unwanted users during and after use of honeypot.
- Many people have their own definition of what honeypot is. They are in their most basic forms, fake information servers which are fed with false information made unrecognizable as files of classified nature.
- Initial configuration of this server is difficult but not impossible to break into them by attacker. Finally, the server is loaded with monitoring and tracking tools s, so every step and trace of activity left by hacker can be recorded.
- This are highly flexible security tools with different applications for security. They have multiple use such as prevention, detection or information gathering. Basic design of honeypot is as shown in Fig. 4.21.

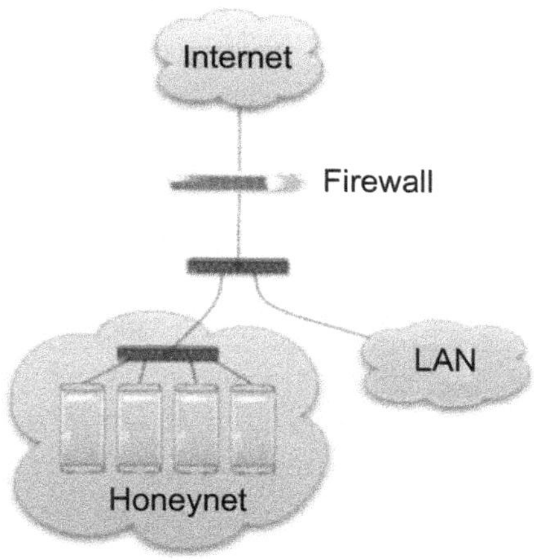

Fig. 4.21: Honeypot

Functions of Honeypot:

1. To divert the attention of attacker from real network considering that main information resource is not compromised.
2. To build attacker profile inn such a way that to identify their preferred attack method.
3. To identify new vulnerabilities and risk of various OS, environment and program which are not identified at the moment.
4. To capture new viruses for future study.
5. A group of honeypot becomes honeynet.

- Honeypots are classifies based on two categories:
  1. According to their implementation environment:
     - Research Honeypots.
     - Production Honeypots.
  2. According to their level of interaction:
     - Low Interaction.
     - High Interaction.

Advantages:

1. Data value.
2. Simplicity.

Disadvantages:

1. Fingerprinting.
2. Narrow field of view.
3. Risk.

Difference between Firewall and IDS:

Sr. No.	Firewall	IDS
1.	A firewall is a hardware and/or software which functions in a networked environment to block unauthorized access while permitting authorized communications.	An Intrusion Detection System (IDS) is a software or hardware device installed on the network (NIDS) or host (HIDS) to detect and report intrusion attempts to the network.
2.	A firewall can block an unauthorized access to network (For example, A watchman standing at gate can block a thief).	An IDS can only report an intrusion; it cannot block it (For example, A CCTV camera which can alert about a thief but cannot stop it).
3.	A firewall cannot detect security breaches for traffic that does not pass through it (For example, a gateman can watch only at front gate. He is not aware of wall-jumpers).	IDS is fully capable of internal security by collecting information from a variety of system and network resources and analyzing the symptoms of security problems
4.	Firewall does not inspect content of permitted traffic, (a gateman will never suspect an employee of the company).	IDS keeps a check of overall network.
5.	No man-power is required to manage a firewall.	An administrator (man-power) is required to respond to threats issued by IDS.
6.	Firewalls are most visible part of a network to an outsider. Hence, more vulnerable to be attacked first, (a gateman will be the first person attacked by a thief).	IDS are very difficult to be spotted in a network, (especially stealth mode of IDS).

Practice Questions

1. What is firewall?
2. Enlist types of firewalls.
3. Explain need of firewall with its basic function.
4. With the help of diagram describe packet filter.
5. What is IDS?
6. Describe the term NIDS and HIDS in detail.
7. What is honeypots?
8. Explain the term vulnerability assessment.
9. What is DMZ? How it works? Explain with example.
10. Describe misuse and anomaly detection detail.
11. Compare firewall and IDS.
12. Explain the term circuit and application level gateways.

■■■

5... Network Security, Cyber Laws and Compliance Standards

Chapter Outcomes...

- Explain the given component of Kerberos authentication protocol.
- Explain working of the given protocol for e-mail security.
- Describe the given component of Public Key Infrastructure (PKI).
- Classify the given cyber crime.
- Explain the specified cyber law.
- Describe compliance standards for information security.

Learning Objectives...

- To understand Basic Concepts of Network Security, Cyber Laws and Compliance Standards
- To learn Kerberos
- To understand IP Security and E-mail Security
- To study Concepts in PKI

5.0 INTRODUCTION

- Network security is the security provided to a network from unauthorized access and risks. It is the duty of network administrators to adopt preventive measures to protect their networks from potential security threats.
- Computer networks that are involved in regular transactions and communication within the government, individuals, or business require security.
- The most common and simple way of protecting a network resource is by assigning it a unique name and a corresponding password.
- Network security is a set of protocols that facilities the use of networks without any fear of security attacks.
- The law (statutory or otherwise) providing answers to these problems or dealing with Information Technology are sometimes loosely referred to as 'Computer Laws' or 'Information Technology (IT) Laws' or comply 'Cyber Laws'.
- Cyber laws yields legal recognition to electronic documents and a structure to support e-filing and e-commerce transactions and also provides a legal structure to reduce cyber crimes.
- Cyber crime or computer-oriented crime is a crime that includes a computer and a network. The computer may have been used in the execution of a crime or it may be the target.

- Cyber crimes can involve criminal activities that are traditional in nature such as theft, fraud, forgery, defamation and mischief all of which are subject to the Indian Penal Code.
- The abuse of computers has also given birth to a scope of new age crimes that are addressed by the Information Technology Act, 2000.
- Access means gaining entry into instructing or communicating with the logical, arithmetical, or memory function resources of a computer, computer system or computer network.
- A program that has capability to infect other programs and make copies of itself and spread into other programs is called virus.
- Cyber law is a term used to describe the legal issues related to use of communications technology, particularly "cyberspace", i.e. the Internet.
- It is a less distinct field of law in the way that property or contract are as it is an intersection of many legal fields, including intellectual property, privacy, freedom of expression, and jurisdiction.
- Today, there are many disturbing things happening in cyberspace. Due to the anonymous nature of the Internet, it is possible to engage into a variety of criminal activities with impunity and people with intelligence have been grossly misusing this aspect of the Internet to perpetuate criminal activities in cyberspace. Hence the need for Cyber laws in India.
- Security compliance is a legal concern for organizations in many industries today. Kerberos is a computer-network authentication protocol that works on the basis of tickets to allow nodes communicating over a non-secure network to prove their identity to one another in a secure manner.
- A Public Key Infrastructure (PKI) is a set of roles, policies, hardware, software and procedures needed to create, manage, distribute, use, store and revoke digital certificates and manage public-key encryption.
- The purpose of a PKI is to facilitate the secure electronic transfer of information for a range of network activities such as e-commerce, internet banking and confidential e-mail.
- Internet Protocol Security (IPsec) is a secure network protocol suite that authenticates and encrypts the packets of data sent over an Internet Protocol network. It is used in Virtual Private Networks (VPNs).
- E-mail is one of the most widely and commonly used Internet service. E-mail was one of the earliest internet applications and is one of the most used. In essence, it is the ability to send messages between two computers: a source and a destination.
- E-mail is the most common delivery mechanism for viruses, worms, Trojan horses, documents with destructive macros, and other malicious code.
- E-mail security describes various techniques for keeping sensitive information in e-mail communication and accounts secure against unauthorized access, loss, or compromise.

5.1 KERBEROS [W-16, 17, 18, 19, S-16, 17, 19]

- Kerberos is a computer network authentication protocol, which allows nodes communicating over a non-secure network to prove their identity to one another in a secure manner.
- Kerberos is often called a third party trusted authentication service. Kerberos keeps a database of all its users and their private keys. Kerberos provides a secure means of authentication over insecure networks.
- Kerberos is a protocol for authenticating service requests between trusted hosts across an un-trusted network such as the internet. Kerberos is built in to all major operating systems, including Microsoft Windows, Apple OS X, FreeBSD and Linux.
- Kerberos is an open standard designed to provide strong authentication by using secret-key cryptography.

Usage:

- It provides mutual authentication - both the user and the server verify each other‘s identity.
- Kerberos protocol messages are protected against eavesdropping and replay attacks.

- It builds on symmetric key cryptography and requires a trusted third party, and optionally may use public key cryptography by utilizing asymmetric key cryptography during certain phases of authentication.
- It provides the tools of authentication and strong cryptography over the network to help us to secure our information systems across our entire enterprise.

5.1.1 Working of Kerberos [W-19]

- In a Kerberos system, there is a designated site on the network, called the Kerberos server which performs centralized key management and administrative functions.
- The server maintains a database containing the secret keys of all users, generates session keys whenever two users wish to communicate securely and authenticates the identity of a user who requests certain network services.
- The Kerberos protocol uses strong cryptography so that a client can prove its identity to a server (and vice versa) across an insecure network connection.
- The Kerberos authentication process uses same at both ends for each exchange. AS_REQ is the initial user authentication request. This message is directed to the KDC component known as Authentication Server (AS).
- AS_REP is the reply of the Authentication Server to the previous request. Basically it contains the TGT (encrypted using the TGS secret key) and the session key (encrypted using the secret key of the requesting user).
- TGS_REQ is the request from the client to the Ticket Granting Server (TGS) for a service ticket. This packet includes the TGT obtained from the previous message and an authenticator generated by the client and encrypted with the session key.
- TGS_REP is the reply of the Ticket Granting Server to the previous request. Located inside is the requested service ticket (encrypted with the secret key of the service) and a service session key generated by TGS and encrypted using the previous session key generated by the AS.
- AP_REQ is the request that the client sends to an application server to access a service. The components are the service ticket obtained from TGS with the previous reply and an authenticator again generated by the client, but this time encrypted using the service session key, (generated by TGS).
- AP_REP is the reply that the application server gives to the client to prove it really is the server the client is expecting. This packet is not always requested. The client requests the server for it only when mutual authentication is necessary.

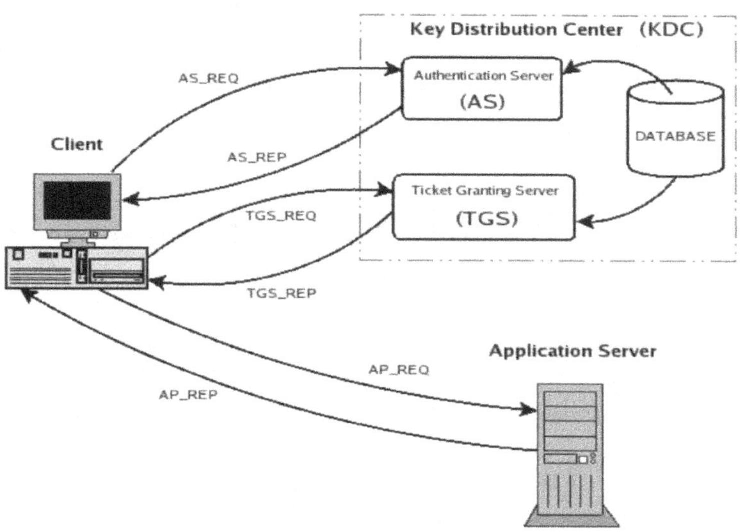

Fig. 5.1: Working of Kerberos

- Kerberos is a standard protocol that provides for mutual authentication over a non-secure network. There are several components in a Kerberos environment:
  - **Client:** The workstation (usually) that desires to access systems or services.
  - **AS (Authentication Server):** A centralized system to which a user initially authenticates.
  - **TGS (Ticket Granting Server):** A centralized system that issues tickets.
  - **SS (Service Server):** A server that provides some useful service.
  - **TGT (Ticket Granting Ticket):** A token that permits access to an SS.
  - **ST (Service Ticket):** An encrypted key.
- Let us illustrate the operations of Kerberos through an example. Let us suppose that an employee, Amar needs to access payroll. The principal database has the secret keys Kp(payroll) and Kj(Amar).
- Fig. 5.2 shows the following flow of information:
  1. The client asks for Amar's ID request. He identifies himself as Amar and indicates that he wants to access payroll. This information is sent to KDC.
  2. KDC Authentication Server (AS) constructs two replies and sends them to the client:
     - **Service Ticket:** This includes the information, Amar, payroll, and a session key (random). The service ticket is encrypted by Kp.
     - **Client Ticket:** This is the service ticket but it is now encrypted by Kj.
  3. The client decrypts the client ticket by using Kj. If this does not happen, then something is wrong.
  4. Client constructs a service request. This consists of the service ticket + request (print check).
  5. Client sends the service request to the payroll server. The payroll server decrypts it by using Kp.

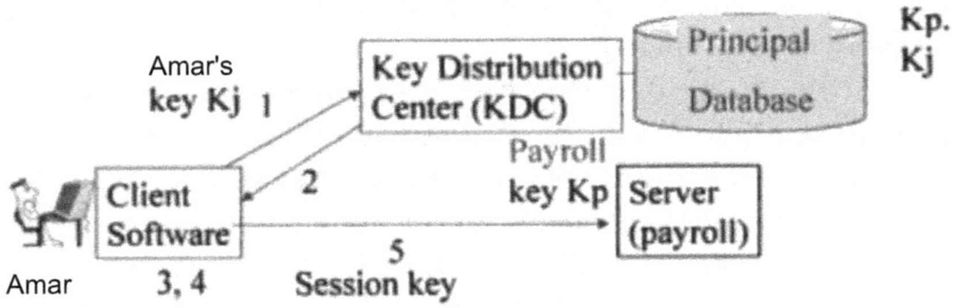

Fig. 5.2: Conceptual View of Kerberos with Example

Advantages of Kerberos:

1. Kerberos protocol provides security even when performed over an insecure network.
2. Kerberos is also designed to protect against replay attacks.
3. Due to the concept of time stamps in Kerberos messages restricts the window in which an attacker can retransmit messages.
4. Kerberos use of symmetric encryption technique which makes Kerberos computationally efficient.

Disadvantages of Kerberos:

1. Kerberos has single point of failure.
2. If attacker attacks on KDC then authorized information of client and server on network would be revealed.

5.2 IP SECURITY [S-17, 18, W-16, 18]

- The IP Security (IPSec) is an Internet Engineering Task Force (IETF) standard suite of protocols involving two communication points across the IP network which gives data authentication, integrity, and confidentiality.
- IPSec gives information related to the encryption, decryption and authenticated packets. It also gives information related to protocols which is required for secure key exchange as well as key management.

Uses of IP Security:

- IPsec can be used to do the following things:
  - For encryption of application layer data.
  - To secure remote internet access.
  - To setup communication with other organizations.
  - To provide security for routers sending routing data across the public internet.
  - To provide authentication without encryption, like to authenticate that the data originates from a known sender.
  - To protect network data.

5.2.1 Overview

- Internet Protocol Security (IPSec) is an open source protocol that secures communications across IP-based networks such as LANs, WANs, and the Internet.
- The protocol is designed to protect data integrity user confidentiality and authenticity at the IP packet level. IPSec is the cryptographic authentication and encryption product of the IETF's IP Protocol Security Working Group.
- It provides a stable, long lasting base for providing network layer security. In TCP/IP protocol stack IPSec resides between internet layer and transport layer.
- IPSec supports all of the cryptographic algorithms in use today, and can also accommodate newer, more powerful algorithms as they become available.
- Main objective of IPSec is to do encryption and seal the transport and application layer data during transmission.

Advantages of IPSec:

1. In a firewall, it gives high security to all traffic crossing the outside boundary.
2. IPSec is present below transport layer, hence transparent to applications.
3. It can be transparent to end users.
4. It can provide security for individual users if desired.

Disadvantages of IPSe:

1. IPSec is very critical than other security protocols.
2. It is complicated to configure.
3. Safety of public keys is required for IPSec. If key is compromised we may experience problems.
4. For small size transmission of packet, IPSec can be an inefficient way to encrypt data.

5.2.2 IPSec Modes

- IPsec has two modes of operation namely, Transport mode and Tunnel mode.
- In transport mode only the IP data is encrypted, not the IP headers. This allows intermediate nodes to read the source and destination addresses.
- In tunnel mode the entire IP packet is encrypted and is then placed as the content portion of another IP packet. This requires other systems at the beginning and end of the tunnel to act as proxies and to send and receive the encrypted packets. These systems their transmit the decrypted packets to their true destinations.
- The encryption of packets is not affected by modes. The packets are protected by AH, ESP, or both in each mode.
- The modes differ in policy application when the inner packet is an IP packet, as follows:
  1. In transport mode, the outer header determines the IPsec policy that protects the inner IP packet.
  2. In tunnel mode, the inner IP packet determines the IPsec policy that protects its contents.
- These modes can be used depending upon the type of communication preferred.

1. Transport Mode:

- This mode is designed for host to host communication. IPSec does not encapsulate a packet received from upper layer.
- The original IP header is maintained and the data is forwarded based on the original attributes set by the upper layer protocol. Transport mode is efficient mode.
- Fig. 5.3 shows the data flow in the protocol stack.

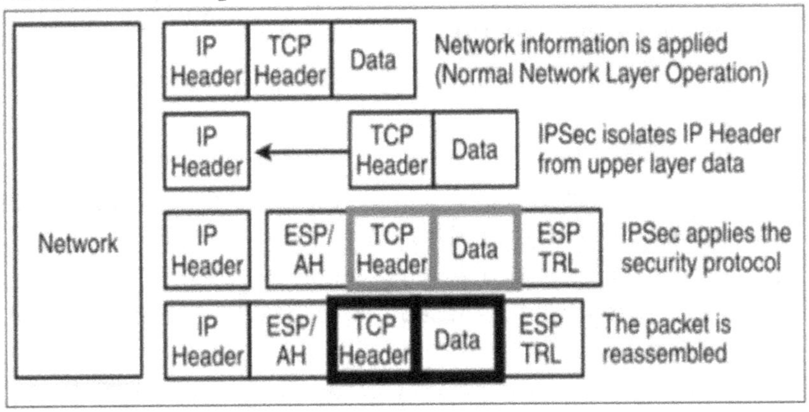

Fig. 5.3

- The limitation of transport mode is that gateway service is not provided

2. Tunnel Mode:

- This mode of IPsec gives encapsulation service as well as other services. In this, the entire packet from upper layer is encapsulated before applying security protocol. New IP header is added.
- Tunnel mode is typically related with gateway activities. The encapsulation provides the ability to send several sessions through a single gateway. Using this mode we can be established between the gateway and individual end system as well.
- Fig. 5.4 shows the data flow in the protocol stack.

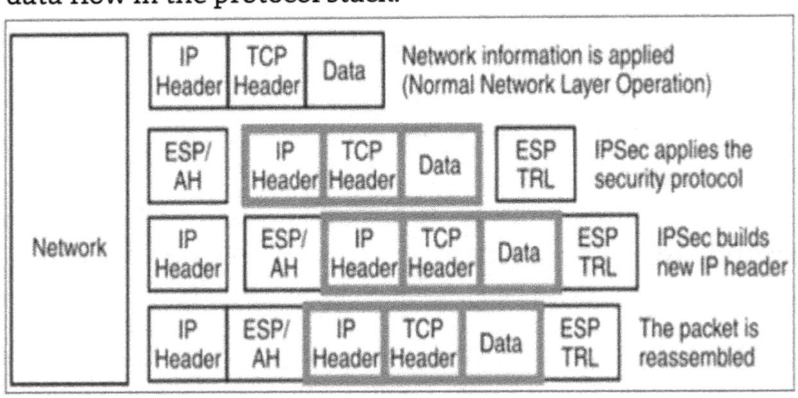

Fig. 5.4

5.2.3 Protocols (AH and ESP) [S-18]

- IP packet has two parts as IP header and actual data.
- IPSec features are implemented in the form of additional IP header called as extension header to the standard, default IP headers.
- Extension IP headers follows the standard IP headers.
- IPSec gives two important services namely, Authentication and Confidentiality.
- IPSec uses the security protocols to provide desired security services.
- IPSec actually consist of two main protocols namely, Authentication Header (AH) and Encapsulating Security Payload (ESP), (See Fig. 5.5.).
- The AH protocol provides system to system authentication and data integrity verification, but does not provide secrecy for the content of a network communication.

- The ESP protocol provides secrecy for the contents of network communications as well as system-to-system authentication and data integrity verification.

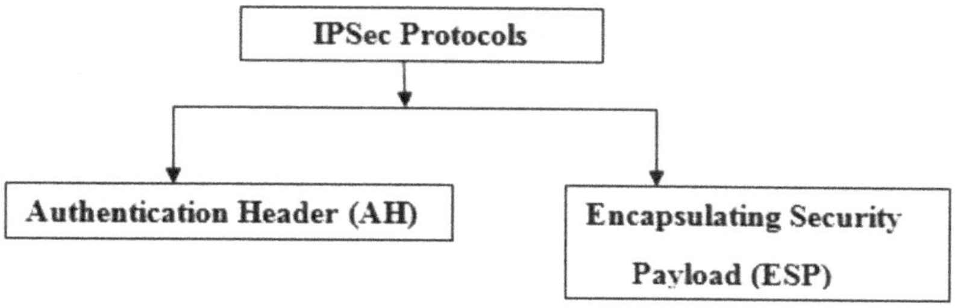

Fig. 5.5: IPSec Protocols

5.2.3.1 Authentication Header (AH)

- AH protocol mainly focuses on authentication. The AH protocol is designed to provide data integrity and IP packet authentication. It also provides data integrity, data origin and an optional replay protection service.
- This protocol provides authentication of all or part of the contents of a packet by the addition of a header. The IPSec AH is a header in IP packet which contains a cryptographic checksum (MD or hash) for the contents of packet.
- AH is simply inserted between IP header and subsequent packet header. The header is calculated based on the values in the packet.
- What parts of the packet are used for the calculation, and where to place the header, depends on the mode operation (tunnel or transport). Operation of AH is very simple. No changes are required to the data contents of the packet.
- Security is completely present in the contents of AH. Structure for AH is shown in Fig. 5.6.

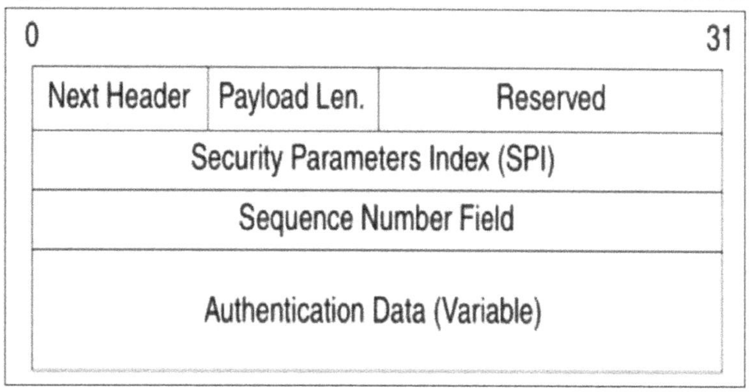

Fig. 5.6: Authentication Header (AH) Format

- Authentication header consist of following fields:
  1. **Next Header (8 Bits):** Identifies type of header immediately following this header.
  2. **Payload Length (8 Bits):** Length of authentication header in 32 bit words minus 2.
  3. **Reserved (16 Bits):** For future use.
  4. **Security Parameter Index (32 Bits):** Identifies Security Association (SA).
  5. **Sequence Number (32 bits):** Monotonically increasing counter value.
  6. **Authentication Data (Variable Size):** A variable length field that contain Integrity Checked Value (ICV).
- The process of AH goes through the following phases:
  1. When IP packet is received from upper protocol stack, IPsec determine the related Security Association SA (SA is agreement between the communicating parties about factors such as IPSec protocol version, modes of operation, encryption algorithm etc.) From available information in the packet; for example, IP address (source and destination).

2. From SA, once we know that security protocol is AH, the parameters of AH header are calculated. The AH header contains parameter shown in Fig. 5.6.

- In AH transport mode the process takes place as shown in Fig. 5.7.

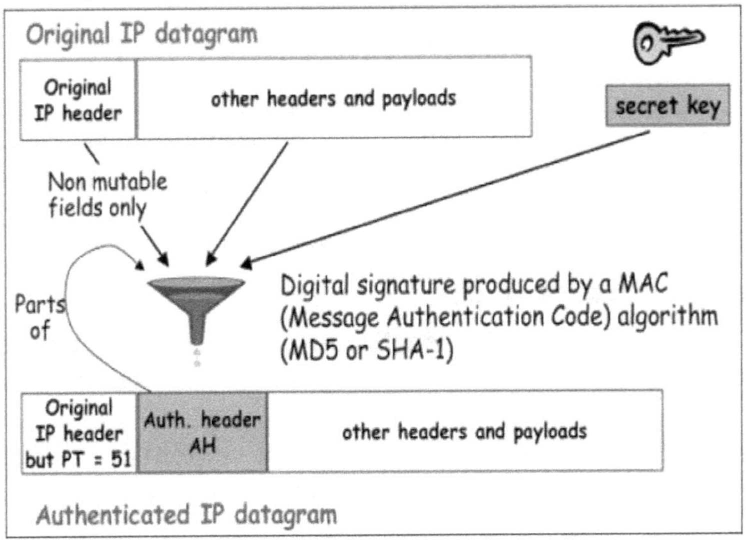

Fig. 5.7: AH in Transport Mode

- In AH Tunnel mode the process takes place is shown in the Fig. 5.8.

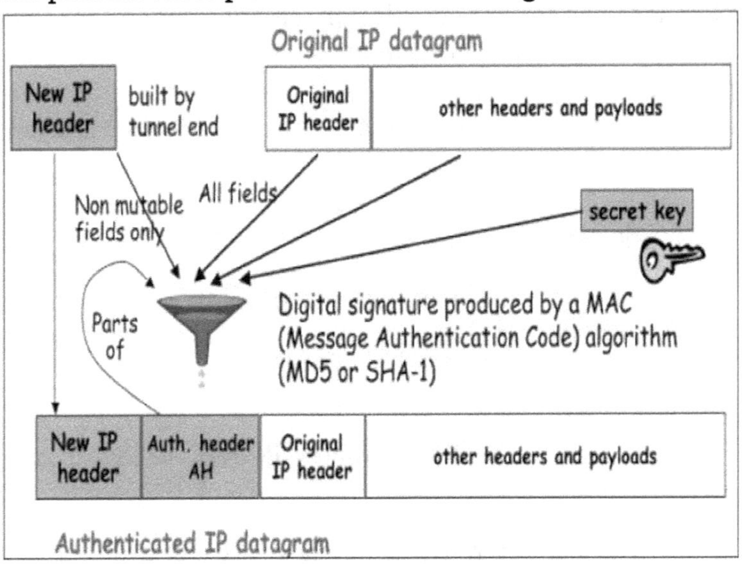

Fig. 5.8: AH in Tunnel Mode

5.2.3.2 Encapsulation Security Protocol (ESP)

- This protocol gives data confidentiality. ESP also offers security services such as confidentiality, integrity, origin authentication, and optional replay resistance.
- The services provided depends on options selected at the time of Security Association (SA) establishment. ESP protocol also defines new header to be inserted into IP packet.
- In ESP, algorithms used for encryption and generating authenticator are determined by the attributes used to create the SA.
- Its processing also includes transformation of protected data into unreadable format. Under normal conditions ESP will be inside AH.
- Structure for ESP is shown in Fig. 5.9.

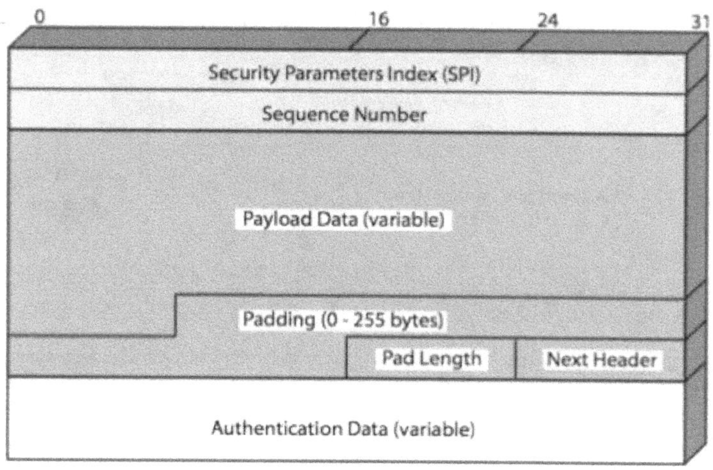

Fig. 5.9: ESP format

- ESP consist of following fields:
  1. **Security Parameter Index (32 bit):** Identifies SA.
  2. **Sequence Number (32 bits):** Monotonically increasing number, provides an anti-replay function.
  3. **Payload data (Variable):** This is transport level segment (Transport mode) or IP packet (Tunnel mode) protected using encryption
  4. **Padding (0-255 bytes):** For various reasons.
  5. **Pad length (8 bits):** Indicates number of pad bytes immediately preceding this fields.
  6. **Next header (8 bits):** Identifies the type of data contained in a payload data field by identifying the first header in that payload.
  7. **Authentication Data (Variable):** Result of applying an authentication scheme to part of packet.
- The process of ESP is as follows:
  1. The first two steps are similar to process of AH as stated above.
  2. Once, it is determined that ESP is involved, the fields of ESP packet are calculated.
- The ESP field arrangement is shown in Fig. 5.10.

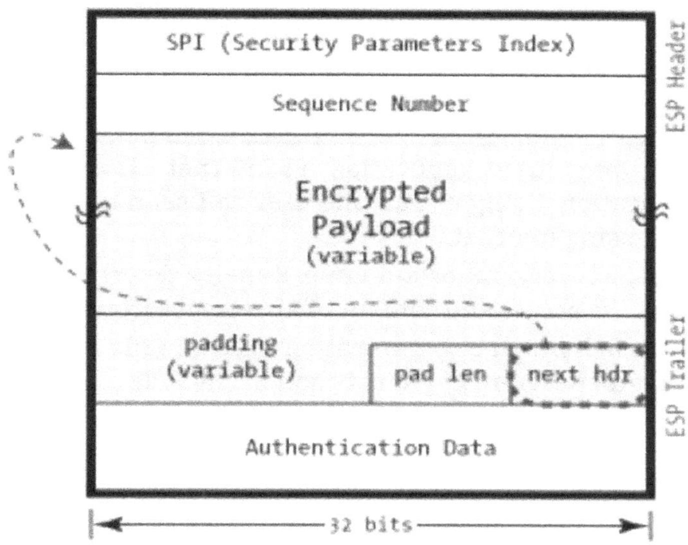

Fig. 5.10

- Encryption and authentication process of ESP in transport mode is shown in Fig. 5.11.

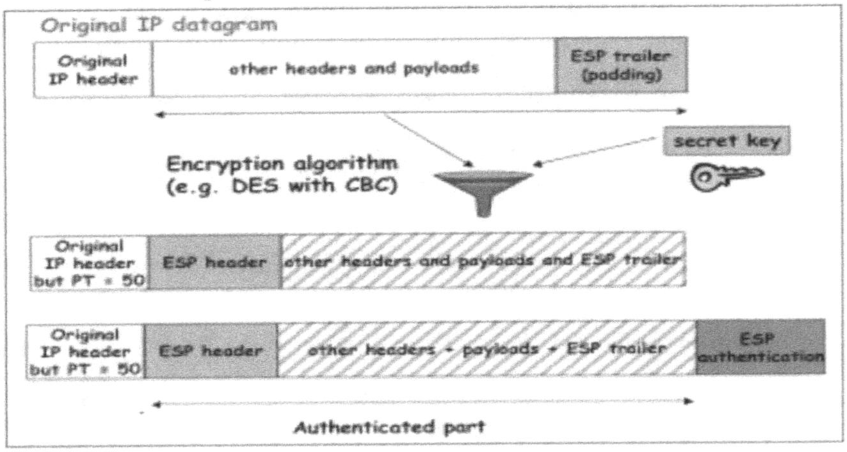

Fig. 5.11: ESP in Transport Mode

- In case of Tunnel mode, the encryption and authentication process is as shown in Fig. 5.12.

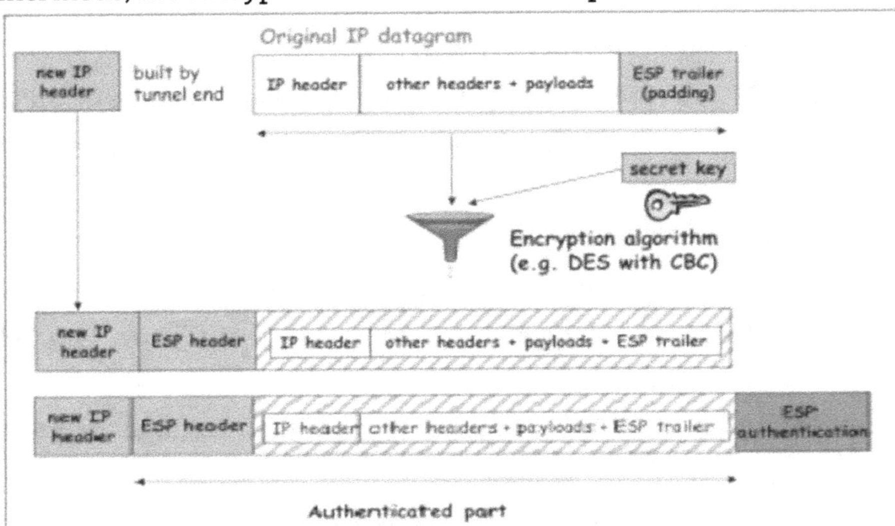

Fig. 5.12: ESP in Tunnel Mode

- Although authentication and confidentiality are the primary services provided by ESP, both are optional.
- The basic concept is to use ESP when one wants authentication and encryption, and to use AH when one wants extended authentication without encryption.

5.3 E-MAIL SECURITY [W-16, 17]

- E-mail (electronic mail) is most used application on internet. Nowadays, e-mail has become very widely used network application. Using e-mail one user can send message (pictures, videos, sound, messages) to another user using internet.
- Protection of e-mail message is very important issue. E-mail security denotes to the collective procedures used to protect the access and content of an e-mail account.
- E-mail security permits an individual or organization to secure the access to e-mail addresses. From an individual standpoint, practical e-mail security actions include:
  1. Strong passwords.
  2. Password rotations.
  3. Spam filters.
  4. Anti-spam applications.

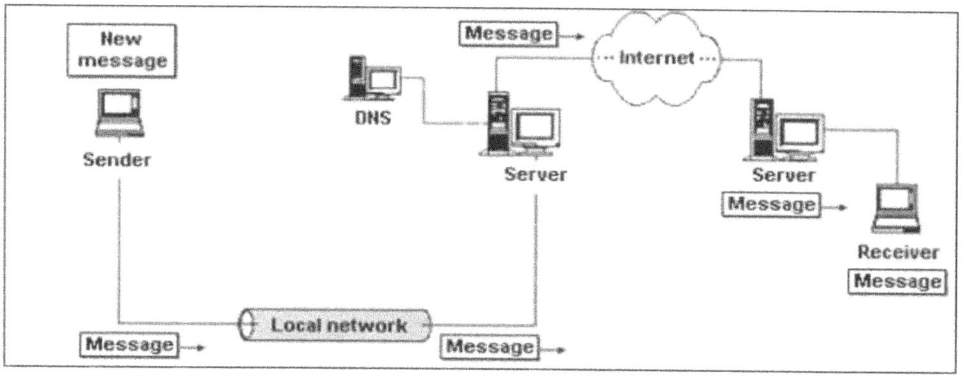

Fig. 5.13

- Fig. 5.13 shows following process for sending e-mail:
  1. A message (Notes or SMTP-based) is created on the clients local network.
  2. The user sends the message via the Domino 6 server.
  3. Lotus Domino executes a TCP/IP DNS (Domain Name System) resolution and finds the target server.
  4. The message is transferred to the target recipients server, and then delivered to the recipient.

5.3.1 SMTP [S-19, W-16]

- SMTP stands for Simple Mail Transfer Protocol. SMTP is a set of communication rules that permit software to communicate an electronic mail over the internet is called Simple Mail Transfer Protocol.
- SMTP also provides:
  - Send one message to one or many receivers.
  - Sending of any type of message is allowed such as text, audio, video etc.
  - It can also send the messages on different networks outside the internet.
  - The main purpose of SMTP is used to set up communication rules between servers.

Components of SMTP:

- Fig. 5.14 shows components of SMTP.

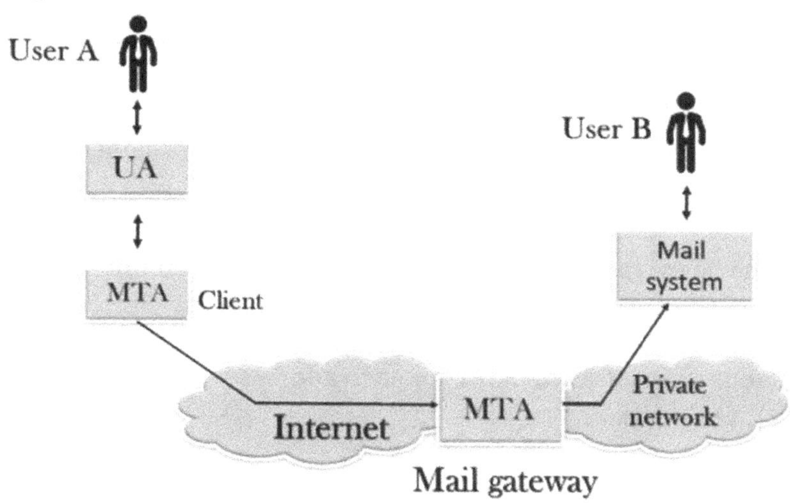

Fig. 5.14

- As message goes from client to server, we will break the SMTP client component into User Agent (UA) and SMTP server component Mail Transfer Agent (MTA).
- Task of User Agent (UA) prepares the message, creates the envelope and then inserts the message in the envelope.
- Task of Mail Transfer Agent (MTA) is to transfers the mail from UA across the internet.

- Instead of just having MTA one at sending side and one at receiving side, more MTAs can be added, acting either as a client or server to relay the e-mail.
- The relaying system without TCP/IP protocol can also be used to send the e-mails to users, and this is achieved by the use of the mail gateway.
- The mail gateway is a relay MTA that can be used to receive an e-mail.

Working of SMTP:

1. Preparation of Mail:

- A user sends an e-mail by preparation mail message using a Mail User Agent (MUA).
- Using Mail User Agent (MUA) we can send and receive mail.
- The message contains two parts: body and header.
- The body is the main part of the message while the header includes information such as the sender and recipient address.
- The header also includes descriptive information such as the subject of the message.
- In this case, the message body is like a letter and header is like an envelope that contains the recipient's address.

2. Submission of Mail:

- After preparation of an e-mail, the mail client then submits the completed e-mail to the SMTP server by using SMTP on TCP port 25.

3. Delivery of Mail:

- E-mail addresses comprise of two parts: username of the receiver and domain name. For example, amar@gmail.com, where "amar" is the username of the recipient and "gmail.com" is the domain name.
- If the domain name of the receiver's e-mail address is different from the sender's domain name, then MSA will send the mail to the Mail Transfer Agent (MTA).
- To relay the mail, the MTA will find the target domain. It checks the MX record from Domain Name System to obtain the target domain.
- The MX record contains the domain name and IP address of the receiver's domain.
- Once, the record is located, MTA connects to the exchange server to relay the message.

4. Delivery and Processing of Mail:

- Once the incoming message is received, the exchange server delivers it to the incoming server (Mail Delivery Agent) which stores the e-mail where it waits for the user to retrieve it.

5. Access and Retrieval of Mail:

- The stored e-mail in MDA can be retrieved by using MUA (Mail User Agent).
- MUA can be accessed by using login and password.

Some SMTP Commands:

1. **HELO:** Identifies the client to the server, fully qualified domain name, only sent once per session.
2. **MAIL:** Initiate a message transfer, fully qualified domain of originator.
3. **RCPT:** Follows MAIL, identifies an addressee, typically the fully qualified name of the addressee and for multiple addressees use one RCPT for each addressee.
4. **DATA:** Send data line by line.

Advantages of SMTP:

1. No coding required.
2. Connects to all system.
3. In case of failure, the message will include an explanation about why the e-mail failed to be delivered.

Disadvantages of SMTP:

1. Some firewalls can block ports commonly used with SMTP.
2. Usually requires more back and forth conversation between servers in order to deliver message.

5.3.2 Privacy-Enhanced Mail (PEM) [S-18, W-16]

- Privacy-Enhanced Mail (PEM) is an Internet standard that provides for secure exchange of electronic mail. PEM does not require the use of a specific algorithm.
- It allows use of several algorithms for data encryption, key management, and data integrity. Three cryptographic functions of PEM are:
  1. Message Integrity.
  2. Sender Authentication (Non-Repudiation).
  3. Encryption.
- The message integrity aspects allow the user to ensure that a message hasn't been modified during transport from the sender.
- The sender authentication/non-repudiation allows a user to verify that the PEM message that they have received is truly from the person who claims to have sent it.
- The encryption (to achieve confidentiality) feature allows a message to be kept secret from people to whom the message was not addressed.

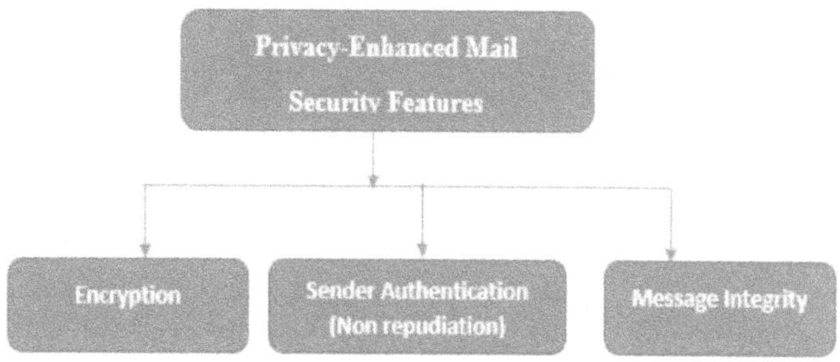

Fig. 5.15

Working of PEM:

- Fig. 5.16 shows working of PEM. Sender and receiver perfom all this steps for e-mail communication. Only receiver has to perform these four steps in reverse direction to get original plain text of e-mail message.

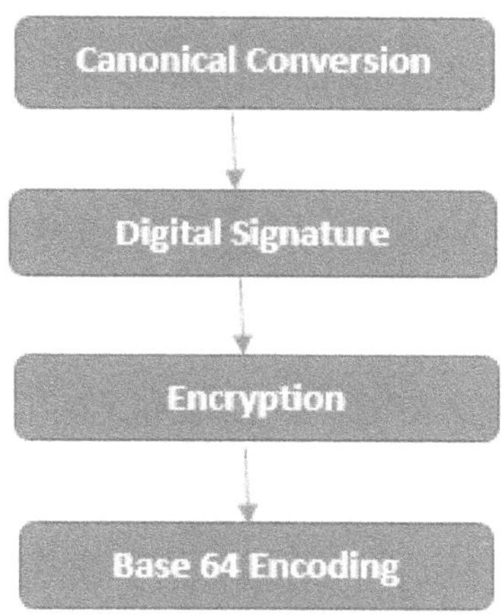

Fig. 5.16: PEM Operation

1. **Canonical Conversion:**

- It is possible that sender and receiver use different computers having different architectures and OS for mail communication.
- For example, in MS-DOS operating system new line is represented by two characters and which is not same in case of UNIX.
- PEM transforms each e-mail message into an abstract, canonical representation.
- This means whatever the architecture and OS at sender and receiver side, e-mail message always travels in a uniform, independent format.

2. Digital Signature:

- In this step message digest of the e-mail message using algorithm such as MD2 or MD5 as shown in Fig. 5.17.

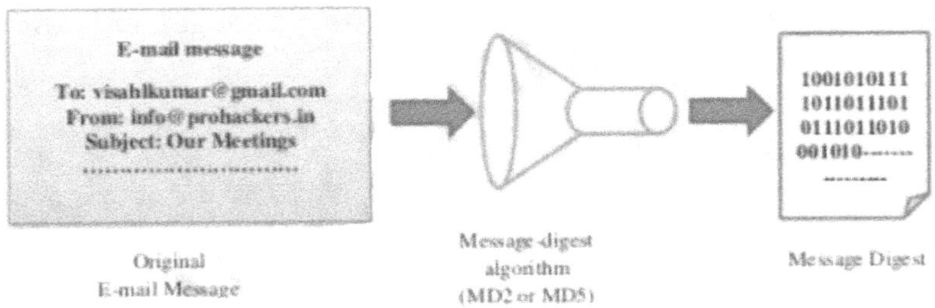

Fig. 5.17: MD Creation of Original E-Mail Message

- Whatever MD created is then encrypted with sender's private key to form the sender's digital signature as shown in Fig. 5.18.

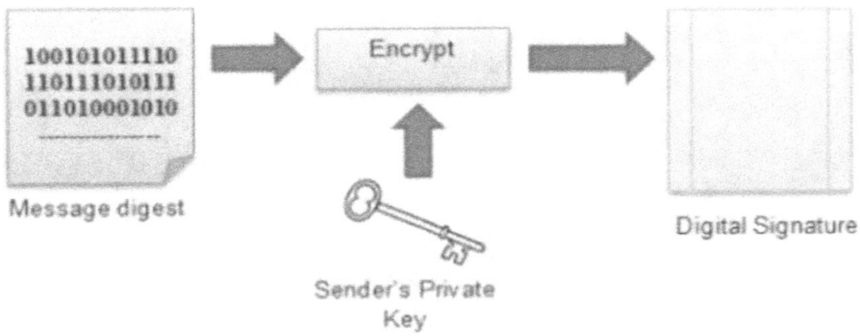

Fig. 5.18: Creation of Sender's Digital Signature Over E-mail Message

3. Encryption:

- In this step the original e-mail message and digital signature are encrypted together with symmetric key. For this encryption DES or DES-3 algorithm in CBC mode is used as shown in Fig. 5.19.

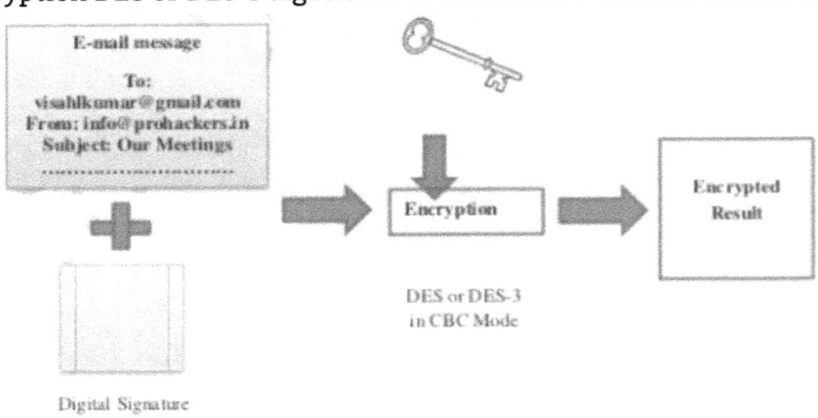

Fig. 5.19: PEM Encryption

4. Base 64 Encoding:

- This is last step in PEM. Base 64 encoding process transforms arbitrary binary input into printable character output.
- In this technique, the binary input is processed in blocks of 3 octets or 24-bits.
- These 24-bits are considered to be made up of 4 sets, each of 6-bits.
- Each such 6-bits is mapped into an 8-bit output character in this process.
- Base 64 coding concept is as shown in Fig. 5.20.

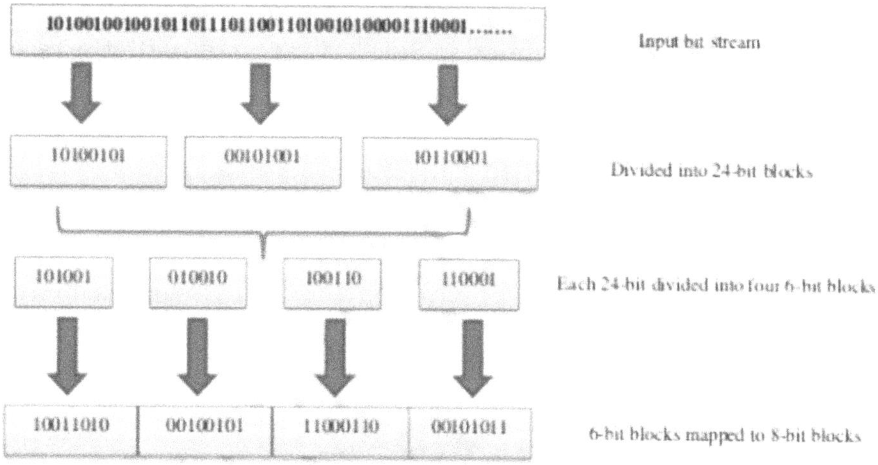

Fig. 5.20: Base 64 Encoding Concept

5.3.3 PGP **[S-16, 17, 18, 19, W-18, 19]**

- PGP stands for Pretty Good Privacy (PGP) protocol which is invented by Phil Zimmermann. PGP was designed to provide all four aspects of security, i.e., privacy, integrity, authentication, and non-repudiation in the sending of e-mail.
- PGP uses a digital signature (a combination of hashing and public key encryption) to provide integrity, authentication, and non-repudiation.
- PGP uses a combination of secret key encryption and public key encryption to provide privacy. PGP is an open source and freely available software package for e-mail security.
- PGP provides confidentiality through the use of symmetric block encryption. It provides compression by using the ZIP algorithm, and E-MAIL compatibility using the radix-64 encoding scheme.

Characteristics of PGP:

1. It uses symmetric as well as asymmetric encryption.
2. For symmetric encryption, PGP uses a block cipher with a 128-bit key to encrypt files or messages.
3. A "session key" is generated automatically for files and messages based on a random number generator.
4. A "session key" is encrypted by using the asymmetric encryption. PGP uses RSA to encrypt and exchange and session key. It uses the recipient's public key to encrypt.
5. PGP can also be used to encrypt files for storage and messages for transmission.

Working of PGP:

- Sender and receiver want to perform following five steps to send and receive an e-mail. Receiver should perform following five steps in reverse direction.

1. Digital Signature:

- In this step Message Digest (MD) of the e-mail message is created using SHA – 1 Algorithm.
- Digital signature is the result of encryption of MD using senders private key.

2. Compression:

- Input message as well as digital signature created in step 1 are compressed together to reduce the size of final message.
- ZIP algorithm is used for compression.

3. Encryption:

- Output from Step 2 are encrypted with the symmetric key.
- For encryption generally IDEA algorithm in CFB mode is used.

4. **Digital Enveloping:**
- In this step Symmetric key used for encryption in Step 3 is encrypted with the receiver's public key.
- Output of Steps 3 and 4 forms digital envelope.
5. **Base 64 Encoding:**
- The output of Step 4 is base 64 is encrypted in this step.

Fig. 5.21: PGP Operation

Advantages of PGP:
1. No compatibility problems.
2. Assured that information that we have send or received has not been modified in transmission.
3. It is free.
4. Worldwide strength and compatibility.

Disadvantages of PGP:
1. Complexity.
2. No recovery.
3. Administering conflicting versions.

5.4 PUBLIC KEY INFRASTRUCTURE (PKI)

- PKI stands for Public Key Infrastructure. A PKI is a set of roles, policies, hardware, software and procedures needed to create, manage, distribute, use, store and revoke digital certificates and manage public-key encryption.
- The purpose of a PKI is to help the secure electronic transfer of information for activities such as e-commerce, internet banking and confidential e-mail.

5.4.1 Introduction

- PKI is closely related to the ideas of asymmetric key cryptography including Digital signatures and encryption services.
- PKI provides assurance of public key. It provides the identification of public keys and their distribution.
- The most unique feature of Public Key Infrastructure (PKI) is that it uses 2 keys includes private key and public key.
- Since the public keys are in open so they are likely to be stolen. It is necessary to find and maintain some way to control these keys. So key management is big task.
- Cryptosystem depends upon how securely its keys are managed. There are two specific requirements of key management for public key cryptosystem:
  1. Secrecy of private keys.
  2. Assurance of public keys.

- PKI provides assurance of public key. It provides the identification of public keys and their distribution. PKI contains components as Public Key Certificate, commonly called as 'digital certificate', Private Key tokens, Certification Authority, Registration Authority.
- PKI is an accepted standard for identifying people through certificates. It includes support for the entire life cycle of certificates and keys, ranging from creation to destruction of certificates and keys.

5.4.2 Digital Certificate (Public Key Certificate) [W-16, 19]

- According to RFC 4949, the term certificate is generally used to refer to, "a document that attests to the truth of something or the ownership of something."
- Digital certificate is similar to small computer file. Similar to our passport which signifies the difference between the person and his characteristics such as full name, nationality, DOB, photograph, signature etc.
- We can say that a digital certificate can be considered as the ID card issued to the person. People use ID cards such as a driver's license, passport to prove their identity. Digital certificate signifies association between person and his public key.
- A digital certificate is an electronic document or container file that contains a key value and identifying information about the entity that controls the key. The certificate is often issued and certified by a third party, usually a Certificate Authority (CA).
- A digital signature attached to the certificate's container file certifies the file's origin and integrity. This verification process often occurs when we download or update software via the Internet.
- Digital certificates are not only given to people but also given to computers, software packages or anything else that need to prove the identity in the electronic world.
- Digital certificates are based on the ITU standard X.509 which defines a standard certificate format for public key certificates and certification validation. Hence digital certificates are sometimes also referred to as X.509 certificates.
- Public key pertaining to the user client is kept in digital certificates by the Certification Authority (CA) along with other important information such as client information, expiration date, usage, issuer etc.
- A Certificate Authority (CA), which issues, manages, authenticates, signs, and revokes users' digital certificates which typically contain the user name, public key, and other identifying information.
- CA digitally signs this entire information and includes digital signature in the certificate. Anyone who needs the assurance about the public key and associated information of client, he carries out the signature validation process using CA's public key.
- Successful validation assures that the public key given in the certificate belongs to the person whose details are given in the certificate.
- The process of creating digital certificate and issuing it to the user is shown in Fig. 5.22.

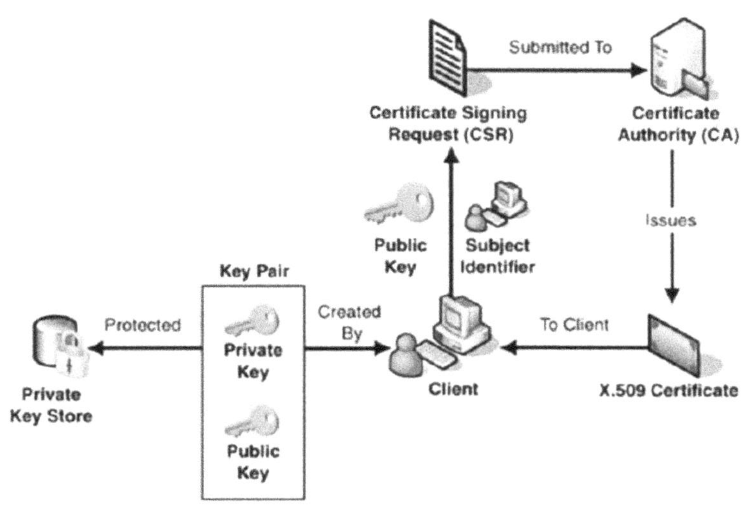

Fig. 5.22: Digital Certificate Creation and Issuing Process

5.4.3 Certifying Authority (CA)

- The main task of CA is to issues certificate to a client and assist other users to verify the certificate.
- The CA takes duty for identifying correctly the identity of the client asking for a certificate to be issued, and ensures that the information contained within the certificate is correct and digitally signs it.
- The CA has authority to give certificate to individual person and organization who want to use that certificates in asymmetric cryptosystem application.
- The **functions of a CA** are as follows:
  1. Generating key.
  2. Issuing digital certificates.
  3. Publishing Certificates.
  4. Verifying Certificates.
  5. Revocation of Certificates.
- To issue a certificate, the CA goes through the following steps, (See Fig. 5.23):
  - The user first generates a public/private key pair.
  - User keeps the private key and sends the public key to the CA with the user identification information (name, SSN, birth date, etc.) in the form of a "certificate request."
  - The CA will verify the user identity through a procedure that may involve a telephone conversation or other mechanisms.
  - If everything is verified, then the CA will issue a certificate with user name, entail address, etc.
  - The CA creates a signed certificate by creating a message digest and encrypting it with his private key. This makes sure that no one can modify this certificate.
  - The certificate is returned to the user, with a copy kept by the CA.

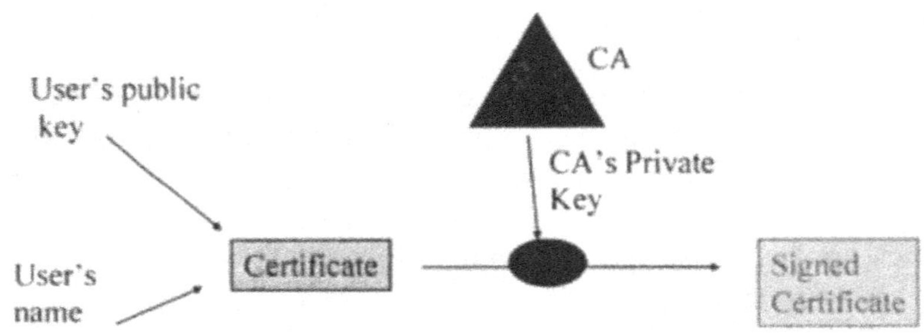

Fig. 5.23: Certificate Authority (CA) and Creation of Certificates

Hierarchy of CA:

- It is not possible practically to have only one authorized CA from whom all users can get digital certificate. If that CA is not available then it may lead to difficulties.
- In such case, the hierarchical certification model is of interest since it allows public key certificates to be used in environments where two communicating parties do not have trust relationships with the same CA.
  - The root CA is at the top of the CA hierarchy and the root CA's certificate is a self-signed certificate.
  - The CAs, which are directly subordinate to the root CA i.e second level CA (For example, CA1 and CA2) have CA certificates that are signed by the root CA.
  - The CAs under the subordinate CAs in the hierarchy (For example, CA5 and CA6) have their CA certificates signed by the higher-level subordinate CAs.
- Verifying a certificate chain is the process of ensuring that a specific certificate chain is valid, correctly signed, and trustworthy.

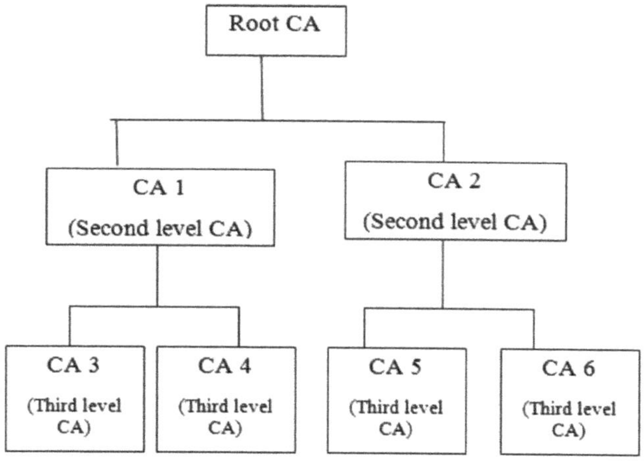

Fig. 5.24: CA Hierarchy

Classes of Certificates:

- There are four typical classes of certificate:
  - **Class 1:** These type of certificates can be easily acquired by supplying an e-mail address.
  - **Class 2:** These type of certificates require additional personal information to be supplied.
  - **Class 3:** These type of certificates can only be purchased after checks have been made about the requestor's identity.
  - **Class 4:** These type of certificates may be used by governments and financial organizations needing very high levels of trust.

5.4.4 Registration Authority (RA)

- Certification Authority uses a third-party Registration Authority (RA) to do the necessary actions on the person or organization requesting the certificate to confirm their identity.
- The RA may appear to the client as a CA. RA does not actually sign the certificate that is issued.
- A Registration Authority (RA), which operates under the trusted collaboration of the certificate authority and can handle day-to-day certification functions, such as verifying registration information, generating end-user keys, revoking certificates, and validating user certificates.

Certificate Management System (CMS):

- In this system certificates are published temporarily or permanently suspended, renewed, or revoked.
- This system do not usually delete certificates because it may be necessary to prove their status at a point in time possibly for authorized reasons.
- This system is run by CA and associated RA's to track their responsibilities and liabilities.

Private Key Tokens:

- Public key of client is kept on certificate and private key is stored on key owners private computer. If an attacker gains access of persons computer then attacker can access users private key.
- For this reason, a private key is kept on secure removable storage token access which is secured through a password.
- Different vendors often use different and sometimes proprietary storage formats for storing keys. For example, Entrust uses the proprietary .epf format, while Verisign, GlobalSign, and Baltimore use the standard .p12 format.

5.4.5 X.509/PKIX Certificate

- The Public-Key Infrastructure X.509 (PKIX) is the working group formed by the IETF to develop standards and models for the PKI environment. The PKIX working group is responsible for the X.509 standard.

- The PKIX standard was proposed in as an improvement for X.509, but when this goal was achieved, the PKIX work expanded beyond its goal and it has developed new standards for using X.509 on Internet.
- X.509 standard defines structure, format and fields of digital certificate. It also gives procedures for distributing public keys.
- In order to extend such standards and make them universal Internet Engineering Task Force (IETF) formed Public Key Infrastructure X.509 (PKIX) working group.
- X.509 is a standard defining the format of public key certificates. An X.509 certificate contains a public key and an identity (a hostname, or an organization, or an individual), and is either signed by a certificate authority or self-signed.
- When a certificate is signed by a trusted certificate authority, or validated by other means, someone holding that certificate can rely on the public key it contains to establish secure communications with another party, or validate documents digitally signed by the corresponding private key.

PKIX Services:

- X.509/PKIX (Public-Key Infrastructure) defines a framework for the provision of authentication services.
    1. **Registration:** It is the process where entity or person makes itself known to a CA .
    2. **Initialization:** It the process of verifying whether the person is contacting to authorized CA or not
    3. **Certification**: In this step CA creates persons digital certificate and returns it to the person, maintain copy of its own record and also may or may not copies it in public diaries
    4. **Key-Pair Recovery**: Key recovery service is provided by CA or by an independent key recovery system.
    5. **Key Generation:** PKIX specifies that person should be able to generate private and public key pairs.
    6. **Key Update:** This service allows creating fresh key pair from expiring key pair by automatic renewal of digital certificate.
    7. **Cross Certification:** It helps in designing trust models so that person that are certified by an different CA's can cross verify each other.
    8. **Revocation:** PKIX supports checking of certificate status in 2 modes (online and offline).

PKIX Model Architecture:

- Above Fig. 5.25 shows association between elements of PKIX model and consist of following elements as:
    1. **End entity:** Person who want to issue certificate.
    2. **CA (Certification Authority)**: Issues digital certificate and Certificate Revocation List i.e CRLs.
    3. **RA (Registration Authority)**: Certification Authority uses a third-party Registration Authority (RA) to do the necessary actions on the person or organization requesting the certificate to confirm their identity. RA may appear to the client as a CA and does not actually sign the certificate that is issued.
    4. **CRL Issuer**: An optional component that a CA can delegate to publish CRL's.
    5. **Repository**: It indicates any method for keeping certificates and CRL's so that they can be retrieved by end entity.

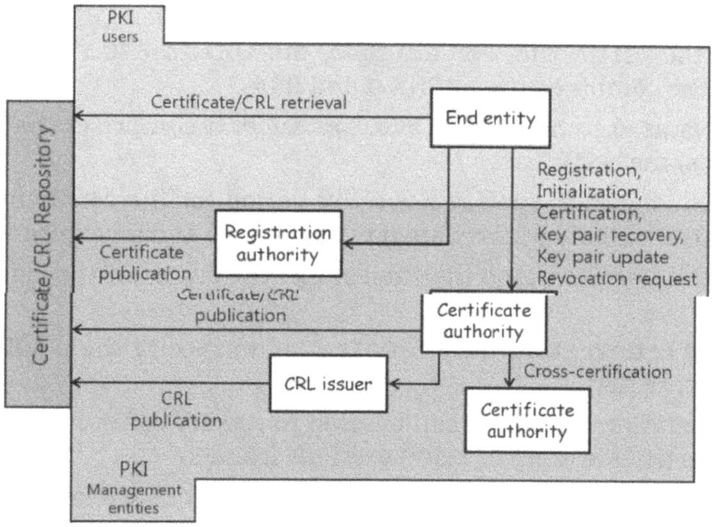

Fig. 5.25: PKIX Model Architecture

5.4.6 X.509/PKIX Certificate Format

- A digital certificate exist in a number of different formats. X.509 is the most common format.
- A digital certificate binds a user, computer, or service's identity to a public key by providing information about the subject of the certificate, the validity of the certificate, and applications and services that can use the certificate.
- Certificates issued in PKIs are structured to meet these objectives based on standards established by the Public-Key Infrastructure (X.509) Working Group (PKIX) of the Internet Engineering Tasks Force (IETF).

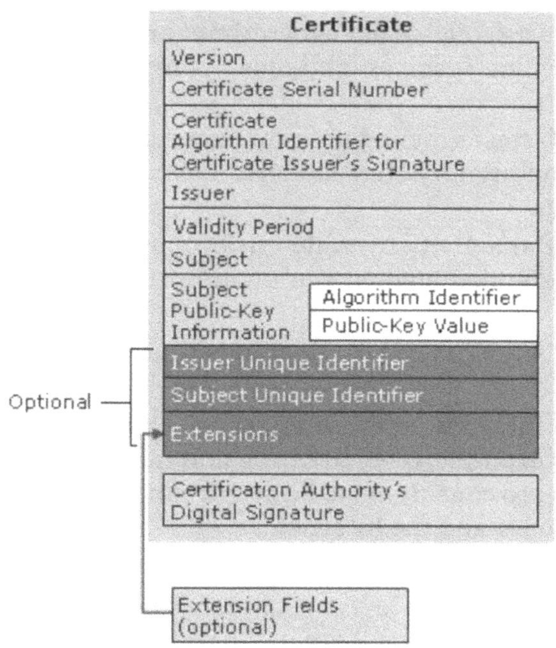

Fig. 5.26

- An X.509 certificate is a data structure that basically consists of the following fields, (remember that any additional extension fields are possible):
  1. **Version:** This field is used to specify the X.509 version in use (i.e. version 1, 2 or 3).
  2. **Serial Number:** This field is used to specify a serial number for the certificate. The serial number is a unique integer value assigned by the (certificate) issuer. The pair consisting of the issuer and the serial number must be unique (otherwise, it would not be possible to uniquely identify an X.509 certificate).

3. **Algorithm ID:** This field is used to specify the Object Identifier (OID) of the algorithm that is used to digitally sign the certificate. For example, the OID 1.2.840.113549.1.1.5 refers to sha1RSA, which stands for the combined use of SHA-1 and RSA.
4. **Issuer:** This field is used to name the issuer. As such, it comprises the DN of the CA that issues (and digitally signs) the certificate.
5. **Validity:** This field is used to specify a validity period for the certificate. The period, in turn, is defined by two dates, namely a start date (i.e. not before) and an expiration date (i.e., not after).
6. **Subject:** This field is used to name the subject (i.e. the owner of the certificate, typically using a DN).
7. **Subject Public Ket Information:** This field is used to specify the public key, (together with the algorithm) that is certified.
8. **Issuer Unique Identifier:** This field can be used to specify some optional information related to the issuer of the certificate (only in X.509 versions 2 and 3).
9. **Subject Unique Identifier:** This field can be used to specify some optional information related to the subject (only in X.509 versions 2 and 3). This field typically comprises some alternative naming information, such as an e-mail address or a DNS entry.
10. **Extension:** This field can be used to specify some optional extensions that may be critical or not (only in X.509 version 3).

5.5 CYBERCRIME [S-16, 17, 18, 19, W-16, 17, 18, 19]

- Cybercrime is a generic term that refers to all criminal activities done using the medium of computers, the Internet, cyberspace and the worldwide web (or web).
- Cybercrime (computer crime) is an illegal behavior, directed by means of electronic operations, that targets the security of computer systems and the data processed by them.
- Computer-related crime is also called as "cybercrime" or "e-crime" or "digital technology crime". In other words, the crime that involves and uses computer devices and Internet, is known as cybercrime.
- Cybercrime is one of the fastest growing areas of crime. More and more criminals are exploiting the speed, convenience and anonymity that modern technologies offer in order to commit a diverse range of criminal activities.
- Cyber security is a potential activity by which information and other communication systems are protected from and/or defended against the unauthorized use or modification or exploitation or even theft.
- Cybercrime encompasses any criminal act dealing with computers and networks (sometimes called hacking or cracking).
- Additionally, cybercrime includes traditional crimes that are now being conducted through the Internet and the Web. For example, telemarketing and Internet fraud, identity theft, sex crimes, and credit card account thefts are considered to be cybercrimes when the illegal activities are committed through the use of a computer and the Internet.
- Criminals are becoming technically literate and their activities are more difficult to track because of the worldwide nature of the Internet.
- Criminal activities can be initiated anywhere in the world using the Internet and other networks.
- A generalized definition of cybercrime may be, "unlawful acts wherein the computer is either a tool or target or both".

Characteristics of Cybercrime:

1. The weapon with which cybercrime are committed is technology.
2. Cybercrime does not have any jurisdictions, no boundaries.
3. Cybercrime has the potential of causing harm and injury which is of an imaginable magnitude.
4. It is extremely difficult to collect evidence of cyber crime and prove the same in court of law, due to anonymity and invisibility of cyber criminals.

5.5.1 Introduction

- Cybercrime is any illegal behavior directed by means of electronic operations that targets the security of computer systems and the data processed by them.
- Cybercrime is the use of computers and networks to perform illegal activities such as spreading computer viruses, online bullying, performing unauthorized electronic fund transfers, etc.
- By definition, cybercrime is a crime related to technology, computers, and the Internet. The majority of publicized cybercrimes that concern governments, industry officials and citizens worldwide.
- A number of components make up the cyber environment, including the Internet infrastructure, the Web, the computer systems, client/server systems, the network, and individual workstations.
- Cyber is a prefix used to describe new things that are being made possible by the spread of computers. Cyberspace is defined as, the global network of interconnected computers and communication systems. Anything related to the Internet also falls under the cyber category.

Need for Cybercrime Security:

- Criminal activity has increased in the area of networking with the advent of worldwide, access to the Internet.
- Cyber crime is any crime with the help of computer and telecommunication technology. Any crime where either the computer is used as an object or subject.

Categories of Cyber Crime:

1. The **computer as a target** using a computer to attack other computer, e.g. hacking, virus/worms attacks, Dos attack etc.
2. The **computer as a weapon** using a computer to commit real world crime e.g. cyber terrorism, credit card fraud and pornography etc.

- There are many categories of cybercrime and security policy issues that must be addressed in today's networking environment. The major issues can be explained as follows: **[W-16]**
  1. Identity theft and fraud.
  2. Pornography and minors.
  3. E-commerce legal issues.
  4. Encryption and computer crime.
  5. Federal code related to cybercrime.
  6. Intellectual property crime.
  7. International aspects of computer crime.
  8. Privacy issues in the high-tech context.
  9. Prosecuting crimes facilitated by computers and by the Internet.
  10. Protecting critical infrastructures.
  11. Searching and seizing computers and obtaining evidence in criminal investigations.
  12. Speech issues in the high-tech context.

5.5.2 Hacking **[S-16, 17, 18, 19, W-17, 18, 19]**

- Hacking refers to the unauthorized access of another computer system. It is the practice of modifying features of assistant in order to accomplish a goal outside of the creature's original purpose.
- The word hacker has now taken on numerous meanings, from a person who enjoys learning the details of computer systems and how to stretch their capabilities to a malicious or inquisitive meddler who tries to discover information by deceptive or illegal means.
- Every act committed towards breaking into a computer and/or network is hacking and it is an offence. Hackers write or use readymade computer programs to attack the target computer.
- They possess the desire to destruct and they get enjoyment out of such destruction. Some hackers hack for personal monetary gains, such as stealing credit card information, transferring money from various bank accounts to their own account followed by withdrawal of money.

- Government websites are hot on hackers target lists and attacks on government websites receive wide press coverage.
- There are different types of hackers. Some of them are explained below: **[W-19]**

1. White Hat:

- This type of hackers is someone who has non-malicious purpose whenever he breaks into security systems.
- In fact, a large number of white hat hackers are security experts themselves who want to push the boundaries of their own IT security ciphers and shields or event, penetration testers specifically hired to test out how vulnerable or impenetrable, (at the time) a present protective setup currently is.
- A white hat that does vulnerability assessments and penetration tests is also known as an ethical hacker.

2. Black Hat:

- This type of hackers is also known as a cracker and he has a malicious purpose whenever he goes about breaking into computer security systems with the use of technology such as a network, telecommunication system, or computer and without authorization.
- His malicious purposes can range from all sorts cybercrimes such as piracy, identity theft, credit card fraud, damage and so forth. He may or may not utilize questionable tactics such as deploying worms and malicious sites to meet his ends.

3. Grey Hat:

- A grey hat hacker is a combination of both white hats and black hats. This is the kind of hacker that is not a penetration tester but will go ahead and surf the Internet for vulnerable systems he could exploit.
- Like a white hat, he will inform the administrator of the website of the vulnerabilities he found after hacking through the site.
- Like a black hat and unlike a pen tester, he will hack any site freely and without any prompting or authorization from owners what so ever.
- He will even offer to repair the vulnerable site he exposed in the first place for a small fee.

4. Elite Hacker:

- As with any society, better than average people are rewarded for their talent and treated as special.
- This social status among the hacker underground, the elite are the hackers among hackers in this subculture of sorts.
- They are the masters of deception that have a solid reputation among their peers as the cream of the hacker crop.

5. Script Kiddie:

- A script kiddie is basically a part-time or non-expert hacker, who breaks into peoples computer systems not through his knowledge in IT security and the ins and outs of given website, but through the prepackaged automated scripts (hence the name), tools and software written by people who are real hackers, unlike him.
- He usually has little to know knowledge of the underlying concept behind how those scripts he has on hand works.

Concept of Cracking: **[W-19]**

- A cracker is someone who breaks into someone else computer system, often on a network by passing passwords or licenses in computer programs or in other ways intentionally breaches computer security.
- A cracker can be doing this for profit maliciously, for some altruistic purpose or cause, or because the challenge is there. The term cracker is not to be confused with hacker. Hackers generally deplore cracking.
- Some breaking and entering has been done ostensibly to point out weaknesses in a site's security system.

- Contrary to widespread myth, cracking does not usually involve some mysterious leap of hackerly brilliance, but rather persistence and the determined repetition of a handful of fairly well-known tricks that exploit common weaknesses in the security of target systems.

5.5.3 Digital Forgery

- Forgery is the criminal act that provides misleading information about a product or service. Forgery is the process of making, adapting or imitating documents or objects with the intent to deceive.
- It is also called as digital tampering. Digital forgery is the process of manipulating documents or images for the intent of financial, social or political gain.
- Digital forgery may involve identity theft and electronic forgery. The majority of digital forgery occurs because digitally altered pictures often appeal to viewer's eyes.
- Now a day's many powerful picture processing software's are available (e.g. Adobe photoshop, Corel draw etc.). Using this software one can alter almost anything in picture.

5.5.4 Cyber Stalking/Harassment

- Cyber stalking is stalking or harassment carried out over the internet. It might target individuals, groups, or even organizations and can take different forms including slander, defamation and threats.
- Harassment by means of e-mail, text (or online) messages or the internet is called as cyber harassment. Cyber stalking is stalking or harassment that takes place via online channels such as social media, forums or e-mail.
- A stalker may be an online stranger or a person whom the target knows. It can take many forms, including following:
  1. Unwanted sexually explicit e-mails, text (or online) messages.
  2. Inappropriate or offensive advances on social networking websites or internet chat rooms.
  3. Threats of physical and/or sexual violence by e-mail, text (or online) messages.
  4. Hate speech, meaning language that denigrates, insults, threatens or targets an individual based on her identity (gender) and other traits (such as sexual orientation or disability).
- Typically cyber stalkers use social media, websites and search engines to intimidate a user and instill fear.
- Usually, the cyber stalker knows their victim and makes the person feel afraid or concerned for their safety.

5.5.5 Cyber Pornography [S-16, W-16, 18]

- Pornography is generally described as the presentation of sexually explicit behavior, as in a photograph, intended to arouse sexual excitement.
- Child pornography is a very inhuman and serious cybercrime offence. Child pornography means any visual depiction, including any photograph, film, video, picture, or computer-generated image or picture whether made or produced by electronic, mechanical or other means, of sexually explicit.
- Child pornography is illegal in nearly all countries, although enforcement varies across the globe. Most countries agree on the basic definition of child pornography as, "sexually explicit material made with actual minors, usually less than 16 to 18 years of age, as subjects".
- It includes the following:
  - Any photograph that can be considered obscene and/or unsuitable for the age of child viewer like film, video and picture.
  - Computer generated image or picture of sexually explicit conduct where the production of such visual depiction involves the use of a minor engaging in sexually explicit conduct.
  - Internet is the most frequently used tool for such criminals to reach children and practice child sex abuse.
  - The spreading use internet and its easy accessibility to children has made them viable victim to cybercrime.
  - There is a type of humans called Pedophiles who usually allure the children by obscene Pornographic contents and then they approach them for sex.

- Then they take their naked photographs while having sex. Such people sometime misguide children telling them that they are of the same age and win their confidence.
- Then they exploit the children either by forcing them to have sex or selling their pictures over internet.

5.5.6 Identity Theft and Fraud

- Identity theft and identity fraud are terms used to refer to all types of crime in which someone wrongfully obtains and uses another person's personal data in some way that involves fraud or deception, typically for economic gain.
- Identity fraud or 'ID theft', involves the use of a person's stolen details to commit crime. They are also called as identity fraud.
- This cybercrime occurs when a criminal gains access to a user's personal information to steal funds, access confidential information, or participate in tax or health insurance fraud.
- It starts with someone stealing the identity, allowing digital criminals to use identifiable data including his/her name, driver's license, social security information and more to commit fraud, steal property, misappropriate goods or use services in his/her name.
- They can also open a phone/internet account in the name, use the name to plan a criminal activity and claim government benefits in the name.
- They may do this by finding out user's passwords through hacking, retrieving personal information from social media, or sending phishing e-mails.
- Identity theft is the act of a person obtaining information illegally about someone else. Thiefs try to find such information as full name, maiden name, address, date of birth, social security number, passwords, phone number, e-mail, and credit card numbers.
- The thief can then use this information to gain access to bank accounts, e-mail, smartphones, identify themselves as someone, or sells the information.
- Fraud is intentional deception to secure unfair or unlawful gain, or to deprive a victim of a legal right. Identity fraud is the use by one person of another person's personal information, without authorization, to commit a crime or to deceive or defraud that other person or a third person.
- A person's personal information may be surreptitiously obtained, commonly described as identity theft, in a variety of ways.
- A fraudster may use another person's basic personal details (such as name, address, username and PIN) to access the victim's online accounts, including banking accounts, e-mail, and social media accounts.

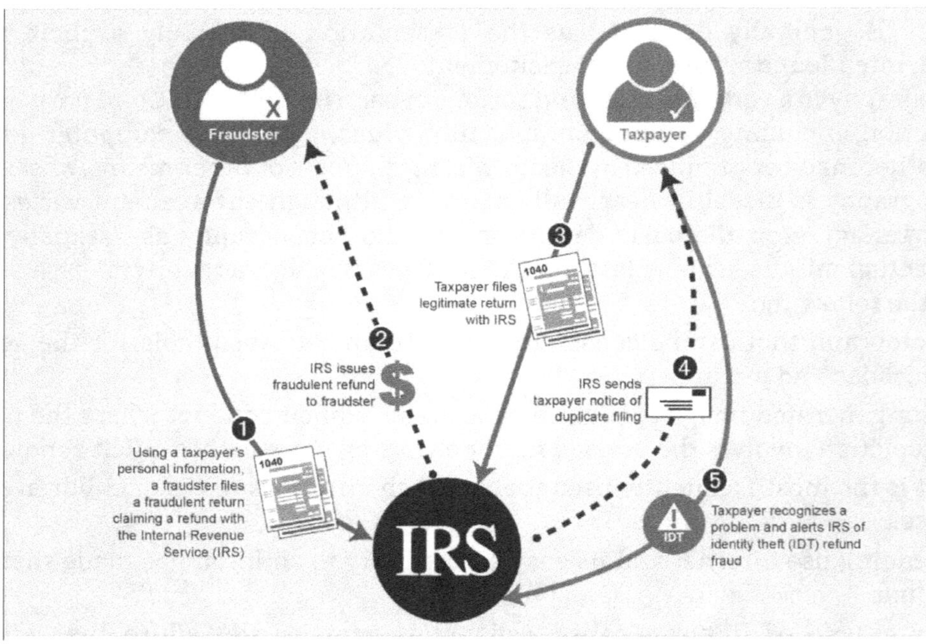

Fig. 5.27

- Example of an identity theft crime:
  1. The fraudster files tax return paperwork in the victim's name, claiming a refund.
  2. The IRS issues a refund to the fraudster.
  3. The victim submits their legitimate tax return.
  4. The IRS rejects the return as a duplicate.

5.5.7 Cyber Terrorism

- Cyber terrorism is an act of terrorism that uses information system or digital technology.
- It describes use of internet based attacks in terrorist activities including acts of deliberate, large scale disruption of computer network, especially of personal computers attached to the internet, by the means of tools such as viruses, worms etc.
- Cyber-terrorism is the convergence of terrorism and cyberspace. A cyber attack would include unlawful attacks and threats against computers, networks, and databases.
- However, when done to intimidate or coerce a government or its people in furtherance of some political or social objective, such actions become cyber terrorism. Cyber terrorism includes attacks that result in violence against infrastructure, persons and property and often lead to death or bodily injury, explosions, plane crashes, water contamination or severe economic damage.
- **Example:** Hacking into computer system, website defacing etc.
- It can either be international, domestic or political. Terrorist group use their own computer technology to attack on victims computer.

5.5.8 Cyber Defamation

- The widespread use of Internet has also given a new face to the crime and a new medium to the bad elements to commit crime.
- Cyber defamation is when defamation is done with computer as a tool. It is intention to harm the reputation of particular person knowing that their conduct is likely to cause harm to the reputation.
- Cyber defamation is publishing of defamatory material against another person with the help of computers or internet.
- Cyber defamation is not a specific criminal offense, but rather defamation conducted via digital media, usually through the Internet.

Cyber Crime Investigation:

- The goal of the investigation is to identify all available facts related to the case. The investigative report should provide a detailed account of the incident, highlighting any discrepancies in witness statements.
- The report should be a well-organized document that contains a description of the incident.
- Computer forensics is the study of computer technology as it relates to the law. This generally means analyzing the system by using a variety of forensic tools and processes, and that the examination of the suspect system may lead to other victims and other suspects.

Cybercrime Investigation Process: [W-16]

- The computer crime investigation should start immediately following the report of any alleged criminal activity. Many processes ranging from reporting and containment to analysis and eradication should be accomplished as soon as possible after the attack.
- An incident response plan should be formulated, and a Computer Emergency Response Team (CERT) should be organized before the attack.
- The incident response plan will help set the objective of the investigation and will identify each of the steps in the investigative process.
  1. **Detection and Containment:** Before any investigation can take place, the system intrusion or abusive conduct must first be detected.
  2. **Report to Management:** All incidents should be reported to management as soon as possible. Prompt internal reporting is imperative to collect and preserve potential evidence. It is important that information about the investigation be limited to as few people as possible.
  3. **Determine if Disclosure is Required:** Determine if a disclosure is required or warranted due to laws or regulations.

4. **Investigation Considerations:** Once, the preliminary investigation is complete and the victim organization has made a decision related to disclosure, the organization must decide on the next course of action.
5. **Obtaining and Serving Search Warrants:** If it is believed that the suspect has crucial evidence at his or her home or office, a search warrant will be required to seize the evidence.
6. **Surveillance:** Two forms of surveillance are used in computer crime investigations are physical and computer.
   (i) **Physical surveillance** can be generated at the time of the abuse, through CCTV security cameras, or after the fact.
   (ii) **Computer surveillance** is achieved in a number of ways. It is done passively through audit logs or actively by way of electronic monitoring.

5.6 CYBER LAWS

- Cyber law is the law governing cyber space. Cyber space includes computers, networks, software's, data storage devices (such as hard disks, USB disks etc.), the Internet, websites, e-mails and even electronic devices such as cell phones, ATM machines etc.
- Cyber law is the area of law that deals with the Internet's relationship to technological and electronic elements, including computers, software, hardware and Information Systems (IS).
- Cyber law deals with:
  1. Cybercrimes.
  2. Electronic or Digital Signatures.
  3. Intellectual Property (IP).
  4. Data Protection and Privacy.

5.6.1 Introduction

- These days Information Technology (IT) is becoming increasingly popular and imminent in the day-to-day life of individuals, companies/organizations and the society as a whole. This is because it has brought more efficiency, accuracy and speedier transactions particularly in business world.
- We find the popularity of data processing equipments and the use of computers in day-to-day transactions like online banking, tele-marketing, use of credit or debit cards and so on, which have made banking very swift, and accurate.
- Such advances in the IT and the potentialities in the business world have attracted many misusers, unscrupulous people and criminals to commit many cyber crimes relating to financial world.
- The cyber crime offenders be fool people through the Internet using different techniques and schemes. And therefore, we find these days a new class of white collared criminals perpetuating fraud on the Internet.
- Cyber law is a term used to describe the legal issues related to use of communications technology, particularly "cyberspace", i.e. the Internet.
- It is less of a distinct field of law in the way that property or contract are, as it is an intersection of many legal fields, including intellectual property, privacy, freedom of expression, and jurisdiction.
- In essence, cyber law is an attempt to apply laws designed for the physical world, to human activity on the Internet. In India, The IT Act, 2000 as amended by the IT (Amendment) Act, 2008 is known as the Cyber law.

5.6.2 Need of Cyber Law

- The computer generated world of Internet is known as cyberspace and the laws prevailing this area are known as Cyber laws and all the users of this space come under the ambit of these laws as it carries a kind of worldwide jurisdiction.
- Cyber law can also be described as that branch of law that deals with legal issues related to use of inter-networked Information Technology (IT). In short, cyber law is the law governing computers and the internet.

- Cyber law is important because it touches almost all aspects of transactions and activities and on involving the internet, World Wide Web (Web) and cyberspace. Every action and reaction in cyberspace has some legal and cyber legal angles.
- All legal issues related to internet crime are dealt with through cyber laws. Following some points describe need for cyber law:
  - The modern thief can steal more with a computer than with a gun. Tomorrow's terrorist may be able to do more damage with a keyboard than with a bomb.
  - Internet has dramatically changed the way we think, the way we govern, the way we do commerce and the way we perceive ourselves.
  - Information technology is encompassing all walks of life all over the world.
  - Cyber space creates moral, civil and criminal wrongs. It has now given a new way to express criminal tendencies.
  - Cyberspace is open to participation by all.
  - "IT" has brought Transition from paper to paperless world.
  - The laws of real world cannot be interpreted in the light of emerging cyberspace to include all aspects relating to different activities in cyberspace.
  - Internet requires an enabling and supportive legal infrastructure in tune with the times.

Advantages of Cyber Law:

- Organizations/Companies are now able to carry out e-commerce using the legal infrastructure provided by the Act.
- Digital signatures have been given legal validity and sanction in the Act.
- It has opened the doors for the entry of corporate companies for issuing Digital Signatures Certificates in the business of being Certifying Authorities (CAs).
- It allows Government to issue notification on the web thus heralding e-governance.
- It gives authority to the companies or organizations to file any form, application or any other document with any office, authority, body or agency owned or controlled by the suitable Government in e-form by means of such e-form as may be prescribed by the suitable Government.
- The IT Act also addresses the important issues of security, which are so critical to the success of electronic transactions.

5.6.3 Categories of Cyber Laws

- There are three major categories that cybercrime falls into: individual, property and government. The types of methods used and difficulty levels vary depending on the category:
  - **Crime against Property:** This is similar to a real-life instance of a criminal illegally possessing an individual's bank or credit card details. The hacker steals a person's bank details to gain access to funds, make purchases online or run phishing scams to get people to give away their information. They could also use malicious software to gain access to a web page with confidential information.
  - **Crime against Individual:** This category of cybercrime involves one individual distributing malicious or illegal information online. This can include cyber stalking, distributing pornography and trafficking.
  - **Crime against Government:** This is the least common cybercrime, but is the most serious offense. A crime against the government is also known as cyber terrorism. Government cybercrime includes hacking government websites, military websites or distributing propaganda. These criminals are usually terrorists or enemy governments of other nations.

5.7 COMPLIANCE STANDARDS

- Security compliance is a legal concern for organizations in many industries today. Regulatory standards like PCI DSS, ISO 27001 etc., prescribe recommendations for protecting data and improving info security management.

5.7.1 Implementing and Information Security Management System

- An Information Security Management System (ISMS) is a set of policies and procedures for systematically managing an organization's sensitive data.
- The objective of ISMS is to provide a systematic approach to managing sensitive information in order to protect it.
- It encompasses employees, processes and information. The ISMS represents the collation of all the interrelated/interacting information security elements of an organization so as to ensure policies, procedures, and objectives can be created, implemented, communicated, and evaluated to better guarantee an organization's overall information security. This system is typically influenced by organization's needs, objectives, security requirements, size, and processes.
- An ISMS is depicted in Fig. 5.28.
- Security threats must be managed and controlled establishing a global policy that is broad security policy with management involvement helps to do this. While doing this, four levels of documentation emerge as shown in Fig. 5.28.

Level 1	Policy, Scope, risk Assessment, Statement applicability	Security manuals
Level 2	Describe Processes-who, what, when, where	Procedures
Level 3	Describes how tasks and specific activities are done	Work instructions, checklist, forms etc.
Level 4	Provides objectives evidence of compliance with ISMS requirements	Records

Fig. 5.28: Four Levels of Documentation in ISMS

ISMS Scope:

- Business security policy and plans.
- Current business operations requirements.
- Future business plans and requirements.
- Legislative requirements.
- Obligations and responsibilities with regard to security contained in SLAs.
- The business and IT risks and their management.

A Sample List of IS Policies:

- Overall ISMS policy.
- Access control policy.
- Email policy.
- Internet policy.
- Anti-virus policy.
- Information classification policy.
- Use of IT assets policy.
- Asset disposal policy.

5.7.2 ISO 27001 [W-17]

- ISO 27001 is a specification for creating an ISMS.
- ISO 27001 is a security standard that outlines the suggested requirements for building, monitoring and improving an Information Security Management System (ISMS). An ISMS is a set of policies for protecting and managing an enterprise's sensitive information, e.g., financial data, intellectual property, customer details and employee records.

- ISO 27001 is a voluntary standard employed by service providers to secure customer information. It requires an independent and accredited body to formally audit an organization to ensure compliance.
- It does not mandate specific actions, but includes suggestions for documentation, internal audits, continual improvement, and corrective and preventive action.
- The focus of ISO 27001 is to protect the confidentiality, integrity and availability of the information. This is done by finding out what potential problems could happen to the information (i.e., risk assessment), and then defining what needs to be done to prevent such problems from happening (i.e., risk mitigation or risk treatment).
- **ISO 27001 Part I:**
  1. Code of practice for Information Security Management (ISM).
  2. Best practices, guidance, recommendations for: Confidentiality (C), Integrity (I) and Availability (A).
- **ISO 27001 Part II:**
  - Specification for ISM.
- ISO 27001 describes following processes:
  - Definition of Information Security Policy.
  - Definition of Scope of ISMS.
  - Security Risk Assessment.
  - Manage the identified risk.
  - Select controls for implementation.
  - Prepare SoA (Statement of Applicability).
- ISO 27001 uses PDCA (Plan-Do-Check-Act) approach and this is used to improve the effectiveness of an organization.

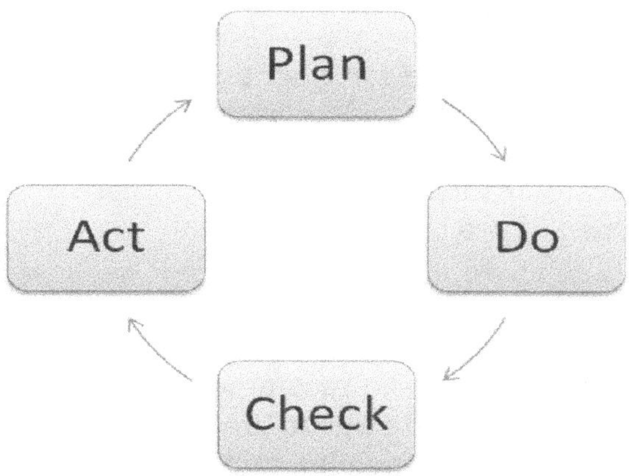

Fig. 5.29: PDCA Approach

- The basic steps of PDCA approach are explained below:
  1. **Plan:** This phase serves to plan the basic organization of information security, set objectives for information security and choose the appropriate security controls.
  2. **Do:** This phase includes carrying out everything that was planned during the previous phase.
  3. **Check:** The purpose of this phase is to monitor the functioning of the ISMS through various channels, and check whether, the results meet the set objectives.
  4. **Act:** The purpose of this phase is to improve everything that was identified as non-compliant in the previous phase.

5.7.3 ISO 20000 [W-17]

- ISO 20000 is a global standard that describes the requirements for an Information Technology Service Management (ITSM) system.
- The standard was developed to mirror the best practices described within the IT Infrastructure Library (ITIL) framework.

- ISO 20000 have two specifications:
  - **ISO 20000-1:**
    - It is the specification for IT Service Management.
    - It defines the processes and provides assessment criteria and recommendations for those who are responsible for IT Service Management.
    - It includes following sections:
      - Scope.
      - Terms and Definitions.
      - Requirements for a Management System.
      - Planning and Implementing Service Management.
      - Planning and Implementing New or Changed Services.
      - The Service Delivery Process.
      - Relationship Processes.
      - Resolution Processes.
      - Release Process.
      - Control Processes.
  - **ISO 20000-2:**
    - It documents a code of practice that explains how to manage IT with regard to ISO 20000-1 audits.
    - It includes all the sections from part 1 except requirements for a management system.

5.7.4 BS 25999

- BS 25999 was a Business Continuity Management (BCM) standard published by the British Standards Institution (BSI).
- BS 25999 is a two-part British Standard Part 1, "BS 25999-1:2006 Business Continuity Management. Code of Practice", took the form of general guidance on the processes, principles and terminology recommended for BCM.
- And Part 2, "BS 25999-2:2007 Specification for Business Continuity Management", specified a set of requirements for implementing, operating and improving a BCM System (BCMS).
- It illustrates what organizations should do to establish demonstrably robust business continuity processes and how they can evaluate their own processes or those of others who they depend on.
- The BS 25999 standard is formed of two parts.
  - **Part 1:**
    - Code of Practice (BS 25999-1:2006):
      - It was published in November 2006.
      - It is in the form of guidance and recommendations that illustrate how to develop and maintain a robust system based on good practice.
      - It establishes the process, principles and terminology of BCM (Business Continuity Management).
      - It provides a basis for understanding, developing and implementing business continuity within an organization and in that organization's dealings with suppliers, customers and other organizations.
  - **Part 2:**
    - Specification (BS 25999-2:2007):
      - Was published in November 2007.
      - It defines requirements for a management systems approach to BCM (Business Continuity Management), against which organizations can be measured formally or informally.
      - BS 25999-2 specifies requirements for "planning, establishing, implementing, operating, monitoring, reviewing and improving a documented Business Continuity.

5.7.5 PCI DSS

- The Payment Card Industry Data Security Standard (PCI DSS) is administered by the PCI Security Standards Council.

- The purpose of the Standard is to decrease payment card fraud across the internet and increase credit card data security.
- Organizations that store transmit or process card holder data must comply with PCI DSS. It can be apply across the whole organization or to a subset of organization that transmit or stores the cardholder data away from the rest of the organization.
- Applied to all peoples, processes and technologies that are involved in the processing, transmission or storage of card holder data.
- The standard consists of 12 core requirements. These requirements are organized into the following areas:
  1. Build and Maintain a Secure Network.
  2. Protect Cardholder Data.
  3. Maintain a Vulnerability Management Program.
  4. Implement Strong Access Control Measures.
  5. Regularly Monitor and Test Networks.
  6. Maintain an Information Security Policy.

Benefits:

1. Peace of mind.
2. Better customer relationships.
3. Universal principles.

5.7.6 ITIL Framework [W-16, S-17]

- ITIL stands for Information Technology Infrastructure Library (ITIL). It is a collection of best practices in IT service management (ITSM). It focuses on the service processes of IT and considers the central role of the user.
- ITIL is an approach to IT Service Management. A service is something that provides value to customers. Services that customers can directly utilize or consume are known as Business services.
- Service management is a set of specialized organizational capabilities for providing value to customers in the form of services.
- ITIL is a set of best practices for delivering IT services - it standardizes the selection, planning, delivery and support of IT services to maximize efficiency and maintain predictable levels of service.
- ITIL is a framework of best practices for developing and deploying IT Service Management (ITSM) in an organisation. The focus is on delivering high quality IT services to support the organisational IT assets, which in turn support the business operations.

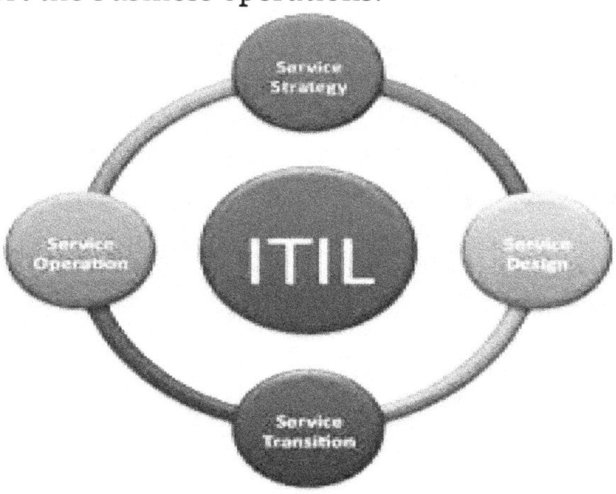

Fig. 5.30: ITIL Framework

- ITIL is organized around a service life cycle which includes:
  1. **Service Strategy:**
     - Life cycle starts with service strategy understanding.
     - What are we going to provide?
     - Can we afford it?
     - Can we provide enough of it?

- How do we gain competitive advantage?
- Perspective
  - Vision, mission and strategic goals
- Position
- Plan
- Pattern
  - Must fit organisational culture.

2. **Service Design:**
   - It ensures that new and changed services are designed effectively to meet customer expectation by understanding.
   - How are we going to provide it?
   - How are we going to build it?
   - How are we going to test it?
   - How are we going to deploy it?
   - Service catalogue management.
   - Service Level Management.
   - Capacity management.
   - Availability management.
   - Service continuity management.
   - Information security management.
   - Supplier and Contract management.
   - Organisational change and communications.
3. **Service Transition:**
   - Through this phase of life cycle the design is built, tested and moved for production to enable the business customer to achieve the desired value.
   - IT includes:
     - Change Management.
     - Service asset and configuration management.
     - Knowledge management and Service Knowledge Management System.
     - Service release and deployment planning.
     - Performance and risk evaluation.
     - Testing.
     - Acquire, build, test and pilot.
     - Service release acceptance test and pilot.
     - Deployment, de-commission and transfer.
4. **Service Operation:**
   - Once, transition phase is completed Service operation then delivers the service on an ongoing basis to see daily overall health of the service.
   - It includes:
     - Monitoring and event management.
     - Incident management.
     - Request fulfilment (Standard Changes).
     - Problem management.
     - Access Management.
     - Service desk.
     - Infrastructure management.
     - Application management.
     - IT Operations.
     - Facilities management.
5. **Continual Service Improvement(CSI):**
   - It measure and improve the service levels.
   - It includes:
     - Measurement and control.

- Service measurement.
- Service assessment and analysis.
- Process assessment and analysis.
- Service Level Management.
- Improvement planning.

○ **Advantages to organization with ITIL framework:**

- Improve resource utilization.
- Be more competitive.
- Reduce re-work.
- Eliminate redundant work.
- Improve availability, reliability and security of business critical IT services.
- Improve project deliverables and time-scales.

5.7.7 COBIT Framework [S-17, 18, 19, W-16, 17, 18]

- COBIT is a framework for Information Technology (IT) management and IT governance.
- COBIT stands for Control Objectives for Information and Related Technology. It is a framework created by the ISACA (Information Systems Audit and Control Association) for IT governance and management.
- It is a supporting toolset that allows managers to bridge the gap between control requirements, technical issues and business risks.
- COBIT has been considered as high level IT governance framework combining in itself IT security, IT audit IT assurance.
- COBIT aims "to research, develop, publish and promote an authoritative, up-to-date, international set of generally accepted information technology control objectives for day-to-day use by business managers, IT professionals and assurance professionals.
- COBIT provides an internal control system or framework to manage business requirements for effectiveness, efficiency, confidentiality, integrity, availability, compliance and reliability of information.
- Control objective is a statement of desired result or purpose to be achieved by implementing control procedures in a particular activity.
- The COBIT framework is based on the principle, "to provide the information that the organization requires to achieve its objectives, the organization requires investing in and managing and controlling IT resources using a structured set of processes to provide the services which deliver the required enterprise information".

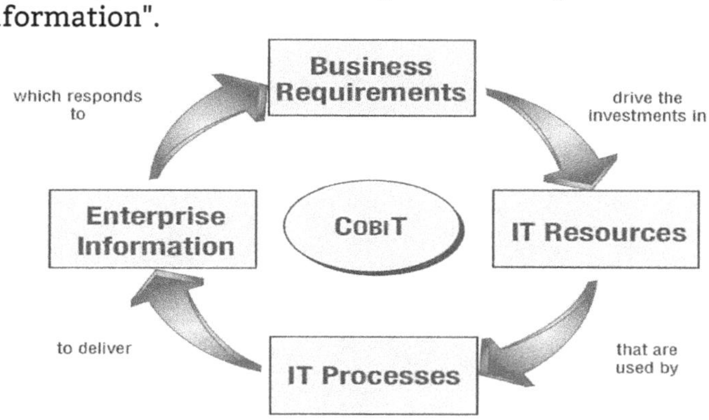

Fig. 5.31: COBIT Framework Principles

- Following are certain criteria that COBIT refers to as business requirements for information:
  1. **Effectiveness:** It means that the information is relevant, timely, correct, consistent and applicable to the business process.
  2. **Efficiency:** It means that the information is optimal for productive as Well as economical use of resources.
  3. **Confidentiality:** It means that the information is protected from unauthorized use.
  4. **Integrity:** It means that the information is accurate and complete and valid for business.

5. **Availability:** It means that the information will be available whenever required by the business process.
6. **Compliance:** It means the information has fulfilled all laws, regulations and contractual arrangements, externally imposed business criteria as well as internal policies.
7. **Reliability:** It means that the information is appropriate for management to operate the entity and apply governance responsibilities.

Practice Questions

1. What is network security?
2. What is cyber law?
3. What is compliance standards.
4. Describe the term Kerberos with its working.
5. Explain the term IPSec in detail.
6. Enlist IPSec protocols.
7. What is AH and ESP?
8. Describe IPSec modes in detail.
9. Define the terms: (i) Network security, (ii) AS, (iii) Cybercrime, (iv) Cyber law.
10. What is identity theft and fraud?
11. What is PKI?
12. What is CA and RA? Explain functions of them.
13. Explain the terms: (i) SMTP, (ii) PEM, (iii) PGP.
14. Define the term digital forgery.
15. Explain the term pornography.
16. Give need for cyber law.
17. What is hacking? Explain its types.
18. What is X.509/PKIX? Explain its format.
19. What is digital certificate? Explain in detail.
20. Describe the terms: (i) Cyber terrorism, (ii) Cyber defamation.
21. With the help of diagram describe the following frameworks: (i) ITIL, (ii) COBIT.
22. What is IMIS? How to implement it?
23. Describe the terms in detail: (i) ISO 20000, (ii) ISO 27001, (iii) PCI DSS.

■■■

www.ingramcontent.com/pod-product-compliance
Lightning Source LLC
LaVergne TN
LVHW062203171026
850499LV00044B/1839
* 9 7 8 9 3 8 9 8 2 5 4 6 6 *